Children, Young Adults, and the Law

A Dictionary

CONTEMPORARY LEGAL ▥▥ ISSUES

Children, Young Adults, and the Law

A Dictionary

Lauren Krohn Arnest

A B C ◆ C L I O

Santa Barbara, California   Denver, Colorado   Oxford, England

Library of Congress Cataloging-in-Publication Data

Arnest, Lauren Krohn.
   Children, young adults, and the law : a dictionary / Lauren Krohn Arnest.
     p. cm. — (Contemporary legal issues)
   Includes bibliographical references and index.
   Summary: A dictionary of terms related to the legal rights of children and young adults.
   1. Children—Legal status, laws, etc.—United States—Dictionaries.   2. Young adults—legal status, laws, etc.—United States—Dictionaries. [1. Law. 2. Children's rights.] I. title. II. Series.
KF479.A68A76 1998   346.7301'35'03—dc21   98-24194

ISBN 0-87436-879-0 (alk. paper)

03 02 01 00 99 98   10 9 8 7 6 5 4 3 2 1 (cloth)

ABC-CLIO, Inc.
130 Cremona Drive, P.O. Box 1911
Santa Barbara, California 93116-1911

This book is printed on acid-free paper ∞.

For my nieces, Kellyn and Langley

Contents

Preface

The law relating to children in the United States is a recent phenomenon. Only in the late nineteenth century did it come to be considered any concern of the law at all as to how children in our society were treated or raised. Today, as the nation stands on the threshold of the twenty-first century, no area of the law is more comprehensive or dynamic. In scarcely more than 100 years, the usual glacial pace of legal development has given way in this area to downright frantic eruptions.

No one set of laws governs the treatment and rights of children in the United States. Laws at all levels, from municipal ordinances to federal statutes, are directed at the way children are treated, both within and outside of their families. All states have laws governing child support and child custody, preventing child abuse and neglect, mandating school attendance, and processing the cases of juveniles caught breaking criminal laws. A number of federal laws influence the way states handle these matters by offering, or threatening to withhold, federal funding if states do, or do not, incorporate certain principles in their own requirements concerning children. In addition to statutes, court decisions in every state and at the federal level all the way up to the Supreme Court define the relationship of adults and the government to our youngest citizens, as well as set forth the entitlements that children have as constitutional "persons" in their own right.

This plethora of laws makes it difficult to write a general compendium such as *Children, Young Adults, and the Law*. Nevertheless, I have attempted to describe most of the important legal issues affecting children and to distill the most common approaches of all the various jurisdictions that have laws on these subjects into short entries. In addition to general topics, the book includes descriptions of the most important federal statutes and Supreme Court cases that deal with children's rights. Each of the approximately 200 entries is also copiously cross-referenced to other entries that expand upon or relate to the topic under discussion. Cross-references appear in bold type. The book also contains a short historical overview of the law's development, a table of cases and statutes referred to in the text, and a bibliography for further research.

As in any project of this scope, there are many people without whose aid and indulgence my efforts would have foundered. I am particularly grateful to Donald T. Kramer, Robert M. Horowitz, and Howard A. Davidson for their excellent reference work *Legal Rights of Children* (1994), which helped frame the issues for my own research; to my friend Diane Redleaf, a practitioner of children's law in Chicago, for steering me to the many organizations nationwide that dedicate themselves to advancing children's causes; and to my husband, Mark, for lending his considerable writing expertise to polish my prose. I also thank Mr. Henry Rasof, lately of ABC-CLIO, for conceiving of a general work for nonlawyers discussing the legal issues affecting children—the work that became *Children, Young Adults, and the Law.*

Children, Young Adults, and the Law

A scant century ago, a manuscript entitled "Children, Young Adults, and the Law" would probably be considered too meager in subject matter to warrant publication. Today, the topic is so huge that every year volumes are published that can only begin to shed light on the various aspects of the field. What has happened in American society to bring about this change? Do we value our children more than our forebears did? Or have we so abdicated personal responsibility that laws must pervade every aspect of our lives in order to guard civilization from breakdown?

Perhaps the answer is a qualified "yes" in both cases: if we do not exactly revere our children more than in past times, we are at least more obsessed with them. And, as other voices of moral authority (i.e., organized religion) have faded in our modern age, the secular law has stepped in to fill the void.

The term *children's rights* really concerns two major ideas. The first is the notion of special protection. The need to protect children from harmful environments and influences, regardless of their source, was the first recognized legitimate aim of the law in dealing with children. Very much later, the second notion arose: the idea that children had some claim to autonomy in important areas of their lives.

In any discussion of children's rights, it should be understood that three separate interests are always involved: first are the interests of parents in raising their children as they believe is proper. Second are the interests of the community, as represented by the government, in promoting the general welfare. Finally, the interests of the children themselves, as autonomous beings, may be considered. For most of American history, the interests of the parents prevailed. In the latter decades of the nineteenth century, the community decided it had an interest in the protection and upbringing of

1

children. Only in the last thirty years has the law recognized anything like rights to autonomous decision making on the part of children themselves. In areas of the law in which the children's separate interests are considered, the law has become concomitantly more complicated. Legislatures and courts must always conduct a delicate balancing act among the three interested parties in matters affecting children. In addition, as divorce has become more common, the interests of the two parents in any matter involving their children may diverge, thus adding yet another dimension to any legal proceeding. A short history elucidates these developments.

1650–1830: FATHERS IN CHARGE

In early American society, a man was the sovereign authority within his household. Women and children were his chattels to manage as he would. Women enjoyed slightly more attention from the law than did children, perhaps because of the issues that had to be settled when the property a woman brought into her marriage merged with the property of her husband. Moreover, adult single women did function autonomously in society when there was no father, husband, or brother to claim authority over their affairs. But for the most part, women were considered perpetual "invalids" whose lives had to be arranged from cradle to grave—unlike male children, who would come into their own existence, legally speaking, upon reaching a certain age. Thus, the need to address the legal status of children was not pressing: they would soon be adults, and subject to adult laws.

When laws did specifically concern children, their purpose was usually to back up patriarchal authority. In Massachusetts Colony, a law known as the "Stubborn Child Law" was passed in 1646 that invoked government participation in disciplining unruly children. The sanctions for disobedience of one's parents under that law could include the death penalty. In other colonies, an occasional statute forbade excessive punishments inflicted by men on their children. But, far from representing a humane policy of respect for the dignity of the latter, these laws rather underscore the extent of children's subjugation: only the most extreme bodily injury was forbidden, and the laws were rarely enforced. For the most part, early American society adhered to the view that childhood was a necessary evil that must be gotten through as quickly as possible. Stern measures were important to ensure that the passage to adulthood was accomplished without frivolous detours that could imperil one's ability to become a virtuous and industrious citizen.

Beyond this, children as a class were virtually invisible to the law. Having no property of their own to bring to the family, the law left them to the status of property themselves. Following customs forged as far back as biblical times, a child was considered the creation of its father, to sell or destroy at his whim. The tradition of English common law that took root in America preserved this view. Fathers were entitled to determine how their children would be "employed" and to receive the fruits of their labor, whether they worked in the home or were "bound out" as apprentices to others. Children were seen as important economic assets whose work was vital to the survival of the family. Moreover, hard work was considered beneficial for the child's development and a deterrent to idle mischief. If a child was orphaned or abandoned, society's response was to place him or her in a new work unit—either in a workhouse or as an indentured servant. A father's dictate could reach even beyond the grave: children could be "disposed of" in his will in exactly the same way as a horse or piece of furniture.

At the same time that a father enjoyed these prerogatives with regard to his children, the laws of most colonies imposed no countervailing duties on him. There was no legal obligation to provide for a child's material support or education.

Politicians are fond of citing the breakup of the "traditional" family as the reason for the plight of our children today and the ills of modern society in general. This notion is simplistic at best, and probably downright mistaken. First, the "traditional" family is difficult to define. Only in the 1890s did it become fashionable for women to stay at home and be supported, and only in the 1920s did a majority of American homes mirror the male breadwinner and female homemaker stereotype.

Moreover, although divorce was uncommon in America before the twentieth century, broken homes were by no means rare in the past. Death of a parent from conflict, accident, or disease was common in America's early days. In addition, it was far easier then for disaffected parents simply to disappear and start a new life in a distant territory without familial burdens. Many did just that. Furthermore, financial exigencies often meant that children under teen age were forced to leave their homes and make their way alone. The result was that a large percentage of early American children spent time growing up in stepfamilies or as indentured servants in other households.

Even in intact families, children were not the hub around which all familial endeavors rotated in the same way as is idealized today. Perhaps the ever-present risk that disease would snatch a child away prematurely kept parents emotionally remote until they could be sure that the child had escaped the usual invisible killers. Or perhaps the difficulty of eking a living from land that had never known the plow kept frontier parents too exhausted to dote on children. Yet, even in affluent families, parents frequently did not interact closely with their children, as servants were employed to care for them. Older children might be sent away to school, whence they might close their letters home with the formal—and distant—request that a father "give my regards to my mother, your wife."

It would be arrogant, however, for us in the closing years of the twentieth century to assume that parents in past centuries loved or treasured children any less than we do. Laws on caring for children were few, but there were strong moral imperatives from the community or the church for parents to treasure their progeny and provide for their material welfare and education. A stroll through any colonial-era graveyard dispels the notion that children were not loved: the poignant agony of families who lost youngsters two centuries ago is evident in the tiny weathered monuments with their carved cherubs and sad verses.

Before the twentieth century, no laws mandated that children were to attend school. Public schools were rare and operated only sporadically in some areas. Yet parents must have understood the importance of education. Anyone who reads letters sent home from soldiers in the Civil War will be amazed at the eloquence and proper locution of even the simplest tradesmen. Clearly, education was considered important.

In short, the American family has always been too diverse to submit to generalizations. Undoubtedly, practices we would today view as fearsome abuse and neglect of children were commonplace in America's early days. On the other hand, American society grew and thrived in those days in a way that experts opine could not have happened if most families had been "dysfunctional." Regardless of the true situation for any particular early American child, one fact can be stated with certainty: the idea that someone outside the family could interfere in the way parents dealt with their children was preposterous. And the idea that children had legal "rights" enforceable against their parents or the world in general would have been laughable. It should be remembered that, at the time, the notion of legal "rights" was rarefied and restricted. Until well into the nineteenth century, only white men who owned property had any real political rights. Rights for poor men, women, and people of color were much slower in coming.

1830–1900: THE CHILD SAVING MOVEMENT

The first decades of the 1800s brought great demographic changes to the young republic. Society became less rural, and the cities swelled with young people from outlying territories eager to find fortunes in the metropolis. Immigrants from other countries also arrived in the cities in large numbers. Many of them found jobs in the newly built factories, working many hours per day for little pay. The children of these immigrants, if they were not themselves employed in the factories, often were abandoned to the streets and were prey to all sorts of unsavory influences while their parents worked. Gangs of these idle children formed in some cities and were considered a threat to civilized society. In response, social activists and religious organizations created orphanages and "houses of refuge" where neglected children could be brought—ostensibly to rescue them from the squalor of their homes and the streets' evil influences. In 1838, a Pennsylvania mother voluntarily committed her daughter to one of these institutions, contending that the child was "incorrigible." When the child's father sued to have her released, the court refused, saying in effect that it had the power to override a parent's wishes in the best interest of the child. Because the house of refuge where the child was placed was supposed to "rehabilitate" its charges and not punish them, the court held that it was in the child's interest to remain there. This power to be a "super parent" and overrule a natural parent's wishes the court called *parens patriae* (Latin for "parent of the country"). It was a term that would become a familiar litany in later years. [*Ex parte Crouse* 4 Whart. 9 (Pa.1838)]

By the time the Civil War ended in 1865, the problem of homeless, orphaned, and neglected children in the cities increased dramatically. The impulse that had established the houses of refuge in Pennsylvania grew and became known as the "child saving" movement. It was the first children's rights movement and was focused on "saving" neglected children from immoral influences and dissolute lifestyles.

Initially, the child savers were individuals and private charities, including religious organizations. However, as the movement grew, public officials were called upon to lend their aid and imprimatur to the child savers' activities. In 1874, the first legal case involving a challenge by a third party on behalf of a child to remove the child from her home achieved notoriety. The child was a certain Mary Ellen Wilson, eight years old, who was chained, starved, and beaten by her adoptive parents. The plaintiff in the case was the founder of the Society for the Prevention of Cruelty to Animals, who successfully argued before the court that, as a member of the animal kingdom, the child was entitled to protection from cruel treatment. [*In re Custody of a Child Called Mary Ellen*, Copy Warrent 2RS572/65 (Abraham Lawrence, Justice, April 10, 1874]

The irony that an organization existed to prevent abuse to animals, but not to children, was not lost on the child saving movement. The reformers redoubled their efforts. The first children targeted for "saving" had been true orphans. Now, children living in any "unfit" conditions were likely to be removed from their families by child saving reformers. Unfortunately, zealots within the movement often defined "unfit" parents as anyone from the "wrong" ethnic group, religion, or socioeconomic stratum. Undoubtedly, some children from perfectly good homes were removed from their families. "Saved" children were placed in poorhouses or houses of refuge, where the conditions they lived in were arguably not much better than the ones they were accustomed to. Some of them were rounded up and put on trains headed to the West, where they were dumped in frontier towns with a small amount of money in their pockets or virtually "sold" to families there as indentured servants.

With all the attention focused by the child savers on the squalid lives of poor children in broken homes, the legislatures in many states acted in an effort to prevent the need for the child saving movement. The first laws requiring fathers to provide material support to their children were passed. Interestingly, the laws were mostly designed to save the public treasuries from having to support the poor youngsters, rather than for the benefit of the children themselves. Many of the laws were weakly enforced—the fathers themselves being destitute, or having flown the locale. Moreover, none of the laws required fathers to support illegitimate children.

In addition, the reform movement sold the public on the necessity for universal, obligatory education. The activists rightly saw education as the only route for poor children to lift themselves out of the perpetual cycle of poverty in which their families were mired. Public schools were established in all states, with mandatory attendance laws not far behind. The apparatus of the state now undertook to ensure that children attended school. By 1918, every state in the union had such laws.

A corollary to children's attendance at school was their absence from factory jobs. The reform movement called attention to the dismal conditions in the nation's factories, where young children toiled for up to twelve hours per day, six days per week, for miserable pay. Not only were the conditions dangerous and dehumanizing, but they robbed children of the chance to be educated. Several states passed laws outlawing child labor. However, unlike other goals of the child saving movement, this one ran directly up against the interests of powerful forces: business owners. States with child labor laws invariably watered them down with all sorts of exceptions that allowed factory owners to continue to exploit this source of cheap labor. It was not until federal legislation against child labor was finally approved by the Supreme Court in 1941 that child labor truly became a thing of the past in the United States.

The child saving movement also did not neglect children for whom "saving" had seemingly come too late: those accused of criminal acts. Up until this point, children who committed crimes were treated exactly the same way as adults. That is, they were tried, convicted, and punished in exactly the same courts and prisons as adult criminals. Most American courts applied some version of English common law, under which any child over the age of seven was held to the same standard of criminal responsibility as an adult. (Under the age of seven, it was presumed that a child could not form the necessary "intent" to commit a crime and was therefore not to be held responsible for it. However, this presumption could be rebutted by showing that the young child actually did understand the wrongful nature of his or her act and the likely consequences to come of it.) Not only were children housed in the same jails and prisons as hardened adult criminals, but there was no law preventing their execution for criminal acts committed while they were still below the age of majority.

The child saving reformers promoted the view that young criminals could be turned from the path of crime with special treatment. Processing them like adults abandoned them to the darker forces, resulting in their further abuse and corruption in adult jails. Rather, a strictly paternal, but benign, system should be instituted that would gently guide young miscreants to become law-abiding citizens. One mistake should not be the unmaking of a young person's life, said the reformers. In 1899, Illinois became the first state to create a juvenile justice system in which minors who committed crimes would be dealt with separately from adults, with rehabilitation rather than punishment as the goal. In exchange for any claims on constitutional due process rights, juveniles would be firmly, but leniently, guided by judges, social workers, and reform school administrators to see the error of their ways. News of their misdeeds would be hidden from the public, so that no stigma would follow them to undo their new lives of virtue. In the succeeding thirty years, all states adopted such systems. The fact that the actual success of the new systems fell far short of the ideal did not deter the nation's juvenile courts from dutifully gnashing the wheels of their "justice" together to process minor malfeasants, until the Supreme Court's decision in *In re Gault* in 1967 shed some light on how these courts really operated.

For all its shortcomings, the child saving movement marked a sea change in the nation's view of its youngest citizens. For the first time, children were the beneficiaries of legal attention: specifically, they were entitled to "custody," which included protection from abuse and the chance for betterment through education. Also for the first time, the status of the nation's children was a fit concern of the public—first through its benevolent private organizations, and then through government action. Nevertheless, children were not considered to possess rights in the same way as adults. Children were still viewed as property; however, now they were a shared commodity between the polity as a whole and their individual parents. The idea of children possessing rights and exercising them was still foreign—but stirrings could be heard. In 1891, a child attempted to sue his mother for placing him in a mental institution against his will. [*Hewllette v. Georgia* (1891)] The court dismissed the case, but not before inventing what became known as the family immunity doctrine: children were not permitted to sue their parents because this would destroy the "peace of society" and "family repose." Thus, although parents' rights were not limitless, the child was not the one to challenge a parent's authority. That was left to the state. Moreover, children were not in any position to challenge the state's newfound authority over them. For children, subjugated to their parents and now to the state, little had changed.

1900–1954: THE PROGRESSIVE ERA AND BEYOND

The era between 1900 and 1940 saw a refinement and exaltation of the idea that children's welfare is the business of society in general. In the 1800s, private charities had spearheaded the effort to improve children's welfare. When the new century dawned, government at all levels was poised to take over as the protector of children. The slogan of "parens patriae" could well be applied to the whole age. To underscore the government's new interest in the nation's youngest citizens, President Theodore Roosevelt called reformers together in 1909 to convene the first White House Conference on Children.

Swept up with reforming zeal, society looked askance at the relegation of poor children to workhouses because their families could not support them. States began to provide limited financial support for children living in single-parent families: more specifically, certain widows were now entitled to "mothers' pensions" from the state that would allow them to raise their children at home without having to enter the workforce and place their children in a poorhouse or have them "bound out" as indentured servants. Eligibility for these payments was very limited. First, only white women qualified to receive them. Minorities and women of color were excluded, as were women believed to have violated societal mores—such as by being divorced, having a child out of wedlock, or working outside the home. Women who applied for such assistance were obliged to open their homes for public officials to inspect. Women who failed to keep a tidy house or suffered from some other defect in "character" were likely to lose any chance at public assistance. In 1935, the U.S. Congress created the program known as Aid to Families with Dependent Children (AFDC). Basically, the AFDC was a federal version of "mothers' pensions." Like those state programs, it too was initially limited to white widows of "good character." It was many decades before the program opened itself to all on a color-blind basis and stopped imposing outdated views of moral behavior as a prerequisite to eligibility.

The early decades of the century also saw the universal adoption of compulsory school attendance laws and the institution of juvenile courts in all states. Lawsuits to establish paternity and, thus, to obligate fathers to pay for the support of their illegitimate offspring saw a sharp upswing. For the first time, women who found themselves in the unfortunate situation of bearing a child out of wedlock were less apt to hide themselves in shame and take on the entire burden of raising the child without calling the father to be accountable.

Perhaps the highest-profile effort on behalf of children to come from the federal government was in the area of labor reform. State laws dating from the 1800s that prohibited child labor had proved remarkably ineffective. Federal legislators took up the challenge. Their first two attempts ended in failure. Federal laws that banned the sale of goods made with child labor in interstate commerce and that imposed a federal tax on such goods were declared unconstitutional. In 1924, Congress adopted the Child Labor Amendment to the Constitution and sent it out for ratification by two-thirds of the states as required in the Constitution. Despite lip service to the idea, foot-dragging among the states left the amendment with only fourteen ratifications in as many years. Finally, in 1938 Congress passed the Fair Labor Standards Act, which banned child labor nationwide in businesses that affected interstate commerce. The law was upheld by the Supreme Court three years thereafter. So great had been the opposition by business interests to this effort on behalf of children, that probably only fear that low-paid children would take adult jobs during the Great Depression of the 1930s finally persuaded the Supreme Court to uphold the law.

The decade of the 1920s saw a number of developments that would have an impact on children's rights later in the century. General prosperity made it possible for the majority of American families to conform to the pattern of a male breadwinner supporting a wife and children. It also meant that families had more leisure time for self-reflection. Advances in hard science and technology also ushered in the dawn of social sciences. For the first time, "childhood" as such became the object of study by persons employing something like the scientific method. In Europe, the school of Sigmund Freud went so far as to develop a method of child rearing that, by allowing the child to exercise his or her will freely, was supposed to prevent "repression," which allegedly caused neuroses in adult life. (The disastrous, yet hilarious, consequences of experiments with this method are detailed in Laura Purdy's book *In Their Best Interest? The Case against Equal Rights for Children*, Ithaca, NY: Cornell University Press, 1992. She also discusses an earlier dalliance with the child-rearing advice of Jean-Jacques Rousseau in the eighteenth century. Rousseau's method: give boys complete freedom, restrict girls ruthlessly.)

Other influences of the decade included a heightened sense of patriotism after the end of World War I, with emphasis in the schools on the superiority of the American system of law, in which individual freedoms are preserved. The women's suffrage movement had just been victorious in winning the vote for females. It was inevitable that children, caught up in the spirit of the times, would want to assert their own rights. In 1923, a certain teenager by the name of Miss Pugsley defied an Arkansas school rule forbidding the use of cosmetics and "provocative" dressing and was expelled. She sued, alleging that the school had violated her "rights." In the court's opinion rejecting her claim, it is unclear which behavior the judges found more scandalous—Miss Pugsley's flamboyant dressing or her claim to have rights. The court ruled that school regulations need only be "reasonable" and not "arbitrary" in order to be legal. It was a standard that lasted for fifty years in American courts. [*Pugsley v. Sellmeyer* (1923)]

Meanwhile, a few rear-guard actions were being fought in the courts against the notion that government could dictate some requirements in how children would be raised. One of the first school cases to reach the Supreme Court, *Meyer v. Nebraska*, 1923, seemed to hand a victory to parents. In that case, the Court invalidated a law forbidding the teaching of foreign languages in the public schools because it interfered with parents' rights to determine what their children would learn, among other reasons. On the surface, this seemed to reinforce parental rights. However, the Court also stated offhandedly that the state had power to interfere with parents' rights if the interference was reasonably related "to some purpose within the competency of the State to effect." Thus, while handing parents a victory with one hand, the Court also reserved the right to government to determine how far the freedom to rear children would extend. It was a familiar tactic of the Court already for a century: grant authority, and by so granting make it clear that it is within the power of the Court to grant, with the hidden corollary that the Court may also someday refuse to grant. The Court did not mention the *children's* rights to learn foreign languages at all in the *Meyer* case. After all, everyone knew that children had no rights.

Two years later, in *Pierce v. Society of Sisters*, the Supreme Court again seemed to hand a victory to parents when it decided that a state could not require children to attend public schools. The law was invalid, said the Court, because it impinged on the rights of parents to direct their children's upbringing. However, the Court again obliquely asserted states could prescribe some sort of compulsory education—they just could not insist that it be a public education. And, again, children's interests as such were not mentioned.

Activity in the area of children's legal issues virtually ceased during the period of the Great Depression in the 1930s. All evidence indicates that the lot of children grew worse during this time, with parents abandoning their families or taking out their frustrations in the form of physical abuse of family members. Yet, despite the preoccupation of the nation with World War II in the 1940s, several important Supreme Court decisions were made in the area of children's rights.

In 1941, in the case of *United States v. Darby*, the Supreme Court finally upheld the constitutionality of the Fair Labor Standards Act, which prohibited children under the age of sixteen from working in jobs that affected interstate commerce.

Three years later, in 1944, the Court heard a challenge to a state's labor laws forbidding children from selling wares in a public place. Finally relying on its carefully constructed authority to declare a state's interest paramount in child-rearing issues, which it had obliquely asserted two decades earlier in such cases as *Meyer* and *Pierce,* the Supreme Court declared the statute constitutional. A mother who had enlisted her minor daughter to help her sell religious tracts on public streets was found in violation of the law. The *Prince v. Massachusetts* ruling is remarkable in several respects. First, the Supreme Court explicitly recognized the parens patriae doctrine, initially espoused by a court in 1838 and used by many lower courts since that time to justify decisions favoring government intervention in child-rearing matters. Second, and most interestingly, for the first time the nation's highest court actually considered the wishes of a child. The Court noted that the child in the *Prince* case felt it was her duty to distribute the literature, and it stated in passing that the child was exercising her "right" to religious expression. Nevertheless, the child was not a party in the case, so this curious statement by the Court had no effect on creating or recognizing the independent rights of children to religious freedom.

Also in 1944, the Supreme Court *did* come within a hairbreadth of recognizing that children have a constitutional right to religious expression. In *West Virginia Board of Education v. Barnette,* the Court struck down a law requiring that students in the public schools recite the familiar "Pledge of Allegiance" to the flag. The case arose over the refusal of several Seventh-Day Adventist children to take part in the pledge because it contradicted their religious beliefs. Pursuant to the law, they were expelled, and their parents were then prosecuted for failure to send their children to school. In declaring that no law could compel one to "speak what was not in his mind," the Court seemed to be addressing the children's situation. However, because the children's interests were identical to those of their parents, and the actual parties were the parents with their children, it could not be said that this case truly recognized an autonomous right to freedom of expression on the part of children. That recognition would have to wait another twenty-five years.

After 1945, marriage rates began to increase in the United States, but so did the number of divorces. By 1946, divorce rates were double what they were in 1941. Countless theories for this development were advanced. Mostly, the blame was laid on women: working women, mothers-in-law, and, above all, mothers themselves. In 1946, psychiatrist Edward Strecker advanced the theory that too much "mothering" by the nation's females was emasculating the nation's young men. Strecker's book *Their Mothers' Sons* (1946) was just the first in an explosion of "how-to" books on raising children that appeared in the next decades. The nation's obsession with its children had begun. In the 1950s, Dr. Benjamin Spock published his first books on child care that soon became the manuals for a whole generation of parents in bringing up their children.

As the 1950s dawned, the "baby boom" was in full swing. The paraphernalia of childhood was everywhere. Yet children remained without rights as we know them. It was a time of prosperity. Historians tell us that record numbers of babies were born. Interestingly, the teenage birthrate was almost double in 1957 what it is today, but most young men could afford to marry, so that illegitimate children living in poverty were not the problem then that they have become today.

1954–1980: EXPANSIONIST ERA

In 1954, the U.S. Supreme Court handed down a monumental decision in *Brown v. Board of Education*. That case held that "separate but equal" school facilities for whites and blacks violated the guarantee of equal protection of the laws in the Constitution. Strictly speaking, *Brown* was more a "civil rights" case than a "children's rights" case, and it is in that context that it is most remembered. However, because the plaintiffs were schoolchildren, the holding was a tacit admission that children had constitutional rights: the right to equal treatment under the law with other children.

The *Brown* decision thus inaugurated a new area in the field of "protective" rights for children—namely, that children were entitled to some protections that rose to the level of federal constitutional guarantees. Before this time, protective rights for children were invented by legislatures, such as the laws requiring school attendance or forbidding child labor. If such laws did not violate the Constitution, they were allowed to stand, but they were permissive in nature. In other words, the Constitution did not demand that children be given the protection that these laws afforded. Now, in *Brown*, for the first time, the Court declared that children had a constitutional right to an "equal" education, and that "equal" required the right to an "integrated" education. (In later decisions, however, the Court would find that the right to an "equal" education did not include equal funding of schools in different districts.)

Following *Brown*, the Supreme Court was very active in finding other "protective" rights for children that are embodied in the Constitution. Two areas of the law in particular were singled out by the Court for recognizing such rights. The first involved the status of illegitimate children. Having decided in *Brown* that children were at least entitled to some equal treatment with other similarly situated children without regard to race, the Court examined whether "birth status" should be a valid criterion for discrimination. In decision after decision, the high Court found that it was unfair to punish illegitimate children for the circumstances surrounding their births by denying them the same benefits received by their legitimate peers. Thus, the Court struck down laws that prevented illegitimate children from claiming material support from their fathers, from inheriting from their fathers, or from receiving the proceeds of life insurance policies, pensions, or welfare payments. Perhaps most importantly, the Court invalidated state laws that set unrealistically short limitations periods for children to bring a lawsuit to determine paternity. The result is that today virtually all legal distinctions between legitimate and illegitimate children have been removed. Such children are entitled to exactly the same level of support from both their parents. Moreover, illegitimate children can sue to have the identities of their fathers established at any time, even after the deaths of the fathers.

The other area of "protective" constitutional rights that occupied the Supreme Court following the *Brown* decision involved the procedural rights of juveniles within the juvenile justice system. The juvenile courts of the states had been creaking along for sixty years as the decade of the 1960s dawned. Intended to provide special protection to children by segregating them from adult criminals, ushering them under the benevolent guidance of special judges and child welfare personnel, and concentrating on their rehabilitation rather than punishment, the juvenile courts were actually hiding woeful inadequacies and abuse. The reality was that decisions in juvenile court were often arbitrary and perfunctory, and resulted in years of incarceration for children without the right to appeal.

We can only imagine that the experience of one Gerald Gault, age fifteen, when he was subjected to the tender mercies of juvenile court in Arizona was more typical of juvenile court justice than it was aberrational. Gault was arrested for allegedly making obscene remarks on the telephone to a neighbor. He was taken into custody one afternoon while his parents were at work and subjected to police interrogation without any notice of the charges against him and without being informed of his right to remain silent or to consult a lawyer or his parents. The boy confessed to making the lewd remarks. Gault's parents were not informed that he had been arrested and only found out that their son was at a juvenile detention center that evening when they were told by another boy's mother. At the detention center, they were informed only that a hearing in Gault's case would be held the next day before a juvenile court judge.

At that hearing, held in the judge's chambers, the only evidence presented was the arresting officer's statement that Gault was a "delinquent," who needed the court's "protection." The woman who made the complaint was not there and neither was Gault's father. Six days later at another hearing, matters were little improved. Gault's father was in attendance, as well as both officers who had arrested him and investigated the complaint against him. However, the complaining witness was still not present. Moreover, no one was compelled to swear to their testimony, no formal opportunity was presented to cross-examine the officers, Gault's parents were not informed that they had the right to hire a lawyer for their son's defense or be provided a lawyer if they could not afford one, and no record of the proceedings was made. Following the hearing, the judge ordered Gault to be committed as a juvenile delinquent to a detention center until he was twenty-one years old—a period of six long years. The judge provided no written reasons for his decision, and no appeal was permitted under Arizona law.

Gault's case reached the Supreme Court in 1967. The high Court declared for the first time that juveniles must be given due process of law in juvenile court. Although the procedures need not conform exactly to what is required in adult court, this due process must at least include adequate notice of the charges to both the juvenile and his or her parents, notice that the juvenile has a right to remain silent and a right to representation by a lawyer, a hearing in which evidence is presented, the opportunity to call witnesses and to cross-examine hostile witnesses, a record of the proceedings, a reasoned opinion, and the right to appeal the judge's decision. It cannot be overstated to what degree this ruling was an about-face for the juvenile justice system. Prior to *Gault*, juvenile courts actively discouraged reliance on strict procedures and the participation of attorneys, believing that such things detracted from the flexibility and "nonadversarial" atmosphere required by the supposedly benevolent authorities in charge to do their jobs.

In the years following the *Gault* decision, the Supreme Court expanded children's due process rights even further. Today, federal law requires that virtually all the rights afforded to adult criminal defendants must be offered to children as well, including the requirement that conviction be based on proof beyond a reasonable doubt. The main exceptions are that children still do not have the right to be free pending trial, the right to a public trial (in the belief that confidentiality is still important so that a delinquent youth will not be unfairly stigmatized as he or she attempts to reform), or the right to a trial by jury. It should be noted, however, that many state laws not only offer these particular rights to accused children but also provide greatly expanded opportunities for children in the juvenile court and welfare systems to be represented separately from their parents' interests by a guardian ad litem—a lawyer appointed just for them.

Nevertheless, critics of the juvenile court system note that, despite these advances, juvenile courts' efforts to rehabilitate juveniles before they are irretrievably ruined are still woefully ineffective. In many cases, juvenile offenders are still merely warehoused in reformatories, halfway houses, and institutions, instead of receiving the careful attention they require. In addition, a new punitive attitude among a populace fed up with stories of teenage atrocities is demanding a greater emphasis on the punishment, rather than the rehabilitation, of juveniles. Juvenile sentences are in some cases more onerous than those imposed on adults for the same criminal acts.

The exposure of the inadequacies of the juvenile justice system almost inevitably had the effect of turning attention to another massive institution for children, which many of them doubtless would liken to prison: the public school. Because children are required to attend school and education has been recognized as an extremely important interest, challenges to school discipline also made their way to the Supreme Court in the years following 1954. In *Goss v. Lopez*, 1975, the Court determined that students must be given some sort of due process, including a chance to state their case and counter evidence against them, before they may be expelled or suspended from school. On the other hand, the Court also ruled that corporal punishment (spanking) in the schools does not in itself violate the Constitution, and that other laws would serve to check excessive force used by school personnel to discipline students. In addition, the right to be free from unreasonable searches and seizures in the public schools applies to juveniles. However, according to the Court, such searches may be conducted when "reasonable" cause for suspicion exists, rather than the higher standard of "probable" cause. Moreover, notice to students in advance that some areas of school property may be searched (such as lockers) or that consent to drug testing is required as a prerequisite to participating in some school-sponsored programs negates any expectation of privacy that students might otherwise have in those areas.

The Supreme Court was not the only institution occupied with expanding the protective rights afforded to children in the decades following 1954. State legislatures and state courts were also actively considering children's issues. Liberalized divorce laws have led to an upsurge in "broken homes" during the last fifty years. Initially, mothers were invariably given custody of minor children, pursuant to either law or custom. The arrangement almost always led to a lowered standard of living for the children, as women still were not on par with men in earning power, and many fathers reneged on their full obligations for financial support. Moreover, fathers who wished to escape their responsibility had only to move out of state (enforcement of support orders were greatly complicated across state lines). In the past thirty years, federal and state laws have vastly simplified support enforcement procedures across state lines, and now a nationwide system of parent locator services makes it very difficult to evade enforcement efforts by disappearing. At the same time, many more fathers are winning custody of their children, as it is generally regarded that a legal preference for giving custody only to mothers is impermissible gender discrimination.

As the twentieth century comes to a close, a large percentage of the nation's children will spend time in single-parent homes or with at least one stepparent. Custody and visitation issues in these families have spawned an industry in both the public and private sectors of lawyers, counselors, and case workers who help oversee court-ordered living arrangements for these children. Also increasing is the number of children entirely without homes, due to either abandonment or action by child welfare agencies to terminate parental rights. Abuses in the use of foster homes that often were merely successive warehouses for problem children are being corrected, and adoption laws liberalized.

In 1961, a study published by C. Henry Kempe et al. entitled *The Battered Child Syndrome* shed light on another problem that had been quietly swept under the national rug for generations: child abuse by parents and relatives. First in a trickle, then in a flood, state authorities began investigating and prosecuting cases of abuse. State legislatures passed laws greatly expanding the investigative powers of child welfare agencies and requiring mandatory reporting of suspected cases of child abuse. The authority of the state to intervene to remove endangered children from their homes and place them in foster care was also increased. Laws were passed that relaxed the rules with regard to children's testimony in court. Children were allowed to testify out of the presence of the defendant in some cases or by videotaped deposition in others. Undoubtedly, this development helped convict numerous bona fide child abusers. Unfortunately, it also led to prosecutorial abuses in some cases. Children were manipulated and coaxed into testifying to having been subjected to acts that did not occur and were then shielded from cross-examination. The methods used by the children's interrogators were not adequately investigated for bias or leading questioning. Some defendants were falsely convicted, their children removed from their homes, their liberty revoked, and their lives and reputations ruined.

On the other hand, many cases of true child abuse were overlooked by overworked or inattentive child welfare officials. To what extent do children have a *constitutional* right to protection from abuse by their relatives? This was the issue considered by the Supreme Court in *DeShaney v. Winnebago County Department of Social Services* (1989). Four-year-old Joshua DeShaney was severely beaten and permanently disabled by his father, even though a state welfare agency had been alerted to the danger. Despite continued warnings by concerned adults and welfare workers themselves, the agency did nothing to protect DeShaney until it was too late. He and his mother sued the state, contending that his constitutional right to equal protection had been violated. The Supreme Court disagreed. Children's right to protection by the state did not extend so far, said the Court. DeShaney might seek compensation from state officials under other laws, but not the Constitution. The expansionist period in children's protective rights was not to go on forever.

From the sheer number of laws and resources devoted to the protection and care of American children in the last decades of the twentieth century, it is hard to avoid the conclusion that children's welfare has dramatically increased in a society that is perpetually obsessing over its young. In truth, progress is difficult to assess. In terms of material comfort, things have probably improved for most American children. In the ways that matter to a life of quality and reflection, the verdict is out. Children are no longer slaving in factories for ten or twelve hours a day, but there is evidence that some of them are voluntarily working too many hours to give much attention to education or play. Children are also voluntarily entering associations that entangle them in adult concerns, such as having sexual relations and becoming parents themselves. It is difficult to legislate protective laws to prevent this type of behavior. Teenagers who wish to circumvent such proscriptions will always find a way to do so. Thus, for all our masses of legal regulations designed to protect children, it is unclear whether the welfare of children has really improved.

RIGHT TO AUTONOMY

Well into the 1960s, the only "rights" any courts or legislatures had recognized for children were the so-called protective rights: the entitlement to material support, education, and freedom from abuse. In 1969, a most astonishing development took place. The U.S. Supreme Court for the very first time explicitly recognized that persons under the age of majority have some rights to make autonomous decisions in their lives. The case was *Tinker v. Des Moines Independent School District.*

To understand why, at this moment and no other, this remarkable step was taken, it is instructive to reexamine the tenor of the decade. In the 1960s, children born in the "baby boom" era were just beginning to enter teen age—the time when self-awareness expands to awareness of a wider world. Because of the huge bulge the baby boomers made in the population and the natural sense of self-importance of adolescents, it was inevitable that juveniles would become the focus of attention of the nation in a way they never had before. The general prosperity of the 1950s continued into the next decade, freeing children from distracting concerns about their families' financial health and putting a television into virtually every home in America. The influence of television as a means for fostering and disseminating a "youth culture" cannot be overstated. Not only were teenagers a huge percent of the population, but now they were made aware of that fact through the unifying power of the broadcast image. In addition to spreading the signature music, dress, and attitude that youth was to adopt, television also brought grim images into the home. The flickering grainy footage of civil rights marchers being beaten in the South and the first strange and disturbing scenes from rice paddies half a world away in Vietnam made their way into each American home. Adolescents felt a swelling sense of power and sophistication. They brought their ideas to school. To these coddled sons and daughters of a prosperous age, there was no doubt in their minds that what their parents had told them was true: they were special, and one could not be special without rights.

The facts in the *Tinker* case were simple. Several high school students were suspended from school for wearing black armbands to protest American involvement in the Vietnam War. Through their parents, these students sued in federal court claiming that their First Amendment rights to freedom of speech had been abridged. Astonishingly, the U.S. Supreme Court agreed. One must keep in mind that up to this point no High Court decision had recognized that children had any First Amendment rights at all. Now the Court declared that students are "persons" under the Constitution. They had the right to freedom of expression in the public schools, subject to restriction only if their expression "materially interferes" with the educational purpose of the schools. In *Tinker*, the Court decided that the school rule banning armbands was merely an attempt to avoid discussion of a controversial subject, rather than a necessary precaution to avoid undue disruption of the educational process.

Some commentators have dismissed the significance of *Tinker* by noting that the students' political views were the same as those of their parents (since the parents were the ones who brought suit on their children's behalf), questioning whether the Court's decision would have been the same if the students' opinions diverged from their parents'. However, no inquiry into the political beliefs of the students' parents was made by the Court, and the Court's decision did not spell out any qualifications on the students' right to express themselves that were dependent on agreeing with their parents. *Tinker* was truly as revolutionary as it seemed to be: children are constitutional persons with some control over their own destinies.

In the years following *Tinker*, the Supreme Court has revisited the issue of student speech on numerous occasions. Decisions since 1969 have spelled out the limitations on expression by students in school: schools may ban obscene, indecent, or "age inappropriate" expressions, especially in school-sponsored publications or events. Schools also have discretion to choose courses for the official curriculum and reading material for inclusion in school libraries. However, schools may not remove materials from school libraries that are already in the collection. The latter infringes on students' constitutional right to hear. Students also have a right to express themselves through symbolic speech, such as the black armbands, and to express their individuality through hairstyles and dress, subject only to restrictions necessary to prevent "material disruption" of the educational process or to promote health and safety.

One of the biggest issues in the last decades of the twentieth century is the extent to which schools may ban religious expressions by students. Since the 1962 decision of the Supreme Court in *Engel v. Vitale*, school-sponsored prayer is forbidden because it constitutes a government "establishment" of religion that is banned by the First Amendment. However, federal law now mandates that entirely student-initiated religious expression that takes place during breaks or off school hours must be tolerated to the same extent as expressions or activities revolving around other issues.

Having recognized children as beings with some autonomous constitutional rights, the Supreme Court inevitably assured that it would be required to define the rights of juveniles whenever any new rights for adults were recognized. The Court's 1972 decision recognizing a woman's right to an abortion in the first trimester of pregnancy was one such example. Did the right extend to minors? In 1976, the Court answered this question in the affirmative. *[Planned Parenthood v. Danforth]* Girls under the age of majority do have a right to privacy that includes the right to make certain decisions involving reproduction. In addition to the decision to end a pregnancy, minor females have the right to receive contraceptive devices and advice, said the high Court in 1977. *[Carey v. Population Services International]*

In succeeding years, the Supreme Court has further delineated the limits of the right for girls to have an abortion by passing on the constitutionality of numerous state statutes that attempt to restrict the right. Presently, the Court has approved laws that require a pregnant minor to obtain a parent's or judge's consent for the abortion.

Following the lead of the Supreme Court, many states have also recognized juveniles' rights to make some independent decisions in their lives. These policies are reflected in laws that allow some children the right to consent to medical treatment (or to refuse medical treatment) and to petition to become emancipated from their parents. States also routinely consider the wishes of children in custody disputes between their divorced parents. In addition, many states have abolished the "family immunity doctrine" that prevented children from suing their parents for injuries caused to them by their parents. The traditional justification for the doctrine—that lawsuits between family members would stir up familial disharmony—seemed ludicrous as a child's desire to sue his or her parents already indicates an extreme degree of disharmony in the family.

The actions of the Supreme Court in expanding protective rights for children and recognizing some constitutional rights to autonomous decision making have seemed inconsistent to some. For example, the Court's insistence that government could protect children from exposure to material that is merely "indecent" (but not obscene) *[Ginsberg v. New York, Bethel School District No. 103 v. Fraser]* yet its failure to make the government responsible to protect children from abuse by their parents—especially when the state has already been warned of the danger *[DeShaney v. Winnebago County Social Services]*—is somewhat paradoxical. Likewise, the Supreme Court has held it proper to protect children from their own immature decisions by upholding parental or judicial notice requirements for juveniles seeking an abortion *[Bellotti v. Baird]* yet at the same time has allowed states to impose the death penalty on persons who committed capital crimes while still under the age of majority. [*Stanford v. Kentucky* (1989)]

Other observers are critical of the recognition of any rights to autonomous decision making by children, claiming that children do not have the maturity to make important choices that will affect their lives and that leaving them to their own devices could mean irreparable harm for them later. Fears such as these should be allayed. What most of the movement for autonomous rights of minors is about is merely the extension of a very ancient principle of fairness embodied in American law: persons should not be grouped into categories for separate rights and privileges based on some arbitrary or immutable characteristic, such as race, gender, or age, without allowing each individual so classified to prove that the restrictions imposed by law should not apply to him or her. In most important decisions, children are subject to judicial investigation before they are permitted to exercise their rights. For example, many states impose consent requirements on juvenile abortions, require a doctor to make a reasoned evaluation of the maturity of a minor before allowing him or her to consent to medical treatment, or require a court hearing to declare a child emancipated.

Moreover, minors are unlikely to claim rights unless they are mature enough (or at least as mature as some adults) to use them. It would not occur to most seven-year-olds to assert a right to live independently. However, some sixteen-year-olds can clearly handle the challenge and should be permitted to try.

One of the most remarkable developments in the course of legal rights for children in the twentieth century is often overlooked. Yet, it perfectly illustrates how being able to comprehend that one should have a right to something usually is evidence in itself that one is mature enough to exercise that right. In 1971, the Twenty-Sixth Amendment to the U.S. Constitution was ratified. This amendment gave the right to vote in federal elections to persons over the age of eighteen. Formerly, one had to be twenty-one years of age to vote. The change came in response to the overwhelmingly powerful argument that a person who was old enough to be sent to die for his country in Vietnam should certainly have a say in the making of a national policy that could result in his death. The change in the federal voting age from twenty-one to eighteen spurred most states to change the age at which they recognized a person to be an adult from twenty-one to eighteen also. In this most remarkable development of all, the children of the twentieth century rolled back by three years the age at which adulthood begins. Yet, the world has not come to an end.

As the start of a new millennium looms, it is anyone's guess what the nation's children will come up with next. And the law will be there to respond.

ABANDONMENT A parent's intentional absence from the life of his or her child without good cause. A form of **child abuse**, abandonment is grounds for termination of **parental rights** in all states.

Like many legal concepts, the definition of "abandonment" is rather vague and flexible. Traditionally, a finding of abandonment required evidence not only that the parent was physically absent from the child's life on a prolonged or repeated basis but also that the parent specifically desired to give up his or her rights to the child. In recent years, the focus of family courts has been more on the effect of the parent's behavior on the child than on the parent's intent. Complete desertion of the child is not required for a finding of abandonment. Under the old approach, even very minimal contacts with a child or simple assertions of a desire to maintain parental rights were enough to prevent a finding of abandonment. Under the more modern view, minimal or very sporadic contacts and stated intentions to be a good parent may not be enough to prevent a finding of abandonment.

With increasing frequency, absent parents who maintain some contact with their child may have parental rights terminated if there is no good reason for the absence; if they fail to provide meaningful financial support for their child's care, though able to do so; and if they exhibit profound indifference to the child's welfare. Some courts find abandonment when a parent, though physically present in the child's life, has physically abused him or her. [See **child abuse; physical abuse**.] Neglect of a child's basic needs may also constitute abandonment. One court even found that a mother's "studied indifference" to the welfare of her child constituted abandonment even though the mother was physically present. Thus, in at least one jurisdiction, the withholding of expressions of love and affection from the child is sufficient in itself to be considered abandonment.

The specific facts of each case are crucial when courts make a ruling on abandonment. No set fact pattern will trigger a finding of abandonment. However, a few factors may be cited as very indicative that abandonment has occurred:

1. The parent makes statements indicating a desire to give up parental rights and responsibilities, coupled with corresponding behavior.

2. The parent leaves the child with others for prolonged periods of time, even though there is no pressing reason to do so. Prolonged periods may be measured in months or even years.

3. The parent fails to communicate meaningfully with a child who is living with others. A few phone calls or cards sent over a prolonged period (usually six months, sometimes longer) is generally not viewed as sufficient to maintain "meaningful" communication with a child. Even sporadic visits are generally not enough.

4. The parent fails to contribute financially to the maintenance of the child, although able to do so. This factor alone is rarely sufficient to establish abandonment, but coupled with other signs it is important evidence that abandonment has occurred.

5. The parent fails to take steps to reclaim a child living with others. This includes refusing to take recommended steps toward becoming a fit parent that have been ordered by a child welfare agency.

Many states will allow a truant parent to "revoke" abandonment and prevent termination of parental rights even up to the very moment a decision is reached in a termination hearing. However, the evidence that the parent has really decided to take responsibility for the child's welfare must be compelling. Self-serving statements are not enough. The parent must show that changes for the better have already taken place in his or her life, such as finding and holding a job or staying away from alcohol or drugs.

Can a parent abandon a child before it is born? Some states hold that a father who manifests the same indifferent behavior that constitutes abandonment toward the pregnant mother will be found to have abandoned the child when it is born. An unwed father who does not voluntarily take steps to acknowledge his paternity after his child is born may also be found to have abandoned the child and have his parental rights terminated.

ABILITY GROUPING From their earliest kindergarten experiences to high school graduation, children in the United States are subject to ability grouping, or placement in educational groups depending on their perceived intelligence or ability. The basis for such placement might be test scores, grades, or merely a teacher's "feeling" about the suitability of a child for a particular group. The group a child is placed in may have great implications for his or her future: for example, by influencing whether he or she will go on to higher education. This, in turn, may profoundly affect his or her socioeconomic status as an adult.

Oddly, there have been few legal challenges to the practice of grouping children according to ability. However, a number of lawsuits have raised objections to particular methods used for grouping children. For example, tracking programs, instituted to steer children with perceived abilities or lack of abilities into separate educational programs, have been invalidated when they appeared to be motivated by an intent to discriminate against black or minority children by placing them perfunctorily in less academically challenging programs. Other successful objections to tracking systems include allegations that the educational opportunities offered in lower groups were lacking, that there were no provisions made for "graduating" children out of lower-track placements, and that the use of standard "IQ" tests for placement purposes is unfair because of inherent cultural bias in the tests.

On the other hand, a challenge to the formation of a special "talented" high school program on **equal protection** grounds was dismissed by a federal court in California. The plaintiffs alleged that the program was discriminatory because its use of past academic achievement as the criterion for admission had a disproportionate tendency to exclude minority and low-income students. The court noted that neither getting into nor being excluded from the special program stigmatized students in the same way as did being placed in a "low achievement" group.

ABORTION RIGHTS   Always emotionally charged, the issue of abortion is especially controversial when the female involved is a minor. Not only are the usual insoluble religious issues in play, but the future of an inexperienced young girl hangs in the balance. Beginning with the decision in *Planned Parenthood of Central Missouri v. Danforth* in 1976, the Supreme Court has been very active in defining the rights a pregnant minor female has to decide for herself whether to abort a child. In *Danforth*, the Court struck down a state statute that gave parents absolute authority to veto their minor daughter's wish to have an abortion. However, because minors' inexperience might lead them to make unwise decisions in this important area (as indeed has already happened when any minor female is pregnant), a young girl's right to have an abortion may be made subject to more restrictions than an adult's.

A state may require a minor female to obtain the consent of, or at least notify, one of her parents before having an abortion. Laws requiring the consent of, or notice to, both parents risk invalidation on constitutional grounds because they do not take into account the reality of broken families in which one parent lives at a distance or has disappeared altogether. The law may designate the custodial parent as the one from whom consent is required, or to whom notice is given.

If a state imposes either a parental consent or notice requirement, it must also provide a way for a pregnant minor to bypass her parents entirely and obtain consent for an abortion from a neutral third party, usually a judge. The reason for the bypass option is a recognition that some parents may react explosively or in a way detrimental to their daughter's physical or emotional health if they are informed that she is pregnant and wants an abortion. A minor in such a situation must have the opportunity to obtain consent from a court instead. Moreover, the court procedure must be confidential and anonymous. This means that the proceedings are kept secret and the name of the child is not revealed to anyone.

Access to the court procedure must be quick. Unreasonable delays that would jeopardize the minor's ability to make a decision within a reasonable period during the pregnancy are not allowed. But, a state is not required to furnish a minor female with free legal representation by an attorney at an abortion hearing.

Generally, a court or other neutral third party to whom a pregnant minor turns for consent to an abortion must determine whether the girl demonstrates sufficient maturity to make the decision to end her pregnancy herself with the advice of her doctor. To this end, the court may examine evidence of the girl's ability to make independent judgments in other areas. Her work experience, grades in school, ability to handle personal finances, participation in extracurricular activities, and experience living away from home are all relevant. In addition, the court will require evidence of the child's realistic understanding and appreciation of the medical procedures involved, her options upon deciding either to have her baby or to end her pregnancy, and the gravity of the situation in which she finds herself. The fact that the minor has good relationships with other adults, including her doctor, in whom she may confide is also important. Usually, the court will not require the girl to show good cause why she cannot seek the advice of her parents on the matter.

If the court determines that a minor female seeking an abortion without notice to her parents is mature enough to make the decision herself, the girl must be allowed to do so. The Supreme Court has held that states may impose a waiting period on minor females before the abortion procedure takes place in order to encourage the child to seek adult advice on the matter. However, the waiting period cannot be so long as to effectively prevent the girl from acting on her decision. A waiting period of forty-eight hours has been held reasonable, while one lasting twenty-two days has been struck down as unconstitutional. A state may not require that a minor's abortion be performed in a hospital licensed for general surgery, nor may it require that a parent or guardian accompany the child when she goes to the clinic performing the abortion.

If the reviewing court decides that the girl is not mature enough to make her own decision regarding whether to terminate a pregnancy, the minor has two options. She may then seek the permission of her parents for the procedure, or, in some states, she may ask the court to determine whether the abortion is in her own best interests. Despite the fact that the child has been determined to be too immature to decide for herself to have an abortion, the court may yet decide that it is in her best interests to do so.

Assuming that a mature minor decides to go ahead with an abortion after obtaining her parents' or a court's permission, the girl's rights will still be subject to any valid restrictions that state law may make on an adult female's right to an abortion. As is well known, the case of *Roe v. Wade* (1973) established the right of women to terminate a pregnancy without undue intrusion by the state. Under *Roe*, a woman's decision to have an abortion is a private affair between her, her doctor, and any one she trusts to advise her during the first trimester of pregnancy. After that point, the state may pass laws restricting the woman's access to an abortion. In the second trimester, a state may forbid abortions except in cases of rape, incest, or danger to the mother. In the last trimester of pregnancy, the state's interest in preserving the life of a viable fetus may outweigh the woman's right to choose to end the pregnancy. During the last three months of a woman's pregnancy, therefore, the state may forbid an abortion. A minor female is subject to all these restrictions as well as to any special restrictions resulting from her underage status.

ACKNOWLEDGMENT STATUTE   A law setting forth a procedure by which a man may formally acknowledge that he is the biological father of a child born out of wedlock. Procedures for this acknowledgment vary. In some states, the law will view a child as the "acknowledged" biological son or daughter of a man who continuously states that he is the father and demonstrates this by building a close relationship with the child. In other states, a written document is required that includes the man's signature and a notarization. The effect of acknowledgment is generally to legitimize an illegitimate child. [See **illegitimacy.**] An acknowledged child will have the right to inherit from the man who claims to be his or her father, unless a **paternity action** proves that the man is not the biological father. Similarly, a man who acknowledges a child as his own will have a duty to support that child.

ADJUDICATION   The phase of a **delinquency proceeding** that roughly corresponds to the "trial" in adult criminal court. Since the 1967 ruling in *In re Gault,* the rights enjoyed by juveniles who are tried in **juvenile court** for acts that would be crimes if committed by an adult have steadily increased. Today, juveniles must be afforded representation by a licensed attorney, must have the right to confront and cross-examine witnesses against them, and must have the right to call and examine witnesses in their favor. They may not be judged guilty except upon proof beyond a reasonable doubt. Despite this progress, there are still some constitutional rights afforded adult criminal defendants that are not available to youths during adjudication. Foremost among them is the right to a **jury trial**. Juveniles also have no constitutional right to a **public trial,** although a strong argument may be raised that this is an advantage because they are not stigmatized by their youthful mistakes. Approaching the close of the twentieth century, approximately eleven states have chosen to go beyond the requirements of the Constitution and offer all accused juveniles the right to trial by jury. A few states limit this right to habitual offenders, or give the juvenile judge the discretion to order a jury trial. Seven states grant juveniles the right to a public trial. Only two states, Alaska and Wisconsin, offer both a jury trial and a public trial to juveniles. See also **burden of proof; counsel rights.**

ADOPTION   A procedure that creates the legal relationship of parent and child between two people who are not biologically so related. The relationship between the parties to a finalized adoption is virtually the same, legally speaking, as if the adopted child had been born to the **adoptive parents.** Thus, the adopted child and the adoptive parents have the same rights and duties with respect to each other as they would have had if the relationship had been biological. At the same time, the parental rights and duties of the adopted child's **biological parents** usually are terminated. However, if the adoptive parent is the spouse of a biological parent, that biological parent will continue to have all the rights and duties of parenthood with respect to the child that he or she had before the adoption.

Adoption was not recognized by the English common law, from which the common law of the United States is derived. Therefore, the institution of adoption has had to be created by statute in all fifty states. Because it is entirely statutory, adoption rules differ from state to state. However, some general requirements and procedures are common to all jurisdictions: All states require the written consent of the parties to the proposed adoption before it may proceed. This includes the child's biological parents, the proposed adoptive parents, and the child, if the child is of a certain minimum age. See **adoptive consent.** In addition, in all states an adoption hearing must take place before a judge, and a court decree is necessary to establish that an adoption is valid.

Children eligible for adoption may be found through an adoption agency. Alternatively, one wishing to adopt may know biological parents who will agree to let him or her adopt their child, often even before the child is born. This is known as a private adoption. Agency adoption has the advantage that the legal availability of the child is usually assured, the child's background and health have been screened, a better match between the child's characteristics and those of the prospective parents can be made, and the identities of the adoptive and biological parents are strictly guarded from each other. Thus, adoptions through an agency run less risk of legal impediments, such as the biological parents' revocation of adoptive consent. Moreover, if impediments do arise, or if the child has some undisclosed handicap, the adoptive parents may be able to sue the adoption agency for negligence or fraud. These safeguards are not available in the case of private adoptions.

On the other hand, parents adopting through private connections may obviate the long waiting periods for a child that are typical with agency-assisted adoptions. In addition, the child is likely to be younger and, hence, able to adapt more easily to his or her new parents. A private adoption is generally the only route for parents seeking to have a child through a surrogate means. [See **surrogate parent.**] And, of course, the adoption of a stepchild by a stepparent does not require the services of an adoption agency.

In all states, an adoption proceeding is initiated by the adult or adults wishing to adopt. This prospective parent (or parents) files a petition in a court having family law jurisdiction. The petition supplies information about the proposed adoptive parents as well as the child to be adopted. A judicial hearing is then held, during which the qualifications of the prospective parents are considered. Frequently, the court seeks the recommendation of the state child welfare agency or other expert body that has studied the suitability of the petitioners as parents for the particular child. This recommendation is not binding on the court. However, the court usually considers it compelling evidence in deciding whether to grant or deny the adoption petition. Whatever decision is reached must be based on the best interests of the child. See **best interests of the child rule.**

In most states, a probationary period during which the child lives with his or her proposed adoptive parents is required before an adoption becomes final. In states without such a trial "live in" period, the adoption may be nullified within a certain time following the decree if problems develop. During the probationary time, a state agency monitors the progress of the parties to see how they are adapting to the new family situation. Difficulties in the relationship may prevent the adoption from going through or (in cases where there is no trial period) cause it to be nullified. When the adoption is final, the records on the proceeding are sealed, and none but the most compelling interest will generally be sufficient to disclose their contents. See **adoption records.**

Once an adoption is finalized, the new relationship is permanent and generally may not be undone. A few states allow for a period of time after the adoption decree during which the child's biological parents may revoke their consent to the adoption. (Most states allow a period of time following the giving of written consent but before the final decree during which parties may change their minds and cancel the procedure.) An otherwise final adoption may occasionally be canceled if the consent of the biological parents was irregular in some way—if it was obtained by fraud, duress, or undue influence, or if proper notification of the pending adoption was not given to one, or both, of the biological parents. See **adoptive consent.**

May an adoptive parent change his or her mind and give the child back? Generally, the answer is "no." The law strongly discourages this, because it runs counter to the policy of providing children stable homes in a parent-child relationship. Nevertheless, a few states permit adoptive parents to undo the adoption. Normally very special circumstances must be shown, such as proof that the adoptive parents were deliberately or negligently misled about some important characteristic of the child, usually his or her mental and/or physical health.

In very rare cases, persons not involved in an adoption at all have been allowed to challenge it. For example, biological relatives of a child who were interested in adopting him themselves were permitted to void an adoption to a third party where they could show that they had no notice that the child was about to be adopted. In other cases, relatives of the adoptive parents were able to cancel the adoption of a child because it adversely affected their expected inheritance. Generally, states have set statutes of limitations beyond which no attack on an adoption decree will be permitted, regardless of the reason.

Absent some challenge to an adoption that would result in its cancellation, the general rule is that all contact between an adopted child and his or her biological family is terminated when the adoption becomes final. Biological relatives traditionally have had no right to visit or contact a child once he or she has been adopted. However, in recent years interest has grown in so-called open adoptions, in which adoptive parents agree to allow biological parents to retain visitation rights with the adopted child. This arrangement is legal in some states, but not allowed in others. In at least one state, biological parents may reserve the right to visit their child as a condition to consenting to the child's adoption by **foster parents.** In addition, some states specifically have passed **grandparent visitation statutes** that allow courts to order visits from an adopted child's biological grandparents when it is in the child's best interest. See also **inheritance rights.**

As the twentieth century comes to a close, there are concerns that the cost of adoption is pricing many middle-class families out of the picture. It is estimated that an adoption in the United States costs about $20,000 in 1996. An effort is under way in Congress to provide tax incentives for people who wish to adopt. (*The Wall Street Journal*, 2 May 1996, A15)

ADOPTION AND SAFE FAMILIES ACT OF 1997 In November 1997 the federal Adoption and Safe Families Act (ASFA) was signed into law by President Clinton. It effectively replaced the Adoption Assistance and Child Welfare Act of 1980 and represents a fundamental change in philosophy from the earlier law. While both the 1980 and 1997 laws were designed to prevent "foster care drift"—that is, the tendency of foster children to languish in one foster placement after another, the laws have profoundly different ideals on the proper disposition for such children.

Under the 1980 law, return of the child to his or her biological family was the primary aim of foster care. Removal of children from their own families could occur only as a last resort when efforts to rehabilitate the biological family had failed. Adoption of foster children by third parties was made difficult because of the requirement that all efforts be focused on returning the child to his or her biological parents before other alternatives could be considered. During the decade of the 1980s and 1990s criticism of this system mounted. Without doubt, the emphasis on return of children to their biological families had cost many children their lives when they were returned to abusive parents. The belief that there are simply some adults who lack the capacity to raise children was validated by studies showing that counseling and other rehabilitative measures are rarely successful in stopping child abuse. Mooveover, it appeared to some observers that states frequently pronounced a dysfunctional family "healed" simply to save the money that keeping the family's children in foster care would entail. The opponents of the 1980 law also objected to what they considered the states' rewarding of depraved and irresponsible behavior by providing subsidies and services to parents who had been found abusive. Meanwhile, suitable adoptive parents waited in vain for children to welcome into their families.

The 1997 act addresses these concerns by shifting the primary consideration in child welfare from the rights of biological parents whose abuse or neglect has necessitated removal of their children to the health and safety of the children. It is no longer assumed that a child's biological family is always preferable to a permanent foster or adoptive home with nonrelatives. Although the 1997 law still requires that reasonable efforts be made to preserve and reunify families, the focus is now on the safety of the child. Where the 1980 act required child welfare agencies to plan for and try to implement a foster child's return to his or her family before any alternatives could be considered, the 1997 act allows concurrent planning for permanent adoption of the child to take place. This way, if the effort to return the child to his or her biological family fails, no time is loss in getting the child into a suitable permanent adoptive or foster home. The 1997 act also requires states to terminate the parental rights of any child who has been in foster care for fifteen of the most recent twenty-two months, thus further accelerating the process of removing children from abusive or neglectful homes and placing them permanently in adoptive families. In addition, the 1997 act requires states to actively identify, recruit, and approve qualified adoptive families for foster children. And, a state is no longer permitted to delay an adoption if an approved adoptive family resides outside the jurisdiction of the agency responsible for the child.

Another serious problem addressed by ASFA is the all-too-frequent placement of children removed from abusive biological families with equally abusive or neglectful foster or adoptive parents. To prevent this, ASFA requires criminal record checks for all prospective foster or adoptive parents prior to placement of any child with them. A felony conviction for child abuse or any crime against a child (including child pornography), child neglect, spousal abuse, or any violent crime automatically results in rejection as a foster or adoptive parent. In addition, drug-related felony offenses within the last five years preclude a person from becoming an adoptive or foster parent under the 1997 act.

ASFA, like the 1980 act before it, continues to provide financial incentives for states to move children out of foster care into adoptive families. It continues to encourage the adoption of children who are difficult to place because of their ages, ethnicity, need for a sibling to be adopted into the same family, or physical, mental, or emotional handicaps. Parents who adopt these children are entitled to monetary subsidies to help defray the costs of the children's special needs. Payments to third parties, such as doctors or special education instructors who provide services to these children may also be made directly from federal funds.

ADOPTION RECORDS   Records pertaining to an **adoption,** including the adoption decree, the adopted child's original birth certificate, and transcripts of the adoption proceedings. Other evidentiary documents, including reports of the child welfare agency that investigates the suitability of the parties for parenthood, may also be part of the records.

Once an adoption is final, all contact between the adopted child and his or her **biological parents** is usually severed. [See also **inheritance rights;**

visitation rights.] To ensure this clean break and a new beginning for the child, adoption records in all states are "sealed" and the information contained in them is kept strictly secret. Thus, unless the adoption parties already knew each other, the adopted child will not know the identities of his or her biological parents, and neither set of parents will know the identities of the other. Traditionally, this secrecy was presumed to promote and strengthen the adoption process. First, it protects all the parties to the adoption from embarrassing disclosures about themselves, because adoption records often contain intimate details of the parents' (both adoptive and biological) lives and the circumstances surrounding the child's birth. Second, secrecy ensures that the biological parents of the child will not meddle in the child's upbringing by the **adoptive parents**. Secure in the knowledge that secrecy will be kept, parties to an adoption presumably are more inclined to enter into the agreement.

In recent years, the assumption that secrecy serves the interests of all the parties to an adoption has been challenged. The sociological trend emphasizing identity with one's "roots" and advances in medical science have both militated for a more open policy on adoption records. Adopted persons in particular cite a strong natural urge to know more about their origins. The law is gradually responding to these changes. At the same time, courts and legislatures are trying to balance the competing needs of many involved in adoptions who wish to erase the traces of former identities or emotional and conflicted periods in their lives. Thus, in some states, access to adoption records has actually been made more restrictive.

In general, a court order is necessary to gain access to information in adoption records. In some states, only a "compelling need" will convince a court to grant such an order. In others, "good cause" or even mere "cause" is sufficient. It is not clear exactly what reason for disclosure will unlock access in any of these jurisdictions. Mere curiosity is not sufficient in any case, while a need for medical or genetic information is usually enough. Some states require a specific and well-documented medical reason for the disclosure. However, courts are increasingly recognizing a psychological need to know as adequate for an order to grant access to records.

In order to balance the needs of the various parties to an adoption, state legislatures have also attempted creative solutions. In some states, information sought for medical or family history purposes is provided to an adoptee requesting it. Yet, the identities of the biological parents are kept secret. In other states, voluntary or mandatory adoption registers are in place. An adoption register allows each party to an adoption to register with a neutral intermediary, supplying information about him or her and stating whether or not contact with the other parties to the adoption is desired. If an adoptee registers requesting information about, or contact with, his or her biological family, the register will attempt to determine whether the biological family has also registered and agreed to the contact. Generally, the neutral agency does the contacting, and only if both parties agree do the adoptee and his or her biological relatives meet or exchange information. Usually, adoption record information is available only to adult adoptees. However, the identities of biological relatives may be revealed to any adopted child in states that allow adopted children to inherit from blood relatives. [See **inheritance rights.**] In such states, the information is furnished only to help the adoptee claim an inheritance. Similarly, some states will facilitate finding an adopted child for the child's biological relatives who wish to include the child in their wills.

ADOPTIVE CONSENT   Before an **adoption** can take place, all of the interested parties must agree. This includes the proposed **adoptive parent**s, the child's **biological parent**s or legal **guardian** if the biological parents are dead or unknown, and the child himself or herself if of sufficient age.

Adoptive parents make known their consent to an adoption by filing a petition to adopt and initiating the procedure. The child to be adopted must then give written consent in all states if he or she is old enough. This threshold age is as low as ten in some states and as high as fourteen in others. Children younger than the set minimum age may be adopted without their consent, although their wishes will generally be considered by a court in determining whether the adoption is in the child's best interests. See **best interests of the child rule**.

Consent of the child's biological parents (or other legal guardian) is also required, unless extraordinary conditions indicate that the child's interest in being adopted outweighs the biological parents' right to consent. Obtaining a valid and irrevocable consent from them is frequently the biggest obstacle to an adoption and presents the most difficult legal issues in this area. The laws of all states are interpreted to give maximum protection to the rights of biological parents. Therefore, efforts are made to ensure that each biological parent is notified of the pending adoption and has soberly considered whether he or she is willing to give up all **parental rights** to the child, as adoption implies. At the same time, however, the law attempts to accommodate the important interest of promoting stability in the lives of children up for adoption and their new adoptive families. The balance is sometimes difficult to strike.

In order best to protect biological parents' rights, the form by which they are required to give consent to an adoption must be very strictly observed. Such consent must always be in writing. It must at least be notarized, and in some states the signatures of witnesses are also required. In other states, a judge must be present when the written consent is given. There may be different required forms for consent to adoption through an agency or for consent to adoption by known persons. If the biological parent is still a minor, special requirements for consent may apply. Generally, the consent of other biological relatives of the child, such as grandparents, is not necessary.

With increasing frequency, biological parents of adoptable children are young themselves and not married. They may have agreed to give the child up before it is even born, having been convinced by friends, relatives, or the prospective adoptive parents that the child is better off in an adoptive home. The law recognizes the pressures on unmarried parents to give up their unborn children; thus, all states allow parents who agreed to give up a child before its birth to revoke their consent.

In most states, biological parents of an already born child also have a period in which to reconsider their decision. In some states, biological parents have an absolute right to revoke consent within a certain time period. This time period ranges from a few days after the consent is signed to a "reasonable" period after the entry of a final adoption decree. While not defined, "reasonable" in one case was held not to include a three-and-one-half-year delay. In some states, the right to revoke consent is not automatic, but will depend on whether it is in the best interests of the child. See **best interests of the child rule.**

Once consent has been given and the requisite time period for revocation has elapsed, biological parents may act to get their child back only if their consent was obtained by fraud, duress, or undue influence. The definition of "fraud," "duress," or "undue influence" sufficient to void an adoption varies from state to state according to cases before the courts. Generally, the payment of money to a parent in exchange for consent to the adoption of his or her child is considered "duress." The payment of money in exchange for an agreement to give up a child is usually illegal in itself because it is considered to be "baby selling."

If the biological parents (or legal guardian) refuse or fail to give their consent to the adoption of their child, the adoption usually cannot take place. However, all states have provisions allowing adoption even without the biological parents' consent in certain extraordinary circumstances. A parent's consent to an adoption is usually not necessary if the parent's parental rights have been terminated by a court for some reason. Consent also will not be required if the parent is proved unfit [see **unfit parent**] or has abandoned the child [see **abandonment**].

A particularly difficult problem arises in cases in which the child's biological father is absent. In some instances, the identity of the biological father is unknown, or the mother does not reveal it. Generally, the consent of an absent, unwed, biological father to the adoption of his child is not necessary unless the father has, at some time prior to the adoption petition, stepped forward and acknowledged the child as his own and taken steps to assume parental responsibility for the child's care. [See **acknowledgment statute**.] The degree to which the father must show interest in, and responsibility toward, the child in order to retain parental rights—including the right to veto an adoption—is the subject of much judicial uncertainty. Basically, the courts in the various states require differing levels of interest and support. Occasionally, a biological father is even unaware of the birth of his child. This may result from deceit by the mother, who actively conceals the father's identity or conceals the fact of pregnancy from him. If the father later finds out that he is the biological father, but the child has already been placed for adoption, problems can arise. This was the case in the infamous "Baby Jessica" case [*In re B.G.C.*, 496 N.W.2d 239 (Iowa 1992), on appeal, *DeBoer v. DeBoer*, 114 S. Ct. 1 (1993)], in which a court ultimately ruled that a child who had been duly adopted three years earlier must be given back to its biological parents because the biological father was not informed of the child's birth and, therefore, had not been given a chance to veto the adoption by refusing to consent. This case outraged many who felt that taking a small child away from the only parents it had ever known was cruel and not in the least in the child's best interests. On the other hand, the case illustrated the law's extreme deference to the rights of biological parents. Cases like the "Baby Jessica" case are likely to cause continued agony until state legislatures address the issue.

ADOPTIVE PARENT   An adult who, although not biologically so related, has assumed the rights and duties of parenthood toward a child through a valid **adoption** proceeding.

There is no constitutional right for a person to adopt a child. Therefore, state laws may set requirements for adoptive parents, although most laws ultimately defer to the **best interests of the child rule** in deciding whether an adoption should take place. Because a child's best interests depend on his or her unique circumstances, there is usually flexibility in the rules regarding who may adopt. Cases are decided by a court weighing a variety of factors, including society's changing views on what makes a good parent. Generally, an adoptive parent must demonstrate an ability to meet the child's physical and emotional needs by providing a stable, loving, and safe environment. Some other factors a court may consider include age, biological relationship, marital status and sexual orientation, health, character, financial status, established relationship, and race and religion.

Age

In most states, an adult wishing to adopt must be at least ten years older than the child. On the other hand, a prospective adoptive parent must not be so old as to be expected to become infirm during the period of the child's minority. Some state laws have set arbitrary ages—such as thirty-five years old for a woman—beyond which they deem an adult "too old" to adopt a baby. However, adults older than these set ages may adopt older children. Although arbitrary age limits remain, age barriers to adoption have been falling as the "baby boomer" generation (often defined as those born between 1949 and 1964) challenges conventional notions of aging. In addition, the large number of children, particularly minority and handicapped, in need of parents has put pressure on some courts to disregard arbitrary age limits where other factors appear to favor the adoption. Courts have occasionally been known to approve adoptions where the prospective parents were over sixty years of age.

Biological Relationship

All states allow for adoption of a child by biological relatives, such as aunts, uncles, and grandparents. However, states differ in their philosophies regarding the advisability of such adoptions. Some states have a strong preference for adoption by biological relations. In others, there is no automatic right for biological relatives to take precedence in adoption proceedings over other qualified adults who are not related to the child. Nevertheless, if all other things are equal, most courts in all states will give preference to biological relatives.

Marital Status and Sexual Orientation

Formerly, most states allowed adoptions only by married couples. All states now recognize adoptions by single adults who are otherwise qualified. Particularly contentious in the late twentieth century is the issue of whether homosexuals may adopt. Some states flatly prohibit such adoptions, and court challenges on constitutional grounds have not met with success. Homosexual adoptions have been allowed in other states.

Health

The health—both physical and mental—of a proposed adoptive parent is a legitimate consideration in adoption proceedings. Persons not physically capable of caring for a child and mentally unstable people may be excluded from adoptive parenthood.

Character

The moral fitness of a prospective adoptive parent may be examined. Persons who have been convicted of crimes, who abuse alcohol or drugs, have unstable employment histories, are promiscuous, or have resorted to lies or misrepresentations to achieve their objectives are frequently denied the privilege to adopt. However, if the alleged moral failing of the prospective parent does not endanger the child's welfare (including his or her understanding of right and wrong) the adoption may be granted.

Financial Status

While adoptive parents do not need to be rich, an adult's ability to provide the material necessities of life to the child will be relevant to the decision of whether to allow an adoption.

Established Relationship

In many instances, an established relationship with the child to be adopted is a plus in determining an adult's fitness to be an adoptive parent. A person who has already been the child's **stepparent** is in a good position to become an adoptive parent, provided the stepparent's relationship with the child is generally good. Oddly, many states find the established relationship that **foster parent**s have formed with a child to be an impediment to adoption. Because the purpose of **foster care** traditionally has been the reunion of the child with its **biological parent**s, child welfare agencies responsible for foster placement have discouraged the development of strong emotional bonds between foster parents and the children in their charge. Forbidding adoption by foster parents has been one way the law has discouraged foster parents from becoming inextricably close to the foster child. This view, however, is changing. Many states now allow foster parents to adopt the children in their care.

Race and Religion

Controversy over the merits of allowing adoptions across racial lines has arisen in the last decades of the twentieth century. Opponents of transracial adoptions believe that a child adopted by parents of a different race will have difficulty establishing a cultural identity and dealing with the unfortunate reality of racial stereotyping and politics as he or she grows up. One of the ironies of this situation is that the biggest opponents of transracial adoptions are organizations formed for the advancement of minority rights. Their opposition has contributed to a large number of minority children languishing in foster care and institutions when there are, in fact, families (albeit of another race) who would eagerly adopt them. Proponents of transracial adoption contend that loving, stable parents of any race are preferable to the instability and alienation prevalent in foster care. Courts have considered the race and racial attitudes of potential adoptive parents when determining the best interests of a child who is the subject of adoption proceedings. However, the constitutionality of this practice is not settled. Some states have passed statutes to deal with the issue. In California, for example, a statute allows a child to be placed with parents of a different race only if placement with parents of the same race or ethnic background cannot be made after ninety days. In 1997, Congress amended the Multiethnic Placement Act (MEPA) of 1994 to prohibit states from receiving federal assistance for adoption programs if they discriminate against prospective parents on the basis of race.

Generally, the religion of potential adoptive parents is irrelevant to an adoption, unless the biological parents of the child have conditioned their consent to the adoption on finding adoptive parents who will bring their child up in a particular religion. However, if it can be shown that the religious practices of the proposed adoptive parents are detrimental to the child, religion may be considered, as, for example, when the adoptive parents are members of a cult that sexually abuses children.

AGE OF CONSENT   The age at which a minor female is considered mature enough to give her consent to sexual intercourse. Below this age, which is sixteen in most states, the law assumes that the girl is incapable of understanding the full implications of the act and, hence, cannot truly consent to it. In states in which the victim of a **statutory rape** may be either a boy or girl, the age of consent applies to male minors as well.

AID TO FAMILIES WITH DEPENDENT CHILDREN (AFDC)   The largest federal program for financial assistance to poor children and their families, AFDC was begun in 1935. It has been considerably amended since that time, seeing a big expansion in the 1960s and a contraction in the 1980s. The primary focus of AFDC is on needy children, with the major goal of keeping these children in their own homes with their own families. Thus, the financial assistance the program provides is in an effort to strengthen family life and ultimately to aid the children in achieving self-sufficiency when they grow up.

AFDC is administered through state governments, with states providing half of the funding and federal monies making up the rest. States are not required to participate in the program, but all fifty states have chosen to do so. Having opted to participate, the states must comply with all federal regulations pertaining to the act. States may have eligibility requirements that are less restrictive than the federal guidelines, but they may not make it more difficult to receive the benefits of the program. However, the amount of money allotted to eligible families may vary from state to state depending on each state's budget.

To be eligible for AFDC a family must have a needy child who has been deprived of parental support by at least one parent. Illegitimate children as well as illegal aliens are included. The absence of parental support can occur through abandonment, death, disability, or unemployment. The child (or children) must be living with a relative—if not with a parent, with an aunt, uncle, grandparent, cousin, stepparents, or stepsiblings. Families who have suffered a catastrophic event, such as a fire, medical emergency, or other costly disaster, may also be eligible.

In order to qualify as needy, the family's income must not exceed $1,000 per month (in 1994), and the family must not own property in excess of a certain value, including automobiles. The amount of AFDC aid an eligible family receives normally depends on the number of children in the family, the family's income, and the average cost of basic needs where the family lives. Some states have requirements that parents receiving AFDC must be looking for work, participating in a training program, or actually working at a paying job. In states where work or training is required, the state must offer child care for the working parent free or at reduced cost. One reason keeping poor parents on welfare rolls has always been the lack of affordable child care. Many found that they could simply not afford to work. This deficiency has been addressed by the new AFDC child care requirement. Under the present regulations, even if an AFDC parent's job brings in too much money for the parent to remain eligible for AFDC aid, the state must continue to offer child care for at least twelve months after AFDC is cut off in order for the parent to make other child care arrangements and avoid having to drop out of the workforce again.

ALCOHOL   Laws in every state now prohibit the sale of alcohol to anyone under twenty-one years of age. This is three years older than the age of **majority** in most states. The added restriction on young people's ability to purchase intoxicating beverages is considered justified to prevent harm to them caused by drinking or to prevent them from causing harm when drunk. Whether this is fair or not, young people are considered less likely than adults to exercise good judgment when confronted with the opportunity to drink alcohol. Moreover, the ability to recognize the subtle (or not-so-subtle) impairment that even small amounts of alcohol can cause to one's judgment and reflexes is beyond even many adults. State legislatures unanimously decided that the likely preservation of lives and health to be gained by requiring young people to postpone the pleasures of alcoholic consumption outweighed a young person's right to indulge.

Anyone who sells or gives alcoholic beverages to a person under twenty-one, therefore, is committing a criminal offense. In some states, the person who furnishes the liquor is guilty with or without knowledge that the young person was under twenty-one. Other states' laws will not convict the seller unless he or she knew the buyer was underage at the time of the sale. Most states' laws extend not only to licensed sellers but to anyone, including social hosts, who furnish underage persons with alcohol. This includes young people themselves. Adults who give parties at which young people are present may be criminally liable if they serve alcohol to underage guests. Persons who sell or give alcohol to underage drinkers may also be sued in civil court by anyone, including the young drinker, who suffers injury as a result of the young person's drinking. Some states' laws exempt parents who furnish alcohol to their children for consumption in the family home from criminal conduct.

In most states, it is also illegal for a person under the age of twenty-one even to possess alcoholic beverages. Most states also prohibit persons under the age of twenty-one from selling or serving alcohol or even from working in establishments that sell alcohol. In some states, it is forbidden for a person under the age of twenty-one even to be present in an establishment that serves alcohol, unless accompanied by a parent. However, this rule does not apply to restaurants that serve alcohol only incidentally to meals.

Schools may suspend students for being under the influence of alcohol while at school or attending a school function, even if the student did not consume the alcohol at school.

AMUSEMENT SITES Many states and communities have passed ordinances restricting the admission of minors to places of amusement, such as pool halls, dance halls, bowling alleys, and in recent years, video arcades. Various rationales have been advanced for these laws, usually relating to the need to protect youth from bad influences. For example, it is feared that adults will corrupt the morals of minors in such establishments or that the youngsters will be exposed to gambling, drugs, or alcohol. Allegedly, these facilities incite truancy, encourage children to waste money, and even result in impaired psychological development!

Various constitutional challenges have been made to these types of regulations, usually with little success. In the most significant case, which reached the Supreme Court, young people challenged a city ordinance prohibiting persons under the age of eighteen from entrance into dance halls. The plaintiffs alleged that this was a violation of their right to freedom of association guaranteed by the First Amendment, and a violation of their right to be free from unfair discrimination protected by the Fourteenth Amendment to the Constitution. The high Court disagreed. It held that neither free association nor **equal protection** rights were impaired by the ordinance, because patrons of the dance halls were not engaged in any form of "intimate or expressive" association protected by the Constitution. Having found that the ordinance did not really affect a constitutional right, the Court further held it to be rationally related to an important governmental objective in protecting youth from moral corruption. [*City of Dallas v. Stanglin* (1989)]

In similar cases, other courts have consistently found that no constitutional rights are affected by laws setting age limits on entrance into entertainment facilities. Even when courts have found constitutional rights to be affected, they usually hold that the regulations merely set reasonable "time, place, and manner" restraints, which are allowable. Moreover, if the establishment affected by the regulation also serves alcoholic beverages, the interest in preventing teen drinking by keeping youngsters away from locales where it is served may override young peoples' freedom to associate.

In the few cases in which ordinances have been struck down, a contradiction between the stated purpose of the law and its actual effect is usually the reason. For example, an ordinance that prohibited youth from playing pinball, but not video games, was invalidated because there was no proof that pinball was more "harmful" than video games. Another ordinance allegedly passed to discourage truancy from school was struck down because it banned minors' access to video game parlors at all hours of the day—not just during hours that school was in session. A court found a regulation designed to protect youth from squandering their money by limiting the number of video games that could be set up at a single location to be similarly flawed. There was no logical evidence that fewer video games at many separate locations would have any effect on children's tendency to spend their money on them. In addition, regulations that are not clearly written and easy to understand and enforce may be deemed unconstitutional. An ordinance that prohibited minors from "loitering about" was invalidated, because it was unclear what was meant by "loitering about."

One avenue of constitutional challenge that has not yet been tried with respect to restrictions on children entering video game arcades is the notion that playing the games may be a form of nonverbal communication that could come under the protection of the First Amendment. If interaction with video and computer games is found to be expression of some sort, it is possible that more protection may be given to children's rights to play them.

It should be noted that adults who are affected by these ordinances may also be able to challenge their validity. For example, the owners of the halls and arcades targeted for restricted youth access may have legitimate complaints that the regulations requiring them to establish their patrons' ages and eject those that are underage are too burdensome. Parents who approve of the entertainment offered their children at the places covered by restricted access regulations may challenge laws that require parental supervision at these venues on the grounds that this hinders their parental authority to choose their children's entertainment.

In the last years of the twentieth century, an ironic twist to age-restricted access ordinances has arisen. With the rise in youth- and gang-related crime, some shopping malls and entertainment establishments are attempting to ban teenagers from access—not to protect the young people from bad influences, but to protect the adult patrons from feared harassment and criminal acts perpetrated by the youth. For the most part, shopping malls are attempting to do this by redesigning their inner spaces to be less attractive to bands of teenagers, although some malls have resorted to outright bans on youth of certain ages unless accompanied by an adult. The validity of these restrictions is unclear. Normally, a private entity, such as a store or shopping center, is privileged to eject anyone it wishes from its property. However, because shopping malls perform the same function as the traditional town square as a gathering place for citizens, the ability of these entities to arbitrarily exclude certain classes of citizens may be circumscribed by the First Amendment. See also **curfew.**

ARREST   Occurs when a police officer "seizes" and detains a person. Technically, minors below the age at which they may be tried as adults are not "arrested," but rather "taken into custody." This distinction is really only semantic, however. Minors are taken into custody following the same procedures as the arrest of adults. A juvenile can be arrested when a judge issues a warrant after determining that there is sufficient cause to believe the juvenile is involved in a criminal act. Or, a police officer can arrest a juvenile without a warrant if the officer witnesses a crime, or has reasonable cause to believe that a crime has been committed, and the juvenile was involved.

The Fourth Amendment to the U.S. Constitution, which has overwhelmingly been found to apply to children as well as adults, requires that police officers have "probable cause" to make an arrest. Thus, the officer must believe that a crime (or delinquent act) has been committed and that the person being arrested has committed it. "Probable cause" exists when the facts and circumstances known by the officer would be sufficient to cause a reasonably cautious person in the same situation to believe that an offense was committed and that the juvenile suspect had done it. "Probable cause" has a rather elastic definition, depending as it does on the facts of each case and how a court believes a "reasonable person" would act under those circumstances. The legality of an arrest does not depend on whether the suspicion that led to the arrest later results in a conviction in court. "Probable cause" to arrest a person can exist even though the person is later acquitted in a court of law of all charges for which the arrest was made.

Of course, not all encounters a minor may have with police officers constitute an "arrest." The fact that a police officer asks questions does not mean that an arrest has occurred. Nevertheless, it is not necessary for an officer to actually say the words *you are under arrest*—or anything at all for that matter—for an arrest to take place. Generally, one has been "arrested" if one reasonably believes that he or she is not free to walk away from the officer. Thus, if a police officer orders a person to "stop" or to come with the officer, a reasonable person might believe he or she had been arrested. The fact that the officer is in uniform, is carrying or brandishing a weapon, and is speaking in the tones of command rather than request adds to the impression that one's freedom has been restricted. However, when in doubt, it is always proper to simply ask the officer "Am I under arrest?" This puts the burden on the police officer to decide at that moment whether probable cause for detention exists. If the officer says "no," the juvenile is free to walk away from the encounter. However, if the answer is "yes," other protections afforded by the Fourth Amendment come into play. See **interrogation** for a further description of these protections.

ATHLETIC PROGRAMS   The enormous increase in opportunities for, and interest in, women athletes in the last decades of the twentieth century can be traced in large part to **Title IX** of the Education Amendments of 1972, which prohibited gender discrimination in any educational program receiving funding from the federal government. Prior to the passage of this law, the greatest disparity in educational funding was often to be found in school athletic programs, with boys' programs receiving virtually all of the emphasis. This is not surprising, because until relatively recently, females were not only considered incapable of, and uninterested in, participating in sports, but some believed physical exertion by girls was actually harmful for them!

Under Title IX, public schools at the elementary and secondary levels must operate gender-integrated, or coeducational, physical education courses. There is an exception for contact sports, which allows schools to restrict participation in sports such as football and hockey to single-sex teams. In addition, schools may group students within a sport on the basis of relative ability. This often means that boys will dominate the upper levels of many sport programs. However, girls who can compete with boys at this level must not be excluded. Title IX itself is gender neutral. This means that it protects boys in athletic programs as well as girls. Generally, a boy must be allowed to participate in noncontact sports dominated by girls. However, if the boy exceeds the skill level of the girls' team, he need not be allowed to participate unless there is no boys' team. One federal court has ruled that boys need not be permitted on a girls' team even if there is no boys' team in the sport—if the overall athletic opportunities for boys at the particular school are at least equal to the opportunities for girls. The issue of allowing boys to play on girls' teams is problematic because the assumption is that, if boys were routinely allowed on girls' teams, their natural superiority in some sports would quickly lead to the team being dominated by boys, and girls would be left out again.

The biggest controversies involving Title IX's antidiscrimination provisions and athletic programs have not involved girls seeking admission to boys' programs or vice versa. Rather, the biggest issue has been ensuring that girls' athletic opportunities are as extensive as boys' given the relative levels of interest. Of course, many argue that the issue of girls' athletic opportunities is plagued by the "chicken or the egg" issue. There may well be less interest among girls in athletic programs because the opportunities are limited, and vice versa. Thus, making sure that a lower level of participation is not due to past discrimination against girls in athletics is a tricky balancing act. Courts reviewing challenges to public schools' athletic programs under Title IX generally investigate whether the selection of sports and levels of competition comport with the interests and abilities of both girls and boys. If a large disparity exists in the equipment, supplies, schedules, training, and facilities for boys' and girls' sports, a violation is more likely to be found.

Because many extracurricular athletic associations are private organizations and do not receive federal funding, Title IX does not apply to them. They may discriminate on the basis of gender, unless some other law prohibits it. Occasionally, a student will challenge the exclusionary practices of some of these organizations on the grounds that they provide training opportunities for the other gender to help them excel in sports that are offered within the public schools. Generally, such challenges must be brought on the basis of the Constitution's **equal protection** guarantee. Also, some states have so-called equal rights amendments in their constitutions that prohibit gender discrimination in organizations such as athletic clubs.

BAIL The right of a person accused of a crime to be released before trial upon paying an amount of money to the court that is calculated to be high enough to discourage flight. The money is returned when the accused person shows up for trial. Technically, there is no federal constitutional right to bail for anyone—adults included. There is, however, in the Eighth Amendment to the Constitution, a prohibition against *excessively high* bail. This clause may imply that a right to bail exists and was considered so self-evident by the framers of the Constitution that they did not see the need to spell it out. On the other hand, this clause may simply mean that there is no automatic right to bail, but that if a state voluntarily chooses to grant bail, the amount set must not be so high that the accused person could not possibly pay it. Whatever the meaning, it has never been clarified by the Supreme Court.

In most states, there is no provision for bail for juveniles. Courts prefer simply to give the accused child over to the custody of his or her parents or guardians, who are then responsible for seeing that the child appears in court. Generally, courts do not release a minor on his or her "own recognizance," which means merely on the promise to return. They believe—rightly or wrongly—that a youth who has been taken into custody on suspicion of having committed a delinquent act is too irresponsible to trust on his or her own. If a minor's parent or guardian is not available to take custody, the youth might be placed in detention pending trial.

The reason most states do not make a provision for bail for children may be a recognition that most children do not have much money. In order not to violate the Constitution's prohibition on excessive bail, the bail amount for a child would have to be set so low that it would virtually be the same as letting the child go on his or her "own recognizance."

Many states do specifically provide juveniles accused of delinquent acts with a right to bail. The view in these states is that the accused youth's parents will probably be supplying the bail money. Thus, when the minor is released, the parents have even more incentive to control the youth's whereabouts and see that he or she shows up for trial.

BEST INTERESTS OF THE CHILD RULE A legal doctrine under which courts deciding **child custody** cases are obliged to give paramount consideration to the welfare of the child rather than the rights of the parents. Although parents have a constitutionally recognized right to determine the upbringing of their children and to enjoy their company and association, these rights are not absolute. Rather, the right of a child to a safe, wholesome, and caring environment takes precedence over the parents' rights. Thus, when a marriage breaks up, the court will make a determination as to which parent can provide the best environment for raising the child. The child's best interests are also paramount when deciding **visitation rights**, appointments of **guardian**s, placements in **foster care**, **termination proceedings,** and **adoptions**.

The best interests of the child rule represents a distinct evolution of thought beginning in the nineteenth century. Before that time, children were viewed as mere property, virtually without any rights at all. Their ascendancy from the status of chattels to the most important consideration in family law is indeed remarkable and coincides with the recognition of the ability of the state to involve itself in family matters through the **parens patriae doctrine.**

The concept of what is in a child's best interests changes over time. For example, at one time it was considered best for a child to be placed with the parent of the same sex: boys with their fathers and girls with their mothers. Today, this theory is out of favor, with courts holding that either parent can be just as successful in raising a child of either sex. Although theories change with regard to what is best for children, there are some set areas into which courts facing custody disputes will inquire. For example, the stability of the home in which the child will live and the ability of each parent to provide emotional, intellectual, and financial support are important considerations in determining what is in a child's best interests.

BETHEL SCHOOL DISTRICT NO. 103 V. FRASER A 1986 Supreme Court ruling important for defining the limits of freedom of expression in the public schools. The case involved a nominating speech that Matthew N. Fraser made in favor of a fellow student at Bethel High School in Pierce County, California, before an assembly of his fellow students. In the words of the Supreme Court, the speech referred to Fraser's candidate "in terms of elaborate, graphic, and explicit sexual metaphor." Before giving the speech, Fraser was warned by three teachers with whom he had discussed it that the speech was "inappropriate" and that he should not give it. During the speech, reactions in the audience of 600 students ranged from boisterous catcalls to confused embarrassment. The day following the assembly, school officials told Fraser that his speech violated a school rule against "conduct that materially and substantially interferes with the educational process," including the use of "obscene or profane language or gestures." The school suspended Fraser for three days and disqualified him from consideration as a graduation speaker. Fraser sued the school district, contending that his First Amendment rights to freedom of speech were violated and that he did not receive **due process of law** in the manner of his suspension.

The Supreme Court ruled against Fraser:

> The schools as instruments of the state may determine that the essential lessons of civil, mature conduct cannot be conveyed in a school that tolerates lewd, indecent, or offensive speech and conduct such as that indulged in by this confused boy. . . . Indeed, the fundamental values necessary to the maintenance of a democratic political system disfavor the use of terms of debate highly offensive or highly threatening to others. Nothing in the Constitution prohibits the states from insisting that certain modes of expression are inappropriate and subject to sanctions. Inculcation of these values is truly the work of the schools.

In addition, the majority of justices noted the importance of protecting minors from exposure to vulgar and offensive spoken language. Among the audience for Fraser's speech were 14-year-old freshmen. As to Fraser's due process claim, the Court held that a suspension of a few days was not worthy of the full array of procedural protections. The school rule was clear and Fraser should have known that his speech would violate it.

Although Justice Brennan concurred in the Court's ruling that schools could regulate offensive and obscene expression, he expressed incredulity that the speech was really that bad. (The full text of the speech appears in Justice Brennan's opinion. To the jaded eye of a reader in the mid-1990s, the speech seems vulgar but not overtly disturbing.) Brennan noted that the speech was no more "obscene," "lewd," or "sexually explicit" than "the bulk of programs currently appearing on prime time television or in the local cinema."

Justices Marshall and Stevens dissented, finding that Fraser's right to due process was violated. They emphasized that, while three teachers expressed misgivings about the speech, no teacher told Fraser directly that the speech violated a school rule. Moreover, there was no real evidence that the speech did, in fact, "materially or substantially" interfere with the educational process at the school. Only one teacher testified that she felt it necessary to cancel a scheduled lesson and devote one class period to a discussion of the speech. Thus, not only did Fraser not have real notice that his planned speech was a violation of school rules, but it is not clear that the speech actually did violate the rule. As Justice Brennan noted in his concurring opinion, Fraser himself was probably in the best position to judge the effect of his words on an audience of his peers. At least he should know better what would offend them than a group of judges "at least two generations and 3,000 miles away."

BILINGUAL EDUCATION   The Supreme Court ruling in *Lau v. Nichols* established that failure to provide children with an education in a language they can understand amounts to impermissible discrimination on the basis of national origin. Such discrimination is prohibited by both the Fourteenth Amendment of the Constitution and the **Civil Rights Act of 1964.** Following this case, and several federal laws enacted in its wake, school districts were required to implement programs to eliminate language barriers for students of foreign heritage whose English is limited. While this requirement was originally aimed at the children of recent immigrants, it has also been held to apply to Native American children, inner-city children who speak "Black English," and others whose English is poor.

The choice of method for achieving an appropriate language remediation program for non–English proficient students was left up to the states until 1988. Generally, states chose one of two types of programs. The first is known as English as a Second Language (ESL), under which non–English speaking students receive most of their instruction in English, but are enrolled in intensive English-language classes for part of the day. The other program, bilingual instruction, uses the children's native language to instruct in the regular curriculum, and then English lessons are included. Children taught with this latter method were believed by some to be less likely to fall behind in their regular studies. On the other hand, critics noted that children in the bilingual program were segregated from other children, and their ability to acquire English might actually have been impeded. Moreover, bilingual programs were more expensive than ESL programs.

In 1988, Congress resolved the debate between the two types of programs with the passage of the Bilingual Education Act, coming down squarely in favor of **bilingual education,** as opposed to ESL, programs. Although it mandated bilingual programs, Congress also sought to allay some of the criticisms of the approach. In order to prevent participants from feeling segregated, it was suggested that the programs also include children whose native language is English. In some courses, such as music, art, and physical education, the foreign children are mainstreamed with other children in regular classes.

BIOLOGICAL PARENT   A person who supplies the genetic material necessary to conceive a child: sperm from the father and an egg from the mother. Generally, the law prefers that all parental rights and duties regarding any child remain with the child's biological parents. This includes the right to custody of the child and the duty to support him or her. However, there are circumstances under which biological parents may, or must, relinquish all or part of their claims to a child. For example, the biological parents may agree to allow their child to be adopted. [See **adoption.**] Or, the parents may have their rights terminated by the state because of some fundamental failure to care properly for their child. [See **parental rights.**] Biological parents may also transfer part of their rights and duties to others temporarily. [See **foster care.**] Parents who divorce may voluntarily agree as to which of them will have custody of their children. However, a court in an official decree must ratify the agreement. Otherwise, it may appear that one parent "sold" his or her rights to the child in return for some other marital "property." "Baby selling" is illegal in all states. Occasionally, a biological parent may attempt simply to renounce his or her duties toward a child and walk away. If he or she does so, the state will generally step in and terminate the parent's rights in order to place the child with an adoptive or foster family.

BOARD OF EDUCATION, ISLAND TREES UNION FREE SCHOOL DISTRICT NO. 26 V. PICO   A 1982 Supreme Court case that addressed the rights of schoolchildren to access materials in school libraries. The Board of Education of Island Trees Union Free School District No. 26 in New York, acting on the recommendation of a politically conservative organization of parents concerned about education legislation,

removed certain books from the libraries of several schools. The board justified its action, stating that the removed books were "anti-American, anti-
Christian, anti-Sem[i]tic, and just plain filthy." Later, the board appointed
a committee of parents and teachers from the affected schools to read the
books and make a recommendation about their suitability for student reading. This committee recommended that most of the books be retained in
the library. Without explanation, the board rejected the committee's views
and removed all the books.

Five students sued the board for violation of their First Amendment
rights to freedom of information. They alleged that the board members
were motivated in their decision not by concern that the books lacked educational value but by their assumptions that "passages in the books of-
fended their social, political, and moral tastes." This, according to the
students, was impermissible censorship. In a very close opinion, the high
Court agreed with the students. However, only four justices believed that
school boards do not have complete authority to remove books from school
libraries. The fifth justice to vote in favor of the students agreed only that
the means taken by the school board in deciding to ban these particular
books was improper because it appeared to be politically motivated. Thus,
the case was decided by a "plurality" of justices voting, rather than a "majority," in which at least five justices agree on *all* issues.

In writing the plurality's opinion, Justice Brennan was careful to reaf-
firm the broad rights of school boards to determine the curriculum to be
taught in public schools and the books to be used to do so. Moreover, he
carefully distinguished between the situation in which a school board desires to remove books already in the school library and the initial decision
to purchase books for the school library. The board's freedom to refuse to
buy books initially is much broader than its authority to censor books already there, according to Justice Brennan. The plurality opinion then went
on to explain the importance of a school library as a place in which "students must always remain free to inquire, to study, and to evaluate, to gain
new maturity and understanding." And, while school boards "rightly possess significant discretion to determine the content of their school libraries,
. . . that discretion may not be exercised in a narrowly partisan or political
manner." Here, the plurality hinted that if it had been clear that the school
board was simply concerned with material it deemed obscene or too vulgar for young children, the ruling might have been different. However, it
appeared that the board had taken its marching order on the matter from
an organization that was openly political in orientation. The board essen-

tially rejected the recommendations of its own appointed committee when that committee's opinion differed with the opinion of a political organization. The plurality opinion stated: "[I]n brief, we hold that local school boards may not remove books from the school library shelves simply because they dislike the ideas contained in those books and seek by their removal to 'prescribe what shall be orthodox in politics, nationalism, religion, or other matters of opinion.'" [at 872]

Chief Justice Burger wrote a strong dissent in the case. He was joined in his opinion by Justices Powell, Rehnquist, and O'Connor. The dissenters objected to the characterization of the school board's action as "censorship." They pointed out that the "students are free to read the books in question, which are available at public libraries and bookstores; they are free to discuss them in the classroom or elsewhere. Despite this absence of any direct external control on the students' ability to express themselves, the plurality suggest that there is a new First Amendment 'entitlement' to have access to particular books in a school library." [at 886] Moreover, said the dissent, although the government may not impose unreasonable obstacles to the dissemination of information, it does not follow that the government, through a school board, must affirmatively aid the speaker in his communication with the recipient: "In short the plurality suggests today that if a writer has something to say, the government through its schools must be the courier." The dissent did not see that there was any real distinction between the removal of books and the initial purchase of books for a library. Thus, the government does not "contract the spectrum of available knowledge, by choosing not to retain certain books on the school library shelf, it simply chooses not to be the conduit for that particular information." Furthermore, the dissent found it odd that a school board could be the absolute authority for deciding which information students *must* learn as part of the curriculum but that it could not decide which information was *optional* for student learning. "It would appear that required reading and textbooks have greater likelihood of imposing a 'pall of orthodoxy' over the educational process than do optional reading." [at 892]

BREED V. JONES A 1975 case addressing the issue of whether a juvenile could be adjudicated in juvenile court and then tried again for the same offense in adult court. The youth in question claimed that doing so violated his Fifth Amendment rights—namely, the right not to be placed in "double jeopardy." The state of California justified its decision to try the youth a second time in adult court on the grounds that, because juvenile court proceedings technically are "civil" rather than "criminal," the Fifth Amendment did not apply to the first trial. Moreover, because the youth did not face the risk of more than one punishment for the same offense, he was not really facing the double risk the Fifth Amendment was designed to prevent. Furthermore, the state argued that forbidding transfer to adult court after a trial in juvenile court would impair the juvenile system's flexibility to fashion appropriate dispositions for youthful offenders.

The Supreme Court agreed with the youth and rejected California's position. Acknowledging that juvenile court is "civil" in name only, the Court noted that a youth tried in juvenile court is in "jeopardy," or at risk, of losing his or her liberty exactly as is the defendant in adult criminal trials: "We believe it is simply too late in the day to conclude, . . . that a juvenile is not put in jeopardy at a proceeding whose object is to determine whether he has committed acts that violate a criminal law and whose potential consequences include both the stigma inherent in such a determination and the deprivation of liberty for many years." [at 529] Moreover, the fact that the youth faced only a single punishment for the offense did not sufficiently address the issue of the risk: The youth, noted the Court, was "subjected to the burden of two trials for the same offense; he was twice put to the task of marshalling his resources against those of the State, twice subjected to the heavy personal strain which such an experience represents." [at 533]

As to California's argument that an inability to transfer a youth for trial in adult court on the same offense after a trial in juvenile court would impair the flexibility necessary to operate the juvenile system effectively, the Court was more than skeptical. A youth for whom the threat of a trial in adult court looms even after trial in juvenile court will be less likely to admit the charges, thereby necessitating a costly trial in juvenile court and another one in adult court, if transfer occurs. This added cost and procedure is of benefit to no one.

BROWN V. BOARD OF EDUCATION   A 1954 case challenging the "separate but equal" doctrine. In the mid-1950s most school systems in states with significant populations of African Americans were segregated. In many, this segregation was pursuant to laws that required it. This is known as de jure segregation. In other states, segregation in the schools was the result of economic factors: minority students tended to come from poorer families who could only afford to live in certain sections of town. They went to schools in their own neighborhoods, while the more affluent white students went to schools in their neighborhoods. Segregation that is the result of these accidental factors is called de facto segregation.

As early as 1896 a challenge to de jure segregation in public transportation reached the Supreme Court. In that case, *Plessy v. Ferguson,* the Court rejected the claim of a black man that his constitutional right to **equal protection** of the laws was violated by a rule forcing him to sit in a "for Negroes only" train carriage. As long as the facilities offered to him were "equal" to those used by whites, separate accommodations did not violate the Constitution, said the Court. This ruling became known as the infamous "separate but equal" doctrine.

In the next fifty-eight years, separate educational facilities for blacks and whites were challenged on numerous occasions. Six of those cases reached the Supreme Court. In several of those six cases, the Court found that the facilities offered to the black students were inferior to those offered to the white students, and the offending school system was ordered either to admit the black students to the white schools or to make the black schools better. In none of these cases, however, was the validity of the "separate but equal" doctrine questioned.

This assumption began to waiver in 1946, when the case of *Sweatt v. Painter* reached the Supreme Court. The Court decided that a black student must be admitted to a law school reserved for whites because the law schools open to him could not provide an "equal" education. The reason the black law schools could not be "equal" did not have anything to do with their facilities or faculty, however. For the first time, the Court recognized that intangible factors could prevent segregated education from being equal: "[T]hose qualities which are incapable of objective measurement but which make for greatness in a law school" could simply not be rectified in the black law schools, said the Court.

The stage was set for the next step: invalidation of the "separate but equal" doctrine in the public schools. In the 1954 *Brown v. Board of Education* case, black students in four states brought a class action to force their admission into schools reserved for whites. They argued that separate education could never be "equal" education for the very reason that it was separate. The high Court agreed with them. After extolling the importance of an education in all children's futures, the Court said: "To separate them from others of similar age and qualifications solely because of their race generates a feeling of inferiority as to their status in the community that may affect their hearts and minds in a way unlikely ever to be undone."

The Court went on:

> We conclude that in the field of public education the doctrine of "separate but equal" has no place. Separate education facilities are inherently unequal. Therefore, we hold that the plaintiffs and others similarly situated for whom the actions have been brought are, by reason of the segregation complained of, deprived of equal protection of the laws guaranteed by the Fourteenth Amendment. [347 at 495]

The road to this realization had been a long one. But the battle for equality in education was by no means over. In the decade following the *Brown* decision, precious little was done to desegregate the nation's public schools. It was not until the civil rights activism of the 1960s that the courts, Congress, and state legislatures really began the task of dismantling the systems of separate education that existed in most states.

BURDEN OF PROOF   Minors accused of delinquent acts must be proved guilty beyond a reasonable doubt. This is the same standard that applies in adult criminal trials. However, it was not always so. Prior to the 1970 Supreme Court ruling in *In re Winship*, all that was needed to declare a minor delinquent was proof of guilt by a mere preponderance of the evidence. Thus, if it was merely more likely than not that a child committed a crime, he or she could be sentenced as delinquent.

Today, the standard of proof beyond a reasonable doubt applies only to juvenile delinquency matters; that is, only to those matters where a youth has been charged with activity that would be classified as a crime if perpetrated by an adult. It does not apply in **status offense** cases. Moreover, the *Winship* case decided only that proof beyond a reasonable doubt is necessary at the adjudicatory, or trial, stage of delinquency hearings. It is still unclear whether proof beyond a reasonable doubt is required at other stages of a juvenile court proceeding. See also **disposition; preliminary hearing.**

In addition to proof of guilt beyond a reasonable doubt, some states have retained what is known as the presumption of infancy. This presumption holds that children under a certain age are incapable of committing delinquent acts because they lack the ability to form an intent to commit the act with understanding of its consequences and wrongful nature. In these states, the government must present evidence that the particular accused child was capable of this understanding—in addition to proving beyond a reasonable doubt that the child committed the act—before the child can be sentenced as a delinquent. The cutoff age for a child to take advantage of this presumption is usually fourteen years of age, although some states go as high as sixteen. This special protection does not exist at all in some states. Others allow the presumption if the child is tried in adult court, but disallow it in juvenile court proceedings. In situations in which the presumption of infancy does not exist, it is assumed the child did understand the wrongful nature of his or her actions, and the burden is on the accused child's defense advocate to show that the child lacked this capacity.

BUSING   Following the Supreme Court's landmark decision in *Brown v. Board of Education* in 1954, which held that racially segregated schools violated the Constitution, courts and school districts were left with the task of determining how schools could achieve a racially balanced student body. Even where communities embraced the goal of integration, decades of segregation forced on citizens by law had left cities with segregated neighborhoods having their own local schools. The concept of busing students from their largely segregated neighborhoods to schools in other neighborhoods in order to achieve a racial balance was the tool of choice to achieve integration. Federal courts early on held that busing to achieve integration was constitutional.

From the earliest days, however, busing had its detractors. Many considered it harmful. It forced students to spend much precious time in transit that could otherwise be used in educational pursuits. Because the schools were far from their homes, extracurricular activities that took place before or after school were harder to participate in. Because the schools in which they studied were not part of their own communities, students and parents alike had more difficulty forming an emotional attachment to them such that they could become a force for helping the schools develop. Moreover, busing was enormously expensive, and there was little concrete evidence that integration achieved through this means had any positive effects on education for minority students.

By the early 1970s, the bloom was off the rose so far as busing was concerned. In 1972, Congress passed the Education Amendments with a provision that became known as the "Anti-Busing Amendment." This law forbade the use of federal funds "to require assignment or transportation of students or teachers in order to overcome racial imbalance." The stage was set for a showdown between Congress and the judicial branch of government, which had been using court orders to force busing. Rather than fireworks, however, a slow evolution occurred. Courts generally found that the new law was constitutional. However, local school districts that requested federal funding to help achieve integration through busing continued to receive it. Even schools that assigned students to schools outside their neighborhood areas were considered proper recipients of funds because the federal government did not "require" the assignment of children to other schools but merely facilitated an assignment made by the local school district itself.

This continues to be the law today. Moreover, busing of school children may still be ordered and federal funds used to implement it if segregation in a school district is the result of intentional discrimination, either presently or as a vestige of past discrimination. But school districts are under no federal obligation to continue busing children if the districts can prove that segregated schools are simply the result of housing patterns and other economic factors that do not reflect intentional racial discrimination.

CAPITAL PUNISHMENT Capital punishment—the death penalty—may be imposed on minors who were older than sixteen when they committed their crimes. The same standards for deciding to impose the death penalty apply to these minors as to adults who commit similar acts. See also *Stanford v. Kentucky; Thompson v. Oklahoma.*

Although it does not violate the *federal* Constitution to execute persons for crimes they committed when older than sixteen yet still minors, it may violate *state* constitutions or other state laws. When a state's laws give citizens *more* protection than the federal Constitution, the state laws will usually prevail. Thus, in states that ban the death penalty altogether, or that outlaw the execution of persons who were older than sixteen yet younger than another specified age when the crimes were committed, the death penalty may not be imposed.

CERTIFICATE OF AGE A document issued by a federal or state labor agency that attests to the age of an applicant for work. Under the **Fair Labor Standards Act,** employers are prohibited from hiring persons under the age of **majority** for certain jobs. Therefore, in order to protect themselves from unknowingly hiring an underage person, employers usually require a young job applicant to furnish a certificate of age. The document must state the child's name, address, place of birth, and date of birth, and it must contain the minor's signature. The name and address of the child's parents, the name and address of the employer, and the industry and position to be occupied by the minor employee are also required.

If an employer presents such a certificate signed by an agent of the issuing agency, the employer cannot be convicted of illegally using child labor, even if it is determined that the certificate is false.

CHILD ABUSE   A blanket term for acts or omissions by a parent, or one with the legal responsibility to care for a child, that endangers the child's health or welfare to the extent that the criminal laws of the state may be invoked to stop the maltreatment and punish the perpetrator.

Criminal cases involving child abuse were known in America as early as the mid-1600s. However, the law of the time generally viewed children as the property of their fathers, who could deal with them as they saw fit. The rare instances in which parents were prosecuted for child abuse involved cruel and unreasonable punishments that disfigured, maimed, or killed children. Failure to provide a child with adequate food, clothing, or shelter might also be prosecuted in rare cases.

In the late 1800s, social reformers made the welfare of children a priority, believing that the industrial revolution and urban crowding were exposing children to dangerous and immoral environments that could cause them harm. The first case to recognize a civil lawsuit for mistreatment of a child came in New York City in 1874. It was brought by the founder of the Society for the Prevention of Cruelty to Animals—there being no corresponding organization to benefit children! That suit forced the removal of a child from the home of her stepmother, who beat her mercilessly, locked her in a room, gave her inadequate clothing, and forced her to sleep on the floor. Legal cases to improve the lot of specific children increased thereafter. Unfortunately, however, the children involved were often removed from an abusive home only to be "placed out" in inadequate apprenticeship programs, foster care, or so-called houses of refuge that caused them more suffering.

After the turn of the century, the issue of child abuse and the role of the state in preventing and remedying it were largely ignored until 1962. In that year, the publication of a seminal article in the *Journal of the American Medical Association (JAMA)* thrust the issue into public consciousness as never before. [C. Henry Kempe et al., "The Battered Child Syndrome," *JAMA* 181, p. 17 (1962)] Since that time, all states and the federal government have passed laws that attempt to define "child abuse" and set limits on parental authority that harms the welfare of children.

A specific definition of "child abuse" is difficult because of the constitutionally protected and fundamental right that parents have in rearing their biological children as they see fit. The state may not interfere with this right under ordinary circumstances. On the other hand, the state also has a long-established prerogative to act for the welfare of its youngest citizens under the **parens patriae doctrine.** A careful balancing of these two principles is necessary to protect everyone's rights.

Child abuse encompasses a broad range of acts or omissions, including physical violence [see **corporal punishment; physical abuse**]; **neglect** of the child's basic needs, including education and medical treatment; or plain **abandonment.** In order to fit the legal definition of "child abuse," the behavior at issue must have been perpetrated with intent. This usually means only the intent to perform the action or make the omission, and not the intent to cause harm to the child. In other words, a parent's intent to strike a child with a tire iron is sufficient to convict him of child abuse. It is not also necessary to prove that he intended to harm the child by this action. At the very least, all states will find child abuse if the adult knew that harm would result, or was at least reckless in taking the chance that harm would result. Some states will find child abuse if the parent was merely negligent in providing care. However, accidentally caused harm is not child abuse if it could not be prevented by ordinary foresight. The failure to intervene when another is abusing a child that one has a duty to protect may also be child abuse. This situation is common in single-parent families where the parent may be dating an adult who abuses the parent's child. Generally, a single act of mistreatment is sufficient to trigger the laws against child abuse.

Technically, child abuse may be committed only by an adult with the legal obligation and authority to care for the child. Mistreatment by anyone else is usually not termed child abuse, but is dealt with under the normal criminal and civil laws prohibiting violence against others.

Once child abuse is suspected, the apparatus of the state is engaged to investigate. [See **reporting laws.**] If an investigation reveals that child abuse has taken place, or is likely to take place, the state may intervene in the family's affairs. This may mean taking custody of the child and placing him or her into **foster care** temporarily. It may ultimately mean that **parental rights** will be terminated and the child given to **adoption.** The offending adult may be prosecuted in a criminal lawsuit or sued in a civil action and required to pay damages or fines, or to serve a term in prison. In less egregious cases, some course of counseling of the offender, or the whole family, may stop the abuse and enable the child to be returned home. See also **child protection action.**

CHILD ABUSE PREVENTION AND TREATMENT ACT (CAPTA)   A federal law first passed in 1974 and amended in 1984 and 1992, that attempted to establish a comprehensive national policy to remedy the causes of **child abuse** and **neglect.** To this end, the act

authorized the creation of a National Center, an Advisory Board, and an Inter-Agency Task Force on Child Abuse and Neglect. These organizations were empowered to conduct research on the issue of child abuse. A national clearinghouse for information relating to child abuse was also part of the legislation's mandate.

The 1984 amendments to CAPTA expanded the definition of persons who could be liable for child abuse to include anyone "responsible for the child's welfare." This brought into the scope of the act's reach day care centers and residential facility personnel. CAPTA requires states to conform their laws to this definition or risk losing federal funds for child welfare programs.

Another major function of CAPTA is to make federal grant money available to states for the purpose of creating and operating child abuse and neglect prevention and treatment programs. The federal law conditions the receipt of federal funds on the states' making certain changes to their own laws on child abuse prevention, reporting, and enforcement procedures. Grants of federal money are also available to nonprofit private organizations for the study of the causes of child abuse and the creation of experimental and demonstration programs designed to prevent, identify, and treat child abuse and neglect.

CHILD CUSTODY Responsibility for the care and control of a child. Initially, custody resides in both the child's **biological parents**. However, if they divorce, die, abandon the child [see **abandonment**], or are found unfit [see **unfit parent**], a court of law must decide to whom custody will be transferred. This may be to just one of the biological parents, other blood relatives, **adoptive parents**, **foster parents**, a **stepparent**, an unrelated third party, or a state institution. Custody transfers may be permanent or temporary.

Child custody is frequently the most difficult issue facing a family court. This was not always the case. Until the latter half of the nineteenth century, children were considered virtually the property of their fathers. Moreover, under a legal doctrine known as the unity of marriage, when a couple married their legal identities merged into the single identity of the husband alone—giving him all the legal rights in the marriage. Thus, in the rare cases of divorce, the father automatically had the right to custody of the child.

This began to change with the growing popularity of the **maternal preference rule.** By 1900, numerous states had written into their laws that custody should go to the mother in most cases. The change reflected an effort by courts to justify denying custody of children to abusive fathers, as well as the romantic and persistent notion that women are more suited to child care than men.

Today, the majority view is that there should be no automatic preference for one gender over another in choosing a custodial parent. Instead, the focus in custody decisions is on the best interests of the particular child. [See also **best interests of the child rule; tender years doctrine.**] However, like all methods tailored to unique circumstances, determining the best interests of the child is frequently slow, cumbersome, and lacking in precedential usefulness from one case to the next.

Presently, there is a clear preference to keep the child with one or both of his or her biological parents. Therefore, the claims of any other person to custody of a child will usually be considered only if both biological parents have relinquished or have lost their **parental rights,** or have died. However, in rare cases, custody may be granted to grandparents, aunts, uncles, or adult siblings if unique circumstances indicate that this serves the best interests of the child. Custody may also be temporarily taken from biological parents if they are found unfit to care for the child.

A court deciding custody must determine which adult or adults can best meet the physical, emotional, and educational needs of the child. It is not usually a contest between one parent who is "fit" and another who is "unfit" to be a parent. The mere fact that custody is given to one parent, rather than the other, should not imply that the noncustodial parent is unfit or incapable of caring for the child. Divorcing parents can work out a plan for custody themselves, but the plan must be approved by a court.

Courts have great discretion to weigh various factors in determining which is the most capable adult to take custody of the child. Among the factors the court may consider are:

- The identity of the "primary caregiver." This is the parent who has performed most of the day-to-day tasks of nourishing, grooming, disciplining, transporting, cuddling, counseling, and entertaining the child. Frequently, this parent will have an advantage in claiming custody, because the child has probably come to rely on the consistency of this care, and the parent has proved that he or she can provide it. See also **psychological parent doctrine.**

- The physical and mental health of both parents and the child. While having a disability no longer disqualifies a parent from custody of a child, the extent and nature of the disability will be considered. If it interferes with the parent's ability to give the child adequate care, custody may be placed with the nondisabled parent. Similarly, if the child is disabled, the court will examine which parent is best able to render the special care the child requires.

- The ages of the child and the parents. If the child is very young, the **tender years doctrine** may weigh in favor of giving custody to the mother. The age of the parent is usually irrelevant. However, in cases in which grandparents or older relatives are seeking custody, advanced age may be considered a disability if it is accompanied by age-related health problems.

- The relative maturity of the child and his or her relationship with each parent. Estrangement from, or antipathy toward, one of the parents may argue for giving the other parent custody. The child's preferences for custodian will usually be considered. See also **child's custodial preference.**

- The type of home environment offered by each parent. This includes everything from the number of persons in the household to the distance from the child's current school. The cleanliness, calmness, and safety of the home environment may be considered. The fact that a child will be required to spend considerable time with a day care provider, rather than at home, may be a factor. Generally, however, the fact that one parent may offer more sumptuous or spacious living accommodations is not relevant to a custody determination, provided each parent's domicile is adequate.

- The stability of the home environment offered. The court will consider whether the parent constantly changes residences or live-in companions. If the changes force the child to give up friendships or transfer to new schools frequently, custody may be denied.

- The ability of the child to maintain existing relationships with extended family. A court will consider to what extent ties with other family members, such as grandparents, aunts, uncles, and cousins, will be disrupted by giving custody to a particular parent. Also, because existing family ties are considered very important to a child's well-being, courts usually award custody of all children in the family to the same person, so that siblings will not be separated.

- The ability of the parents to provide for the child's intellectual development. One parent's greater emphasis on, and personal sacrifice for, the child's educational opportunities will weigh in that parent's favor on custody issues. The fact that one parent can afford to send the child to private school is not usually relevant, however, since a decree may stipulate that this parent pay for the schooling regardless of where the child lives.

- The parent's ability to give emotional support to the child, including frequent expressions of affection.

- The "moral fitness" of each parent. This factor generates controversy in modern custody proceedings because of the trend toward a nonjudgmental and relativistic view of personal behavior in America at the end of the twentieth century. What used to be regarded as immoral behavior is now frequently considered a lifestyle choice. Therefore, the modern view is that, unless the parent's behavior directly affects the health, welfare, or safety of the child, it is probably irrelevant in a custody dispute. Some states even have laws forbidding consideration of conduct that does not affect the child. Even here, however, judges are not in agreement as to what behavior will affect the child. For example, although a growing number of judges will not disqualify a parent because of homosexual orientation, other judges continue to find that homosexuality is a bar to child custody.

- A parent's sexual relationships outside of marriage. Regardless of orientation, these relationships may be considered an impediment to custody if they are promiscuous, flagrant, or adulterous.

- A parent's use of drugs, alcohol, or other controlled substances. Use of such substances will be considered a negative in a custody battle, particularly if it impairs the ability of the parent to see to the needs of the child.

- Criminal history. The fact that a parent has been convicted of a crime, or is living with an individual who has been convicted of a crime will be counted against giving that parent custody, even if the crime was not of a type that poses a threat to children. If the person with whom the parent is living has been known to have abused children in the past, custody will almost always be denied to that parent—at least while the relationship with that person continues.

- Character. Even if a parent has not been convicted of a crime, evidence that he or she is dishonest, manipulative, slovenly, lazy, irascible, or possesses any other "character flaw" may be added to the mix of factors a court will consider when deciding who is best able to see to the upbringing of the child. Of course, any behavior that renders a parent unfit [see **unfit parent**] is sufficient to deny him or her custody. This includes **abandonment, neglect,** or any form of **child abuse.**

In addition to these factors, there are others that have fallen out of favor, or are even unlawful to consider, but which some courts may take into account regardless. These include:

- The race of the parents. Generally, the race of the parents should be completely irrelevant to a custody determination, and it is likely that consideration of this factor would be considered a denial of the parents' constitutional right to equal protection of the laws. Nevertheless, there are those who advocate that children are best off in the custody of adults of their own race. This issue is most frequently raised when a child of one race is sought to be adopted by parents of another race. However, in cases in which a mixed-race couple divorce, some argue that it is legitimate to consider placing the child with whomever he or she most resembles racially so that the child will have an easier time "fitting in." While this argument may have some merit, courts have held that denying a parent custody following a divorce because he or she has remarried a person of another race is impermissible.

- The national origin of the parents. National origin, like race, is a consideration tainted with the suspicion of illegal discrimination in custody cases. However, some courts will consider the national origin of the parents, particularly if a foreign-born parent intends to return to his or her own country, now or in the future. In that case, the court will consider the circumstances of the child's life in that country, as well as the difficulty of arranging visitation with the other parent. The laws regarding children's rights in that country may also be a consideration.

- The sex of the parents and of the child. Formerly, a common caveat followed by courts in custody cases was that female children should be placed with their mothers and male children, unless very young, should be in the custody of their fathers. This thinking has lost favor today, and it is more likely that courts find any consideration of the gender of the participants not relevant.

- The religion of the parents. Generally, courts may not consider a parent's religion when deciding who should have custody of a child. An exception may be made if the parent's beliefs are likely to pose a risk of harm to the child. For example, the fact that the parent does not believe in medical care for an ill child may militate against him or her being given custody. Similarly, beliefs that border on psychotic and are likely to adversely affect the child may be a negative in determining custody. A mother who believed that devils resided in her child's toys was denied custody. In the cases of older children who have begun to develop their own religious identity, the fact that one parent wishes to impose a different religion on the children may militate against giving custody to him or her.

- The financial status of the parents. The fact that one parent is more financially secure than the other, or can provide a "better life," should not in itself be considered a factor in determining custody. Provided the less wealthy parent can adequately provide for the physical needs of the child, his or her chances of gaining custody should be equal. Theoretically, therefore, a parent on welfare should have as much right to custody of a child as a multimillionaire. Practically, however, relative wealth may be indirectly considered when the court examines the home environment that each parent is able to provide. Moreover, some courts do consider relative financial wealth a legitimate factor in custody cases, although it is never to be the decisive factor.

- The marital status of the parents. There is no automatic preference today to place children in the custody of two-parent families. Thus, the fact that one biological parent has remarried, or intends to remarry, should not influence the court's award of custody. However, again, this is a factor that may be indirectly considered when the court examines the home environment that can be offered by each parent. For example, if the remarried parent is able to devote more time to the child because his or her spouse's income allows him or her to be at home more, the court may consider this a plus. Or, if the child is not required to spend so much time in day care, because the remarried parent or his or her spouse is able to be home at times when the child is there, the court may consider this also.

Once the court has made its determination, "legal custody" of the child will be given to one parent, or to both parents jointly. [See **joint custody.**] The parent with legal custody is known as the custodial parent and has the right to make most of the important decisions in the child's life. In most jurisdictions, the parent with legal custody may determine the child's religious training. He or she may also decide where the child will live and go to school. The custodial parent will also make crucial decisions regarding the child's medical care and will be responsible for most of the child's discipline, and setting the rules by which the child will live day to day. Frequently, the custodial parent is also in a position to dictate many of the terms of visitation that the noncustodial parent will have with the child [see **visitation rights**]. Of course, the noncustodial parent will usually have some time with the child, during which the child may even reside with him or her. While the child is with the noncustodial parent, it is said that he or she has "physical custody" of the child. Actually, whenever *anyone* is **in loco parentis** to a child, he or she has physical custody. This may include baby-sitters, teachers, or state agencies into whose care the child has been given temporarily. Persons with physical custody of a child have limited authority over the child's care and activities. However, they do not normally have the power to make important decisions in the child's life.

Child custody orders may be modified by a court if the parents' circumstances have changed, or if a child who has reached a sufficient level of maturity decides he or she would prefer to live with the other parent, and this is in the child's best interests.

CHILD PORNOGRAPHY   The visual depiction of children engaged in sexual conduct or sexually explicit poses. The production, dissemination, and even possession of child pornography is outlawed by the federal **Sexual Exploitation Act** and by the laws of all states. A visual depiction may include photographs, videotapes, other moving pictures, or drawings if clearly from live models. The delivery of the materials may be by mail or any other method, including fax or computer modem.

Because of the risk of physical and emotional harm to the children who are used to produce these materials and the risk that such materials incite sexual abuse of children in general, the U.S. Supreme Court has made clear that child pornography is not protected as free expression under the First Amendment to the Constitution and may be banned. In addition, the Supreme Court has held that sexually explicit materials depicting children do not have to come within the legal definition of "obscenity" before they may be outlawed. In other words, material that would not be considered obscene if it depicted adults may be found illegal if it depicts children. [*New York v. Ferber* (1982)]

The Supreme Court has also ruled that the government has such a compelling interest in destroying the market for material that sexually exploits children that it outweighs the liberty and privacy interests of those who view it. In other words, laws that punish the possession of child pornography—even when it is entirely within the privacy of one's home—do not violate the constitutional right to liberty or privacy. [*Osborne v. Ohio* (1990)]

Even though sexual materials depicting children do not have to meet the legal definition of "obscene" in order to be outlawed, child pornography laws must define the forbidden conduct fairly specifically, or they risk being too vague for enforcement. However, because of the wide variety of activities that can be considered sexually oriented, the definition may be somewhat flexible. Mere nudity is not child pornography under any state's definition. This is to protect a family's innocent collection of bare-baby-on-a-bearskin-rug type photographs. Beyond this, courts are usually granted discretion to determine whether the depictions of children were directed at sexual titillation. Factors indicating that the material is pornographic include a focal point in the genital area of a nude or partially nude model, a sexually suggestive setting for the model, or a suggestion in the model's expression of a willingness to engage in sexual activity. Of course, depictions of children actually engaging in sexual acts are child pornography.

Under the federal Sexual Exploitation Act, as well as the laws of approximately half of the states, the use of young people under the age of eighteen as models or actors in sexually explicit materials is forbidden. The law is violated whether or not the producers or possessors of the material actually knew that the children depicted were underage. Most other states set sixteen as the age under which modeling in sexually explicit material is illegal. The remaining states recognize seventeen as the cutoff age.

CHILD PROTECTION ACTION A legal procedure through which the state acts to protect children from abuse and **neglect** by intervening in their families' affairs. A child protection action is initiated in a court having jurisdiction over juvenile or family matters. Typically, the case is filed by a child welfare agency after an investigation turns up evidence of **child abuse.** A child protection action is a civil, rather than criminal, type of lawsuit. Activities considered to be child abuse are frequently also crimes, and perpetrators may be tried for the same activities in criminal and civil courts at the same time.

Civil child protection cases have many advantages for a child's long-term welfare over criminal cases against the perpetrators of child abuse. First, the burden of proving child abuse is lighter in civil cases than in criminal cases. Generally, in a civil child protection action it is only necessary to prove that child abuse was more likely than not to have occurred before corrective action may be taken. (In some states, this standard is a bit higher; child abuse must be proved by "clear and convincing" evidence.) In a criminal case, by contrast, guilt must be proved beyond a reasonable doubt.

In child protection actions, the rules of evidence may be more relaxed than in criminal cases. For example, unlike most legal proceedings, "hearsay evidence"—what the alleged child victim said to others about the incidents at issue—may be admitted into evidence. This exception to the rule is justified in the child protection action by the reality that children often make poor witnesses in the courtroom. When children do testify in child protection actions, the judge may allow them to testify in another room or to preserve their testimony on videotape in order to prevent intimidation.

Rules requiring certain persons to keep confidences are also relaxed in child protection actions. For example, the court may order communications between husbands and wives, doctors and patients, and attorneys and clients to be revealed in child protection actions. Normally, these communications are protected and kept confidential. Relaxation of these confidentiality rules is justified in child protection actions by the fact that child abuse is an activity with few witnesses. Crucial evidence may, therefore, not be withheld.

Prior acts of abuse involving other children may be entered into evidence in child protection actions in order to show that the accused adult also abused the child at issue. Normally, evidence of prior events is not permitted in court cases.

Civil child protection actions also differ from criminal cases in the scope of options available to a court once abuse has been confirmed. In a criminal case, the court has only limited options: it may fine the abuser or sentence him or her to prison. The emphasis is on punishment, rather than rehabilitation. In a civil case, the court has a wide range of remedial orders available to it—from requiring counseling and agency supervision for the child's family to total termination of **parental rights.** In between these extremes are many variations. For example, the court may place the child in the custody of a child welfare agency for assignment to temporary **foster care.** The emphasis in child protection cases is first to protect the child from harm, but ultimately to return the child to his or her family after the abusive behavior has been stopped.

A juvenile court typically retains jurisdiction over a civil child protection case even after a decision has been made. This means that if there are changes in the family's situation—for example, if counseling has helped abusive parents mend their behavior—the case may be reopened, and the court may change its orders with regard to the child's placement.

Finally, in criminal cases, courts act only to punish the wrongdoers after the fact. In a civil child protection action, a court may take preventive measures to protect children at risk before abuse occurs. For example, if the juvenile court finds that a parent abused one child in the family, the court may remove all children from the parent's custody, even though those children have not yet been victimized.

Child protection actions, like any cases in which constitutionally protected "liberty interests" are at stake, invoke the entire panoply of due process rights. Those accused of abusing a child must have the right to notice of the charges and the right to a hearing at which they may call and cross-examine witnesses. The child must have a **guardian ad litem** to represent his or her separate interests. A child may not be taken from his or her parents' custody without a hearing and a court order. The hearing must be expedited, both for the parents and out of recognition that the child for whom the action is taken may suffer profound emotional distress caused by the procedure itself. It is essential to have the case decided as soon as possible. Lastly, a method for appealing a court's decision must be made available.

CHILD VICTIMS' AND CHILD WITNESSES' RIGHTS ACT

A federal law enacted in 1990 that permits federal courts to take extraordinary measures to protect the emotional health of children called to testify before them. The act applies only in cases in which the child called to testify has been the victim of **child abuse** or has witnessed a crime committed against another person. Attorneys for the government, the child's parent or **guardian**, or a **guardian ad litem** must apply for the special protections prior to trial. If circumstances warrant it, the court may then order that the child's testimony be taken in another room and televised via two-way closed circuit television. Or, the court may order that the child's testimony be taken in a videotaped deposition elsewhere.

Justifications for the special measures include situations in which the child is too intimidated by the atmosphere in the courtroom to testify and when the child would suffer emotional trauma from being forced to testify there. In some cases, if conduct by the defendant or the defendant's attorney makes it impossible for the child to continue to testify in the courtroom, the special measures for testifying may be ordered. The court may also close a trial to the public during a child's testimony and order the identity of the child withheld.

CHILD'S CUSTODIAL PREFERENCE   A child's preference regarding the parent with whom he or she will live following the parents' divorce is a factor that is increasingly considered by courts when making custody determinations. [See also **child custody.**] Approximately one-half of the states have laws mandating consideration of the child's wishes when determining custody. In Georgia, a child of fourteen has an absolute right to select the custodial parent, unless a court finds that the selected parent is unfit. The remaining states provide that judges in custody cases may take the child's wishes into account at their discretion.

Generally, courts determine custody based on the child's best interests, but must or may consider the child's preference in determining what those best interests are. This approach recognizes the fact that a child's wishes and best interests are not necessarily the same. In spite of the trend toward considering the opinions of children in custody matters, a child's preference for custodial parent will usually be decisive only where other considerations indicate that both parents are equally qualified.

If no statute directs the court how much weight to give the child's preference in a custody dispute, the following factors will be considered:

- The child's age. Although there is no magic age of discretion in most states after which a child is presumed to be mature enough to decide his or her own custody arrangement, courts will assume that an older child has more mature reasons for making a choice and usually will give deference to that choice. This approach also reflects the fact that it is difficult for a court to enforce a child custody order when a teenager wishes to disobey it.

- The child's maturity level and ability to make reasoned judgments, regardless of age.

- The strength and clarity of the child's expression of preference.

- The degree to which the child is a good judge of his or her best interests.

- Whether the child's opinion appears to be the product of parental manipulation. The court must assess whether the child's impression that one parent will be more lenient in disciplinary matters or can give more material favors has unduly influenced his or her preference. Conversely, the court will investigate whether the child's antipathy toward one parent is the result of a campaign of negativity by the other parent.

- Whether the child's choice is unduly influenced by matters extraneous to the parenting ability of the parties. For example, is the child's choice of a particular parent due to a desire to live in a certain city or neighborhood, to attend a certain school, or to be with particular friends? If there is no objective superiority of the preferred environment over the environment offered by the unchosen parent, the court will probably discount the child's preference.

A child's custodial preference is relevant only to the extent that it involves parents. A court is not obligated to consider a child's wishes to live with a nonparent, unless the **parental rights** of the child's parents have been terminated. In fact, some courts believe that, unless the child's **biological parent**s are officially found unfit for parenthood, it is a violation of the parents' due process rights to even consider the child's placement with a third party. See also **psychological parent doctrine.**

While consideration of the child's preferences in custody matters is routine today, the method through which these preferences are elicited from the child can be problematic from a legal standpoint. The "fairest" way to discover a child's custodial preference from the point of view of the parents is to have the child testify in court and be subject to questioning by each parent's attorney. However, courts usually reject this method as too intimidating for the child and, for this reason, unlikely to elicit the child's true opinion on the matter. Therefore, most state laws allow the family court judge to interview the child in the privacy of his or her chambers, even without the consent of the parents. In some states, the parents' attorneys or the parents themselves must be present during the interview. Other states find that the presence of the divorcing parties and/or their attorneys does little to safeguard the rights of the parents and, in any case, is outweighed by the chilling effect it might have on the child's attempt to express his or her true feelings on the matter of custody. In these states, a judge may interview the child in private, without the presence of the parties or their attorneys. However, a written record of the interview must be made and available to the parties if they request it. In other states, interviews of the child are conducted by a child welfare agency, a guidance counselor, or a psychologist, who then files a report with the court detailing the outcome of an investigation of the child's preferences.

CHINS An acronym for "child in need of supervision" that is applied to minors who have committed **status offense**s as adjudicated in **juvenile court.** These children may be placed under the jurisdiction of a child protective agency to ensure that they are receiving adequate care and rehabilitative services.

CITIZENSHIP REQUIREMENTS The U.S. Supreme Court has struck down requirements that children be citizens of the United States in order to attend public schools in this country. In *Plyler v. Doe,* the Court held that it is a denial of **equal protection** of the laws to refuse to educate undocumented alien children in the public schools on the same basis as children who are citizens. This 1982 decision is of particular significance considering the repeated attempts of states with large populations of aliens to discourage illegal immigration through denial of educational opportunities to undocumented alien children. Undoubtedly, the Court will be presented with challenges to such laws again. Whether states will be able to advance reasons in favor of such discrimination that are significant enough to warrant the Court's reconsideration is an issue to be watched in the twenty-first century.

CIVIL RIGHTS ACT OF 1964 A federal law that banned discrimination on the basis of race, color, or national origin in any program receiving federal funding. It was also designed to eradicate racial discrimination in public schools. In particular, Title VI of the act requires school districts to demonstrate compliance with government directives calling for **desegregation** as a prerequisite to receiving federal monetary support.

Despite its sweeping intent, Title VI of the Civil Rights Act of 1964 has played a relatively minor role in influencing public schools to desegregate. The reason for this may be that the courts had already ruled that separate educational systems, no matter how "equal," violated the Constitution's guarantee of **equal protection** under the law a decade before the act was passed. [See *Brown v. Board of Education.*] Thus, much desegregation was achieved by means of court orders directing that certain actions be taken in the public schools—orders that resulted from lawsuits brought directly by private citizens who were suffering from discrimination in the schools.

By contrast, Title VI is enforced by government administrators deciding to withhold federal money if certain steps are not taken by school districts. For one reason or another, this withholding has rarely been resorted to. Between 1969 and 1975, only fifteen school districts were deprived of federal funds because of continuing segregation. The reason for the reluctance to actually cut off federal aid to public schools, despite continued segregation, may simply have been the realization that denying funding would simply make a bad situation worse, and the ones who would suffer from it were innocent children.

Ironically, one of the biggest sources of litigation involving Title VI has been the issue of "set asides," or positions in educational programs that are "reserved" for persons of minority races in an effort to achieve integration. In 1978, the Supreme Court held that one such program that set aside a number of positions in medical school to minority applicants violated Title VI because it was "reverse discrimination" against a white applicant. [*Regents of University of California v. Bakke* (1978)] This decision did not even come close to resolving the issue, however. In the years since, courts have decided both ways on programs that seek to ensure minority enrollments by creating reserved positions.

Although Title VI has been less effective than one might think in fighting race discrimination, a lawsuit based on violations of the act has advantages over a lawsuit based on a violation of the constitutional right to equal protection. In the latter case, it is necessary for the aggrieved party to prove that a school district intended to discriminate in order to find a violation. Under the act, it is only necessary to prove a discriminatory effect of a school policy to find a violation. Thus, discrimination is easier to prove under the act.

COMMUNITY SERVICE   One possible **disposition** for delinquent youths is an order for them to perform community service. Community service is appropriate for young offenders because it impresses a sense of responsibility for their actions at the same time as it benefits the community. The youth also gains job experience and an appreciation for the type of discipline a job requires. By demanding that juveniles affect the world in a beneficial way, community service may also impart a positive impetus to children whose sense of self-worth is so low that they can only perceive of their presence as making things worse.

As with any sentence, whether for adult or juvenile offenders, an order to perform community service cannot be "excessive," but it must bear some relation to the gravity of the original offense. In most states, the number of hours of community service required and the places it will be performed are within the juvenile judge's discretion to determine. However, in some states, a judge may not order a length of time for the performance of community service that is in excess of the time the youth could be placed in secure detention for the same delinquent acts.

COMPETENCY TESTING   The vast majority of states require public schools periodically to test their students to ensure that they have achieved a minimum level of basic skills. A minority of states require students to pass such tests as a prerequisite to graduation or advancement to a higher grade.

Testing of this sort has been challenged on the grounds that it violates the guarantee of **equal protection** under the law imposed on the states by the Fourteenth Amendment to the Constitution. Students have alleged that the testing requirements are unfair because they do not actually reflect what is taught in the schools or because they disproportionately fail members of traditionally disadvantaged minority groups whose poor performance reflects the residual effects of past educational discrimination. At least one court has been sympathetic to these arguments. Hence, to be valid, a minimum competency test should measure achievement only in subjects that are actually taught in the public schools. Moreover, such tests should endeavor to root out cultural biases that would make them easier to pass by students of the dominant middle-class population.

COMPULSORY ATTENDANCE LAW A law that requires children to attend school until they reach a certain age. Compulsory attendance laws also set a minimum number of years that students must attend. The purpose of such laws is to ensure that each child receives a minimal education, in hopes thereby of fostering a well-informed and productive populace. By 1918, all states had adopted some sort of compulsory attendance laws as part of the development of their public school systems.

Compulsory attendance laws are directed at parents, usually making it a violation of the state's criminal laws to fail to send one's child to school between specified ages. Occasionally, however, truant teenagers who are beyond their parents' control have also been subject to sanction for failure to attend school. Parents may withdraw their children from school temporarily only for very important reasons, such as when the health or safety of the child demands removal. If a child is unable to attend school for some pressing reason, such as health concerns (or employment, as for a child actor, for example) some alternative form of tutoring must be instituted.

Despite the great deference given to parents to raise their children as they see fit, laws that require children to attend school are not unconstitutional. A law may not require that a child attend any particular type of school. In *Pierce v. Society of Sisters,* the U.S. Supreme Court invalidated a law requiring children to attend public schools. In the same case, however, the Court reaffirmed the right of the state "to require that all children of proper age attend some school, that certain studies plainly essential to good citizenship must be taught, and that nothing be taught which is manifestly inimical to the public welfare." [268 U.S. 510, at 535]

Thus, states are permitted to set minimum educational standards and require that certain subjects be taught in all schools within the state. These requirements can apply to private as well as public schools, including religious schools and **home schools**. State laws may also require any student not educated in the public schools to take an equivalency examination to prove that he or she measures up in training to requirements set in the public schools as a condition of receiving official academic credit. State laws can also set minimum competency requirements for teachers in all schools within the state. Laws setting educational standards must apply equally to all schools.

Compulsory education laws occasionally collide with the religious beliefs of some parents who object to their children being "corrupted" by exposure to ideas not within the teachings of their faith. Generally, this is not accepted as an excuse not to comply with state educational standards. [See *Wisconsin v. Yoder* for a case in which the Supreme Court excused the children of a certain religious persuasion (Amish) from completing schooling up to the age required by a state law (sixteen).] While allowing great leeway to parents to inculcate their children with their own views, the law of a free society recognizes great value in exposing citizens to a wide variety of ideas in order to promote civilized debate and tolerance of differing views.

CONFRONTATIONAL RIGHTS   A minor being tried for delinquent acts has a constitutional right to confront the witnesses who testify against him or her at the adjudicatory stage of the proceedings. The adjudicatory stage is the phase during which evidence and testimony of witnesses are presented before a juvenile judge. Prior to the Supreme Court's 1967 ruling in *In re Gault*, a juvenile had no right to confront or cross-examine his or her accusers. A juvenile could be committed to a juvenile institution on the word of a witness who did not even have to make an appearance in court.

Generally, the witnesses against a juvenile defendant are cross-examined by the accused's attorney. It is rare that a youth will choose to represent himself or herself.

A corollary to the right of a juvenile to confront accusers is the right to be present at all hearings. An accused juvenile may be excluded from attending hearings only under extraordinary circumstances, such as mental illness. A disruptive juvenile may also be removed from the courtroom.

Although the federal Constitution does not require the right to cross-examination and confrontation to extend to phases of a delinquency case other than the adjudication, most states allow cross-examination at detention hearings, probable cause hearings, dispositional hearings, and waiver hearings. See also **adjudication; disposition; preliminary hearing.**

A youth must inform the court that he or she intends to exercise the right to cross-examine witnesses at the adjudication. It is then the court's duty to ensure that these witnesses are present at the hearing.

CONTRACEPTIVE RIGHTS Young people under the age of majority have a right to privacy regarding their sexual activities that includes the right to obtain contraceptive pills or devices, as well as the right to birth control information and services. In the case of *Carey v. Population Services International*, 431 U.S. 678 (1977), the Supreme Court struck down a New York law that forbade the sale to children under the age of sixteen of nonprescription contraceptives, even though it was legal for them to obtain contraceptives through a doctor's prescription. The state argued that the law was necessary to discourage minors from engaging in sexual activity. The Court, however, found that there was no solid evidence to show that the law had this effect and, therefore, that the minors' rights to privacy in the area of sexual relations outweighed any interest the state had in forbidding the sale of nonprescription contraceptives to them.

Following this lead, numerous other courts have rejected states' arguments that restricting minors' access to contraceptives protects them from immoral influences or strengthens parental authority over their children's lives. Instead, the judicial view in the last years of the twentieth century seems to be that a youth's interest in obtaining contraceptives is protected against state interference. In consistently making these rulings, judges probably have at the back of their minds the inconsistency that would result from recognizing the established right of a young girl to have an abortion [see **abortion rights**] while forbidding her to obtain the means to prevent getting pregnant in the first place.

The Supreme Court has not yet ruled on whether states may require that notice be sent to the parents of a minor who requests contraceptives. However, numerous state and federal courts have ruled that notice to parents may not be ordered over the objections of a child who seeks contraceptives.

While a state may not prevent minors from obtaining contraceptives, the Supreme Court has ruled that the government has no affirmative duty to ensure that those who lack financial resources—including young people—are provided with them. [*Harris v. McRae* (1980)]

CONTRACT RIGHTS   A contract is an agreement between two or more parties that the law will enforce. Children have the right to enter into contracts with adults and enforce them. However, the child retains the right to back out of the contract at any time until a reasonable period after he or she reaches the age of **majority.** This right to back out of a contract is known as the right of disaffirmance. Its purpose is to protect children from their own improvident financial decisions. Generally, anyone who has not reached the age of **majority** has the right to disaffirm contracts. This is true even for emancipated children. [See **emancipation.**] Because of children's right to disaffirm contracts, adults are less likely to enter into contracts with them, lest they change their minds.

An exception to the rule of disaffirmance is made for contracts for the purchase of items that are reasonably necessary for a child's maintenance, and that the child's parents have failed to provide. Contracts for these **necessaries** are not subject to the right of disaffirmance, and a child will be held to his or her side of the bargain to purchase them. In addition, some states also except certain other contracts from the right of disaffirmance. These may be agreements related to marriage, adoption, insurance purchases, loans for educational purposes, and employment. The latter exception was created to allow child entertainers to make binding agreements.

A child may disaffirm a contract by returning the merchandise, by pleading his or her youth in defense to a lawsuit for breach of contract brought against him or her, or by suing to recover the money back from the purchase. The adult with whom the contract is made, of course, has no such right. Upon reaching majority, a child who has made a contract must decide within a reasonable time whether to disaffirm it or to ratify it. A reasonable time is not definitely established, but it is clear that it may be as much as six months. Three years, however, is too long. The young adult may ratify the contract by expressly agreeing to do so, by continuing to perform his or her side of the bargain (for example, by continuing to make installment payments), or by doing nothing. If the young adult does nothing, after a reasonable time the contract will be considered ratified.

If a child chooses to disaffirm a contract, he or she usually is required to return anything of value received from the other party. Thus, the child must return merchandise purchased. If the thing of value no longer exists, or has been all used up, the child is excused from this requirement. For example, if a minor buys a car and then decides to disaffirm the contract after the car is destroyed in an accident, he or she may do so without returning the vehicle. In some states, in addition to returning the item, the minor must pay a reasonable amount representing the use of, depreciation of, or damage to, the item.

When a child misrepresents his or her age in making a contract, courts view the consequences differently in different jurisdictions. In some states, the fact of the misrepresentation is irrelevant. The minor still has an absolute right to disaffirm. Other states hold that a minor who misrepresents his or her age in order to enter a contract will be held to the contract and may not disaffirm it. In between these extreme positions, the remaining states allow the other party to sue the minor for damages caused by the misrepresentation. Usually, these damages may not exceed the amount the child owed under the contract.

CORPORAL PUNISHMENT In the case of *Ingraham v. Wright,* the U.S. Supreme Court determined that the Eighth Amendment with its proscription against "cruel and unusual punishment" does not apply in the public schools. Thus, according to the Court, that amendment does not prohibit the use of spanking, paddling, or slapping to discipline schoolchildren. The high Court did not endorse excessive corporal punishment through this ruling, however. Rather, in the Court's opinion, children do have a constitutionally protected right to be free from bodily restraint and punishment except in accordance with **due process of law.** (The source within the Constitution for this right remains unclear.) The Court also noted that other laws (such as state tort laws against battery or legislation banning child abuse) should serve to check excessive physical force used to discipline students. Thus, hitting public school children for disciplinary purposes is not unconstitutional, but it must be "moderate" and no more forceful than necessary to correct the student.

The *Ingraham* case also determined that schoolchildren are not entitled by the Constitution to notice or a hearing before moderate corporal punishment is administered. The Court noted that most corporal punishment in schools is applied in direct response to infractions of school rules that occur in view of a teacher. Hence, the danger of punishing the wrong child is lessened. Moreover, the value of a swift corrective lies just there—in its swiftness. If a drawn-out procedure of notice and a hearing were required, the disciplinary value of corporal punishment would be all but destroyed. Of course, a state or even a particular school can decide to give schoolchildren the benefit of a hearing before administering corporal punishment or can decide to outlaw corporal punishment entirely. However, the Constitution does not require this.

Although the Eighth Amendment does not prohibit corporal punishment, other constitutional challenges to the practice have been raised, notably through the Fourth Amendment ban on unreasonable "seizures." Most people are familiar with the concept of "seizure" as it relates to the seizure of evidence in criminal cases. However, physical seizures of persons are also included within its scope.

In 1995, such a challenge was made by a student who had been grabbed by a teacher trying to break up a fight. In *Wallace v. Batavia School District No. 101* (1995), a student, Heather Wallace, was attempting to hit another student when teacher James Cliffe seized her by the wrist and elbow and steered her forcibly toward the door. At the door, Wallace told Cliffe to let go of her, which he did. After the incident, Wallace alleged that her Fourth Amendment right to be free of unreasonable seizures had been violated in the incident. The Seventh Circuit Court of Appeals ruled that the only thing "unreasonable" in this case was Wallace's making a "federal case out of a routine school disciplinary matter." The appeals court endorsed a test of "reason" to determine whether physical force used by school personnel against a student is constitutional. This test requires a court to weigh "(1) [t]he need for the application of corporal punishment; (2) the relationship between the need and the amount of punishment administered; (3) the extent of injury inflicted; and (4) whether the punishment was administered in a good faith effort to maintain discipline or maliciously and sadistically for the very purpose of causing harm." [870 F. Supp. at 224] In the *Wallace* case, the need for a quick, decisive seizure to break up a fight with another student was clear. The amount of force—grabbing the wrist and elbow of the student and moving her toward the door—was not excessive. There was no indication that Wallace suffered any real injury. Finally, Cliffe's motives were clearly within reason: he was acting to stop physical violence between students on school property.

While the *Wallace* case presents a clear-cut example of corporal punishment that is reasonable, other situations are not so obvious. As students become more violence-prone toward the turn of the twenty-first century, school personnel are placed in a difficult position: if they do not take swift measures to deal with violent actions by students—some of which require physical restraint—they are vulnerable to charges that they are not doing their jobs in keeping students safe. On the other hand, if they do seize students or apply physical punishment, they risk a lawsuit for violating the punished students' constitutional rights. Critics of corporal punishment also have a point in questioning the value of violent solutions to misbehavior in an era when escalating violence among youth is precisely one of society's biggest problems. Unfortunately, there is little the law can do to clarify exactly when, and how much, force is acceptable. Each situation is unique, and each teacher must have flexibility to respond as judgment dictates. Clearly, however, this area is likely to see continued litigation into the new century.

COUNSEL RIGHTS The right to consult with, and be represented by, an attorney. Under the U.S. Constitution, minors have the right to counsel at the adjudicatory stage of any delinquency proceedings in which their liberty is at stake. The adjudicatory phase is the "courtroom" part of the proceeding, during which evidence is given and witnesses testify and are cross-examined before a judge. The attorney must also be permitted to give closing arguments in the case. The federal Constitution requires counsel for minors only when they are accused of acts for which they could be sentenced to a juvenile institution. However, today a majority of states' laws mandate counsel in the adjudication of any delinquency case, even when punishment does not include the possibility of incarceration. Moreover, many states provide that a minor must be given the option of consulting with a lawyer from the moment he or she is taken into custody. In those states, an attorney must be present at the child's request before any interrogation by the police. Many states also extend the right to an attorney to the phases following adjudication of delinquency charges: the **disposition,** in which sentence is determined and passed; and any appeals of the court's decision to higher courts. In most states, the state must pay for a minor's attorney if the minor or his or her family cannot afford one.

The right to the services of an attorney must be explained to any minor charged with delinquent acts. Failure to adequately explain this right may result in the invalidity of any confession the child makes without an attorney present. In most states, the right to an attorney must also be explained to the minor's parents so that they can advise their child and actually hire the lawyer. Many children would not even know how to find a lawyer, let alone arrange to pay one.

Generally, a minor who has been taken into custody and his or her parents must be informed of the right to an attorney by either an attorney or a judge. A social worker or other layperson is not qualified to explain the right. A videotaped presentation by a judge has been held to be adequate, provided the youth and his or her parents are then required to sign a written statement that they understood the tape's contents.

A minor charged with delinquent acts is entitled to a full-fledged attorney who has passed the bar examination and is licensed to practice law in the jurisdiction in which the adjudication is taking place. Thus, the child must have more than just access to the services of a law clerk, legal intern, or a juvenile "case worker." Moreover, a minor has the right to "effective" counsel. This means the attorney must represent the child's interests in a competent manner. However, it does not mean that the attorney must always "win" or achieve everything the child desires in the case.

The issue of effective representation for minors is complicated by the possible conflict between the minor's desires and "what is best for him or her" as seen through the eyes of an adult. Of course, part of effective representation is to explain to the child why a particular legal strategy is "best" for him or her. But even more problematic is the situation in which the child and his or her parents differ on the best course of action to take. Normally, parents represent the child's interests in any legal proceeding. That is, it is they who direct the litigation. However, where it is clear that the parents' interests are different from those of the child, most states require that an attorney hired to represent the child in a delinquency proceeding ignore the parents' wishes and proceed to give the best representation based on the lawyer's judgment and the child's needs and desires.

A child may choose to do without a lawyer, or "waive" the right to a lawyer. However, courts carefully scrutinize the circumstances under which a minor elects not to have a lawyer. If it appears that the child did not fully understand the right to an attorney, and the usual advantages of having an attorney, or was pressured to give up the right to an attorney, the court may find that the child did not actually intend to forgo professional representation. In that case, an attorney may be appointed for the child regardless of what he or she says.

The right to an attorney may extend to other types of proceedings besides delinquency adjudications. Some states require the appointment of a lawyer to represent a child in custody determinations, termination of parental rights proceedings, child abuse investigations and trials, medical treatment consent issues, and other procedures in which major decisions regarding a child's life and welfare are involved.

COURT RECORDS Records generated by a minor's brush with juvenile court generally are kept confidential, so as not to stigmatize the youth so early in life that rehabilitation seems futile. As the Supreme Court in *In re Gault* put it, it is necessary "to hide youthful errors from the full gaze of the public and bury them in the graveyard of the forgotten past." [387 U.S. 1 at 24 (1967)]

Records that fall within this cloak of secrecy include almost anything compiled as a result of a minor's arrest. Thus, in addition to the expected police reports, fingerprints, and jail photographs, all investigative reports gathered by social workers on the child's background and family relationships and psychological profiles are also confidential. Furthermore, all court pleadings, transcripts, depositions, dispositions, and detention reports are secret.

Although juvenile court records are not accessible to the public, they can be disclosed to various "interested" parties, usually at the discretion of a juvenile court judge. State laws may also delineate to whom records may be revealed. Generally, a court may order the transfer of juvenile records to another court of law before whom the juvenile is appearing, to a state agency preparing a predisposition investigative report on the juvenile in a case pending before another court, to another state agency that is treating the child or offering him or her rehabilitative programs, to an agency of government that is considering hiring the subject of the records for a position directly affecting national security, and also to the victims (and victims' families) of the juvenile's delinquent acts in answer to inquiries about the ultimate disposition of the case. In rare other instances, someone may be able to convince a court that he or she has an important need to see the contents of the juvenile records, for example, in order to construct a defense to criminal charges.

Questions frequently arise about whether one's juvenile court records can be put into evidence in a subsequent criminal trial in an adult court in order to prove guilt. Generally, the rule is that juvenile adjudications cannot be used in later adult trials. However, such records *can* usually be used at the sentencing phase of an adult trial, after a conviction, in order for the judge to pass sentence in an informed manner. Occasionally, someone attempts to use the juvenile court record of a witness in a criminal trial to cast doubt on the credibility of the witness. The U.S. Supreme Court has held in one case, *Davis v. Alaska* (1974), that it was a denial of a defendant's constitutional right to confront and cross-examine witnesses for a court to refuse to allow questions to a juvenile witness regarding the witness's juvenile court record.

The secrecy surrounding juvenile court proceedings and records is, of course, profoundly at odds with the right of the public to know the workings of government agencies and the First Amendment rights of the media to report on these matters. In all other courts, except under very special circumstances, the records are open to the public. In the closing days of the twentieth century, more challenges to the rule of confidentiality are being raised [see **public trial**] as the offenses committed by juveniles have seemingly become more serious. This issue will continue to occupy judicial time in the coming century.

In addition to the rule of confidentiality with regard to juvenile records, most states provide some means of destroying (expunging) or sealing the records after a period of time has passed, so as to forever erase the evidence of youthful mistakes. Usually, a period of two to five years must have passed since the final discharge of the person from juvenile court supervision, and the person must not have been subsequently convicted of any crime or misdemeanor. In most states, expunction is automatic for records of arrests that did not lead to trials, for proceedings in which charges were dropped, or if an adjudication was terminated in the juvenile's favor (that is, he or she was found "not guilty"). In all other dispositions, expunction is not automatic, but requires that a formal request be made in court for the destruction or permanent sealing of the records. Often the petitioner must show that the subject of the records has been rehabilitated and that his or her best interests are served by destroying the records. It has been held in at least one court that it is not a violation of a juvenile's rights for the court not to inform juvenile offenders about their rights to expunction of records.

States differ in exactly what records must be sealed or expunged. In some states, only the documents that were actually used in court must be sealed. Investigative background reports and sometimes police records are not sealed.

The issue of whether a person must voluntarily disclose that he or she had a juvenile court record (after expunction) is also controversial. The entire purpose behind expunction statutes is to "wipe the slate clean" so that youthful mistakes will not follow a person throughout his or her life and hinder leading a productive life. Thus, a few states (Ohio is one) actually have statutes that provide that a person may freely deny having had a juvenile record if asked, provided the record has been expunged or sealed.

Other states have laws making it illegal to discriminate against a person applying for employment, driver's licenses, credit, or housing on the grounds that he or she had a juvenile court record that was expunged.

CRIMINAL NONSUPPORT STATUTE A law in all states making it a criminal offense for a parent willfully to fail to support his or her child. Such statutes are yet another incentive for noncustodial parents to discharge their **support obligation**s to their children. Usually, prosecutors will agree to suspend the prescribed fines or imprisonment of a parent convicted under such a statute if the parent will pay the support owed. A criminal nonsupport action may be prosecuted in addition to a civil contempt of court suit to enforce child support orders issued upon the divorce of parents. [See also **support enforcement.**] Because a finding of civil contempt may also result in incarceration, the two actions are similar. However, a civil contempt case is usually brought by the custodial parent on behalf of the child, to whom the money is really owed. A criminal nonsupport action is initiated by a state prosecutor.

Usually, the state prosecutor must prove that the owing parent was willful or deliberate in refusing to pay support. Since it is frequently difficult to prove a person's intentions, some criminal nonsupport statutes provide that showing that support has not been paid is proof on its face (prima facie proof) of violation of the statute. The owing parent must then rebut this presumption of guilt by proving an inability to pay the required amount. A genuine inability to pay will allow the parent to avoid conviction. However, if the inability to pay the required amount was the result of a ruse to avoid payment, a conviction will follow. An indigent parent accused of criminal nonsupport is entitled to a state-appointed lawyer.

CURFEW A law forbidding people from being on the streets during specified hours after dark. Curfews are very ancient in origin. They are thought to have been in general use throughout Europe in the Middle Ages and were probably introduced into England by William the Conqueror after 1066. The word *curfew* derives from the French phrase *couvre feu* meaning "cover the fires." In ancient times, the town bell would ring, signaling citizens to extinguish their fires and go to bed.

Theoretically, the curfew helped prevent destructive fires and preserve the public peace by encouraging the dispersal of crowds, and it fostered a climate of rest so that labor could resume early the next day. In modern times, curfew laws have been used effectively by totalitarian regimes to prevent insurrections. Although curfew laws were used in the United States during the Civil War in areas under martial law, today it is well settled that a curfew applicable to adult citizens would be unconstitutional except in the most extreme circumstances. For example, conditions of war, anarchy, natural disasters, or mass rioting may justify a limited curfew imposed on all citizens. The freedom to move about is considered one of the most important liberties of American citizens—for its own sake and also because it is so closely connected with the constitutionally protected rights of freedom of association and freedom of speech.

While curfews directed at adults would almost certainly be unconstitutional, the same is not true of curfews aimed at young people. The Supreme Court has made it clear that, although the distinction between constitutional rights available to adults and those available to minors is narrowing, the state may place special restrictions on children under the **parens patriae doctrine.** It is believed that the interests children have in being out at night are usually not as important as the reasons adults have for late hours, and children are more likely to engage in irresponsible behavior than adults when out for entertainment.

Generally, three basic justifications for curfew laws directed at minors have been advanced. First, the government has a legitimate interest in preventing crimes by juveniles, who—it is believed—are more likely to cook up illegal schemes in late-night gatherings. Basically, children are seen to be more susceptible to suggestion by their peers and older children that might lead them into unlawful behavior. This is particularly true where a group dynamic arises in which individual children may not have the independence of judgment or courage of action to refuse to go along with the crowd.

Second, curfew laws are designed to protect children from being preyed upon by unscrupulous adults. Since adult criminals of all types are often abroad at night, children, who are naturally naive, are more likely to be victimized by them at that time. Moreover, some adult criminals specifically seek out children as victims. The fewer children that are on the street during the hard-to-police night hours, the fewer will fall victim to crimes by these predators.

Third, curfew laws are believed to strengthen parental authority by putting the force of law behind parents' concerns in having their children home at a reasonable hour where their behavior can be supervised and directed. See also **status offense.**

Despite these strong justifications, courts have also recognized that young people have similar interests in freedom of movement, association, and free speech to those of adults. Thus, in order to be legal, curfew laws must advance their legitimate objectives with the least possible restriction on these important freedoms.

To be legal, a curfew ordinance must first not be "overbroad." This means that it must not include clearly lawful activity within the scope of its prohibitions. For example, a curfew that made it illegal for children to be out of doors anywhere within city limits would probably be "overbroad" and unconstitutional because it would also forbid a child from sitting on the front porch of his or her home. This is clearly an activity that could cause none of the harm the curfew was designed to prevent.

Second, a curfew must not be so vague that normal citizens would not know exactly what type of activity was forbidden. For example, a curfew that made it illegal to "hang out" after dark might be void for vagueness, because people do not know exactly what is meant by "hanging out." Generally, a valid curfew law must also clearly state the hours and places to which it applies. One curfew law was struck down because it did not include a time when the prohibition on being out on the streets ended, leaving it up to citizens to guess.

Laws that make it illegal merely to "be" in a certain place at a certain time are very likely to be considered overbroad and/or vague. Thus, most curfew laws that have survived constitutional challenges have carefully spelled out the type of behavior that is excepted from the curfew's scope. For example, a valid curfew may state that children going to and from legitimate employment, school, or religious activities during curfew hours are exempted from the curfew. Most laws also make an exception for children who are in the company of their parents or other responsible adults. A valid curfew may also make an exception for children who are on the streets because of an emergency—either seeking help or going to render help to someone. Valid curfews must have reasonable hours. For example, an 8:00 P.M. curfew may be considered unreasonable, while an 11:00 P.M. one would not. A curfew that ended at 10:00 in the morning might be unreasonable, while one that ended at 4:30 A.M. would not be. Also, in order to be lawful, a curfew law must not be drafted so that it gives police too much discretion in deciding whether to enforce it. Courts have struck down curfew laws when they were being enforced in a discriminatory manner against minority youth.

CURRICULUM CHOICE The choice of what and how to teach in the public schools has traditionally been left to state and local school districts to determine. Students may be given a choice of "elective" courses, but generally they have no say in what courses are required for graduation and no option not to take the ones that are required. Similarly, individual parents are not permitted to exempt their children from specific required courses or to choose alternative textbooks for their children's instruction. The general view of the courts is that such objections to the chosen curriculum amount to parents' efforts to prevent their children's exposure to ideas with which the parents do not agree. In a democratic society, this is not a value meriting a high degree of protection. Rather, courts have concluded that the interest in exposing children to values such as independent thought, respect for diverse views, self-reliance, and logical decision making outweighs any rights of the parents to "tailor" a narrow curriculum for their children within the public schools. Parents who object may send their children to private schools more in keeping with their religious or political views.

On the other hand, courts are sensitive to attempts by public school authorities to force children, through means of required classes or exercises, to affirm or deny matters that conflict with the children's religious beliefs. For example, children must be free to decline to say the "Pledge of Allegiance" if they so choose. [See *West Virginia Board of Education v. Barnette.*] In some cases, courts have upheld parents' rights to excuse their children from attending sex education classes, because they conflict with the parents' deeply held views on sexual matters. In one case, a court ordered a school district either to provide segregated boys' and girls' physical education classes or to excuse from participation students who objected to appearing in coeducational classes in minimal exercise uniforms or to seeing other students in such attire.

In the last decades of the twentieth century, some groups have attempted to style certain religious beliefs as "science" and have required their teaching in the public schools. At the same time, these groups object to standard scientific teachings on the grounds that they, too, are "religious" in nature and should be banned from public schools, or at least "equal time" should be given to alternative religious theories. In particular, this battle has raged over the theory of the evolution of life and the role in that process played by natural selection, as espoused by Charles Darwin in the nineteenth century. Some groups claim evolution and natural selection to be tenets of a religion they call secular humanism. As an alternative, they advance what they call creationism, a view holding that the various forms of life on earth appeared fully developed and all at once. In general, courts do not accept these arguments, finding that only the evolution theories qualify as scientific and, thus, are proper subjects for public school education. Basically, a theory is scientific if it corresponds to observed phenomena and its adherents are prepared to reject or modify it if and when the theory no longer so corresponds. The theory of evolution does correspond to observation. By contrast, adherents of creationism reason from their conclusions, choosing to reject observations that do not support the theory or to explain these observations in ways that are equally incapable of being proved false. See also *Edwards v. Aguillard.*

CUSTODIAL CONFINEMENT   The most severe of measures that may be ordered by a **juvenile court** for rehabilitation of a **juvenile delinquent,** custodial confinement is the placement of the convicted youth in an institution to live for a period of time. Custodial confinement roughly corresponds to incarceration of adults, except that punishment is not the aim of the placement. Rather, the juvenile institutions in which delinquents are housed are required to provide rehabilitative opportunities.

State laws differ in setting guidelines for when custodial confinement is an appropriate disposition for youthful offenders. Usually, it is based on the child's age, the offense committed, the youth's previous record, and any aggravating circumstances, such as a youth's intransigent attitude toward reform. Generally, courts must consider less restrictive alternatives for reforming delinquents, and confinement is said to be the last resort. Usually, confinement is appropriate if the delinquent acts were serious and of the type that would be felonies if the perpetrator were an adult or if the youth is a repeat offender. Custodial confinement may even be ordered for **status offense**s, such as habitual truancy, if the court determines that this is the best hope of reforming the child.

Custodial confinement may be in either a secure or nonsecure facility. Nonsecure facilities, as the name implies, have no physical barriers to keep inmates in. These are institutions such as group homes, halfway houses, foster homes, boarding schools, or other facilities at which the child may live in a very structured environment under supervision of personnel charged with enforcing the child's attendance at school and participation in any court-ordered counseling programs, and with enforcing curfew restrictions. Despite the supervision, however, the juveniles assigned to nonsecure facilities may have access to the surrounding community and take part in normal activities.

A secure facility, as the name implies, is one that restricts the movements of its inmates by means of physical barriers. Juveniles assigned to these facilities do not have access to the outside community. Generally, placement in this type of facility is justified only if a court believes that the youth poses a danger to society if he or she is permitted freedom within the community. However, increasingly, children who are repeat substance abusers, have run away from other nonsecure placements, and are beyond parental or any other control may also wind up in a secure facility.

Incarceration in secure facilities for juveniles has been subject to much criticism, as many studies have shown that rehabilitation in such institutions is unlikely. Critics charge that the facilities operate as no more than "storage" for unwanted youth and that any educational programs are subordinated to regimentation and control.

Youths in secure facilities have the same constitutional rights as do adult prisoners; that is, they have the right to a safe and sanitary environment, adequate clothing, and adequate medical and dental care, as well as the right to communicate with family and their lawyers. However, beyond these rights, they also have rights to other services, such as counseling, psychiatric treatment, tutoring, or educational and vocational training, that need not be given to adult inmates. Numerous federal courts have held that these rights to services are part of the **due process of law** guaranteed to citizens by the Constitution and to minors in particular as a result of the rehabilitative purpose behind juvenile courts. The theory behind this is that, since children do not have all the same pre-detention due process rights as adults, they must at least derive some benefit from their status as children. Thus, they are due more than just warehousing in a prison.

In some states, the parents of delinquents sentenced to custodial confinement may be required to pay some or all of the costs of the child's incarceration or to reimburse the state for such costs.

Generally, juveniles may not be kept in the same facilities as adult criminals, unless the youths are carefully segregated within the facility. Many state laws do not allow jailing juveniles in any penal institution that also houses adults. Some courts have gone so far as to hold that such jailing automatically violates a youth's Eighth Amendment rights against cruel and unusual punishment. The federal **Juvenile Justice and Delinquency Prevention Act** also prohibits states that receive federal funds under its provisions from housing juveniles in jails with adult offenders. Exposure of children to adult offenders, even for a short time, is believed to incite suicides and lead to sexual and physical abuse and psychological harm. This could contribute to further criminal behavior rather than prevent it.

CUSTODIAL INTERFERENCE STATUTE   A state law making it a criminal offense to interfere with the lawful custody or **visitation rights** of a parent. These criminal laws have been passed in every state. They were necessitated by the many cases of noncustodial parents kidnapping their own children and taking them across state lines, often leaving no trace of their whereabouts. Usually, child snatching within a state is classified as a misdemeanor, while taking a child across state lines is a felony. In cases in which a child has been taken across state lines in violation of a state custodial interference statute, the Federal Bureau of Investigation may be called upon to help find and return the child.

In most states, only a violation of a court order regarding custody or visitation will result in a criminal offense. In a few states, the existence of a court order is not relevant to the offense. Any concealment of a child or removal to another state in an attempt to defeat the jurisdiction of a court deciding custody is a violation of the law.

Most custodial interference statutes apply to any person who takes a child or prevents a child from being taken by his or her lawful custodian, or a person having lawful visiting privileges. However, a few states' laws are directed at parents only. A parent or other person who takes a child in contravention to a lawful custody decree may be absolved of criminal responsibility if the child was taken to protect him or her from imminent danger. Voluntary return of the child may also save a child snatcher from prosecution.

DELINQUENCY PROCEEDING A procedure in **juvenile court** through which minors accused of committing acts that would be crimes if committed by adults are tried. If such a juvenile is found guilty, he or she is officially a **juvenile delinquent.**

Theoretically, juvenile court is intended to resemble a sort of "clinic" at which troubled youngsters receive help in resolving the problems that led to their antisocial behavior. In reality, however, a delinquency proceeding more and more mirrors an adult criminal trial. As in an adult trial, there are three distinct phases: (1) the **preliminary hearing,** which corresponds to the arraignment in adult court; (2) the **adjudication,** corresponding to the trial phase of an adult proceeding, in which evidence of the accused's guilt or innocence is presented; and (3) the **disposition** phase (corresponding to sentencing in adult court), at which time the judge determines what will happen to the juvenile who has been found guilty.

Although in most important ways a juvenile delinquency proceeding is like an adult criminal trial, there are some important differences. For example, the U.S. Constitution does not require **bail** for juveniles or the right to a **jury trial,** although some states' laws grant these privileges to minors tried in juvenile court. There are also some differences in rules of evidence at juvenile proceedings. [See **burden of proof.**] Most importantly, however, the available options for "sentencing" a juvenile delinquent are greater and usually less punitive than adult offenders. See also **counsel rights.**

DESEGREGATION Since the 1954 Supreme Court decision in *Brown v. Board of Education,* it has been firmly established that children have a right to attend schools that are not racially segregated. In that case, the Court ruled that separate schools, even if perfectly matched in facilities and resources, are inherently "unequal" because, among other things, the stigma they impose on minority students, who are to be "kept away" from the mainstream majority, is detrimental to those students' education.

Of course, the nation's schools did not become integrated overnight after the *Brown* decision appeared. In fact, it was not until ten years after the decision that the Supreme Court and other federal courts really began cracking down on school systems that had not moved to remedy segregated schools. The last forty-odd years have been a period of constant struggle to realize the dream of a color-blind educational system. While great progress has been made in wiping out laws that specifically called for separate schools (so-called de jure segregation), segregation that is the result of more subtle prejudice and economic patterns continues today (so-called de facto segregation). Moreover, the last decade of the twentieth century has seen a peculiar voluntary refragmentization of student bodies within integrated schools. Students seem to be finding more comfort in reinforcing separate ethnic identities than in finding common ground with others. Naturally, no law can prevent voluntary associations such as these from forming.

Presently, the law on segregation is this: if segregation is the result of deliberate governmental policies, the federal government may order remedial actions, such as busing, to force integration. However, if segregated schools are truly the incidental outcome of race-neutral factors, no remedial action will be ordered. In the latter case, the segregation must in no way be the result of racial prejudice. Thus, creatively drawing school district boundaries in order to minimize the number of minority students in certain schools is clearly not "race-neutral" even though there is no explicit policy to exclude certain students. On the other hand, if certain districts are predominantly populated by citizens of one race as a result of economic factors in areas in which there never existed laws that deliberately segregated the races, segregated schools do not in themselves violate the Constitution.

When is a school considered integrated? This is a difficult question, because the Constitution does not demand that there be "equal" numbers of black and white (or other race) students in a school—or even that the percentage of minority students in a school correspond to the percentage of the overall minority population. All the Constitution requires is that schools have a "unitary" school system in which school attendance patterns are not shaped in any way by present, or past, deliberate racial discrimination. The presence of all-black or all-white, or nearly all-black or all-white, schools is usually highly suspicious, however, and may require judicial investigation. Other factors that courts consider—besides the mere numbers of students of various races in attendance—include (1) the racial composition of the faculty and staff, (2) the condition and extent of the facilities and equipment, (3) the richness of extracurricular activities, and (4) the transportation policies of the school.

🏛 *DeShaney v. Winnebago County Department of Social Services* In this 1989 case, the U.S. Supreme Court determined that the duty of the government to protect children from abuse by others does not rise to a constitutional imperative. The *DeShaney* decision is important in defining the extent to which the government will be required to act under the **parens patriae doctrine** for the benefit of minor citizens.

Joshua DeShaney was a four-year-old child living in the custody of his father in Winnebago County, Wisconsin. The Department of Social Services there was alerted to the possibility that Joshua's father was physically abusing him and took some measures to protect the child. They removed Joshua from his father's care, but then returned him upon the father's promise that he would participate in an abuse prevention program. During the next six months, the father failed to live up to his agreement. The department continued to receive reports of abuse, including accounts from Joshua's caseworker, his father's girlfriend, and a local hospital that twice treated Joshua for suspicious injuries in its emergency room. Yet the department did nothing further to protect the child. Finally, Joshua was beaten so severely by his father that he lapsed into a coma from which he emerged profoundly and permanently retarded.

Joshua and his mother sued the Department of Social Services, alleging that the department, as an agent of the state government, had violated Joshua's constitutional rights. Specifically, they claimed that Joshua had been deprived of his liberty without the **due process of law** required by the Fifth Amendment of the Constitution. While expressing sympathy for Joshua and reproaching the county officials who stood by and did nothing to help him, the Supreme Court did not agree that the government had a constitutional obligation to take affirmative measures to protect the child: "The Constitution does not require a state or local government to protect its citizens from private violence or other mishaps not attributable to the conduct of its employees." The Supreme Court also rejected Joshua's argument that the county, by initially intervening in Joshua's case and having knowledge of the danger he was in, had assumed a "special relationship" with Joshua that affirmatively required it to act for his protection.

Although the Supreme Court ruled that Joshua had no constitutional claim against the government, it noted that the child might prevail in a common law tort claim against the department. (A tort is a private wrong that can be addressed through a civil lawsuit for compensation in the form of money damages. Success depends on showing that the one who caused injury had a duty to act carefully and failed to do so. This duty does not have its origin in the Constitution, however.)

Three justices—Brennan, Marshall, and Blackmun—disagreed with the majority's opinion. They pointed out cases in which the Supreme Court previously held that the government did have a constitutional duty to act to protect citizens from the acts of private persons. These involved situations in which the inmates of prisons or mental institutions were injured by other inmates from whom the government did not protect them. The plaintiffs in these cases were helpless to help themselves, being, as they were, totally dependent on the government for their care. Joshua's situation was really no different than these cases, said the dissenters. Just because he was not physically in the custody of the state did not mean that he was not helpless to help himself. The dissenters pointed out that only the Department of Social Services had the authority to help Joshua. All anyone else could do was to report their suspicions and concerns about what was happening to Joshua to that department. No one else could legally act to take him from his abusive father.

DISABLED STUDENTS Prior to the mid-1970s, children with disabilities had been left out of the revolution of rights for school children. Children with disabilities of all types could simply be judged "untrainable" and excluded from public school systems entirely. Or, if they were permitted to attend public schools at all, they were often sidelined into segregated programs that did not address individual needs, or they sat marginalized in regular classes merely waiting until they were old enough to drop out. However, following the ruling in the case of *Brown v. Board of Education,* many pointed out that the guarantee of "equal educational opportunities" for all children should not be denied to those suffering from disabilities.

In the intervening years, a flood of legislation, both federal and state, has addressed the needs of disabled children. Federal laws include Section 1684 of Title IX of the Education Amendments of 1972, Section 504 of the

Rehabilitation Act of 1973, the Education for All Handicapped Children Act (EAHCA), the Developmentally Disabled Assistance Act and Bill of Rights, the Handicapped Programs Technical Amendments Act of 1988, and the **Individuals with Disabilities Education Act of 1990** (IDEA), to name a few.

Today, this comprehensive web of laws provides handicapped children with the following:

- The right to procedural safeguards in decisions regarding the children's identification, evaluation, and placement.

- The right to be educated together with children who are not handicapped to the greatest extent possible. A disabled child may be removed to a separate environment for schooling only if the disability is so severe that the use of supplementary aids and services within regular classes cannot bring him or her significant educational benefits.

- The right to an "appropriate" education, including the design of an individualized education program (IEP) adapted to each child.

These requirements are mandated by federal law in each state that receives federal assistance for educating disabled children. Some states' laws are even more protective of the rights of disabled children. When that is the case, the state law will prevail over the federal one.

In the last decade of the twentieth century, disputes have arisen over just what types of disabilities the many laws protect. It is settled that the laws cover children with mental retardation; hearing, vision, and speech impediments; physical motion deficits of all types; autism; and some specific learning disabilities. The laws also cover serious emotional disturbances. However, as more and more "syndromes" are identified as medical conditions, there is greater and greater pressure to include children that, in another day, would simply have been labeled "difficult," "incorrigible," or "undisciplined." The extent to which bad behavior must be accommodated in the classroom because it is symptomatic of some identified medical condition, and thus within the scope of laws protecting the disabled, is a question that will occupy jurists' time in the coming century. The fact that many parents of normal children are complaining that the special measures taken to educate disabled children are detracting from their own children's education is part of the drive behind these challenges. Increasingly, also, challenges are based on fears for other students' safety when some violence-prone disabled students are allowed in regular classes. The safety issue has been particularly intense with regard to the mainstreaming of children carrying the AIDS virus. Courts have decided both ways on this issue. The Supreme Court, however, has not rendered an opinion.

DISPOSITION The phase of a **delinquency proceeding** during which the judge decides what requirements to impose on the juvenile who has been found guilty of a delinquent act. The dispositional hearing corresponds to the "sentencing" phase of an adult criminal trial. However, there is one important difference: in a criminal trial, the judge's mandate is to choose an appropriate punishment for the offense that will protect society at the same time. In a delinquency proceeding, the judge's traditional focus has been the welfare of the child, and what can be done to rehabilitate him or her. While this is the traditional focus, it should be noted that a strong shift toward punitive measures for misbehaving juveniles has taken place in the last decade of the twentieth century. In some forty-three states, this shift is apparent in the juvenile code itself, where the rehabilitation of the misbehaving juvenile now shares equally with the protection of society as the stated goal of the juvenile justice system. In Minnesota and Washington, society's interests are placed above those of the delinquent youth. Sentences in delinquency hearings in all states are increasingly designed to punish offending youth, with less emphasis on rehabilitation. Because dispositions in juvenile cases are more and more resembling those in adult cases, children's advocates have raised strong arguments in favor of giving children all of the same due process rights in delinquency proceedings as adults have in criminal trials. This area of the law is likely to develop in the coming century.

A judge fashioning an appropriate disposition for a juvenile delinquent must consider the individual situation and personality of the convicted youth. The judge may not simply impose a standard sentence as often happens in adult court. In order to tailor an individualized disposition, the judge calls for an investigative report on the child. This report is usually prepared by a court employee assigned to the case or a child welfare worker. The child's attorney may, and probably should, present an independent report on the same matters in order to counter or correct the court-ordered report's conclusions. These reports typically contain information about the child's family, his or her school situation, and a psychological profile of the child by a psychiatric professional. These reports also include information about prior arrests and convictions. Because these reports contain highly personal information about the child and the child's family, which could cause the judge to become biased, most states do not allow juvenile judges to have access to investigative reports until after adjudication of the child's guilt or innocence. In some states, the report cannot even be prepared before this point. The child and his or her attorney must be given access to any reports prepared by order of the judge. The reports may only be used in fashioning an appropriate sentence for the child's misbehavior.

In addition to investigative reports, the judge must also consider the child's age and the gravity of the offense. Most states also require the judge to consider the youth's opinions on an appropriate sentence. It may seem odd to ask someone convicted of what is a crime in all but name about the punishment he or she prefers. However, keeping in mind the remedial purpose behind a juvenile disposition, it is clear that a youth is more likely to respond positively to a sentence he or she thinks is fair. Usually, the child's attorney presents the child's opinions on sentencing to the judge, along with the attorney's independent evaluation of the alternatives for sentencing and determination of which would be most beneficial to the attorney's client.

The final consideration before the judge makes a decision on disposition is one imposed by a majority of states: the sentence must represent the "least restrictive alternative" for the child. In other words, the disposition must meet the goals of the juvenile justice system with the least restraint on the child's liberty. This does not mean that the judge must give the lightest sentence and then wait until it fails before trying harsher measures. Rather, the judge must decide on the least harsh sentence that he or she believes will have the desired remedial effect on the child's behavior. Ironically, there is no denial of **equal protection** under the Constitution if a juvenile's sentence is longer or harsher than an adult would serve if convicted of a similar offense. However, some states and the federal government have passed laws that prohibit judges from handing down sentences to youths that are harsher than those given to adults.

Possible dispositions for juvenile delinquents include the following:

1. Having the finding of juvenile delinquency suspended—in essence, a pardon, if there are no further violations.

2. Paying **restitution** or reparations to the victims or victims' families.

3. Participating in **community service.**

4. Living on **probation** or under home supervision.

5. Living in **custodial confinement** in a nonsecure residence, such as a foster home or group home.

6. Living in custodial confinement in a secure facility, such as a juvenile reform school or a mental hospital.

7. Being put to death. **Capital punishment** for juveniles over the age of sixteen has not been declared by the Supreme Court to be unconstitutional. Thus, it remains a possibility in states that have not outlawed it themselves.

DIVERSION An alternative to a formal trial in **juvenile court** for youthful misbehavior is known as a diversion. This involves "diverting" the minor's case from the state's apparatus for dealing with juvenile crime to another agency—usually a private concern—that will take on the challenge of rehabilitating the child. These private agencies may help arrange placement for the youth in a foster home or other supervised living situation. Services such as job training and placement, psychological counseling, and remedial education are also offered.

Usually, a decision is made at **intake** whether to prosecute an arrested minor formally in juvenile court or to "divert" him or her to another program. Nationwide, about 50 percent of cases involving juvenile crime are dealt with in informal diversion programs. Although sanctioned by the juvenile justice system in each state, diversion programs often lack effective enforcement mechanisms. Successful rehabilitation depends, therefore, on each juvenile's willingness to participate in good faith. The warning that a relapse could result in formal prosecution often persuades a troubled teen to make a serious effort to comply with the diversion program's requirements.

DRESS CODES Courts have generally upheld the attempts of school authorities to regulate the dress and grooming of public school students. Dress codes (as distinguished from rules regulating hair) have usually been given a pass because they are viewed as necessary to promote discipline, maintain order, and ensure the safety of students. Thus, rules designed to maintain modesty by regulating dress length or banning revealing styles are usually considered reasonable and necessary to the orderly functioning of the school. Schools also have a strong argument in favor of requiring students to wear uniforms in order to discourage rivalries and promote concentration on academic studies, although there have been challenges to mandatory uniforms in public schools.

A more problematic area is reached when school dress codes seek to regulate the types of ornamentation that students wear. As the Supreme Court ruled in *Tinker v. Des Moines Independent Community School District*, students have constitutional rights to the free expression of ideas, which can be conveyed through symbols worn as apparel as well as in words. In *Tinker*, the symbols at issue were black armbands worn by some students to protest the involvement of the United States in the war in Vietnam. In that case, the Supreme Court sided with the students, finding that the school's rule against the armbands was really an attempt to avoid the "discomfort" that arises when controversial topics are broached. However, the Court also stated that rules against wearing certain symbols might be valid if they were really necessary to avoid serious disruption of the school's mission.

In the last decade of the twentieth century, this latter situation may pertain in many schools that are battling violence among students as a result of gang affiliations. Today, some schools have banned the wearing of certain colors, items of clothing (such as baseball hats), lettered sweatshirts, and various other types of insignia that can represent gang affiliations. Challenges to such sweeping regulations are sure to come. Their validity will depend on whether the interest in combating gang violence in the particular school at issue is very pressing and whether the adopted prohibitions will really have the desired effect. In at least one case, a federal court rejected students' challenge to a school rule forbidding students from wearing gang insignia or "displaying any indicia of membership" in a gang while on school property. The rule also forbade "using any speech, either verbal or nonverbal (gestures, handshakes, etc.) showing membership or affiliation in a gang." The students alleged that it was within their First Amendment rights to do all of these things as a message of their "individuality." The court ruled that "individuality" was not protected speech under the First Amendment. Moreover, unlike some other cases when there was no clear evidence that the students' dress would disrupt the educational mission of the school, the school in this case had experienced violence between students caused by rival gang members provoking each other.

Unlike rules regulating what students may wear in school, rules relating to hair length are upheld by courts less often. Because a hair length or style cannot be changed as easily as clothing, courts give more deference to students' freedom to keep it as they please. Usually, challenges to hair codes are based on students' First Amendment rights to freedom of expression or religion, or their Fourteenth Amendment right to be free of unfair discrimination. This latter ground has been used to invalidate rules against boys' wearing long hair while girls are permitted to do so. Despite the greater freedom of students to choose hairstyles, schools may set reasonable rules requiring cleanliness and hygiene of hair. If long hair presents a health or safety risk, schools may be justified in requiring that it be cut, or at least safely tied back or restrained by a hair net. Generally, to justify a rule regulating hair length or style, including facial hair, a school must show that the rule really will promote discipline or the teaching of hygiene, or instill discipline and prevent disorder.

As the twentieth century draws to a close, public school students are stretching the bounds of decency in ornamentation. Body piercings that are both excessive in number and bizarre in location, tattoos, and even brands are all the rage among certain sets of teenagers. The legality of school rules regulating these affectations is yet to be determined.

DRIVING PRIVILEGES All states allow young people under the age of eighteen limited privileges to operate a motor vehicle. In most states, young people may obtain a driver's license at age sixteen. In many states, a teenager must first acquire a learner's permit with restricted driving privileges before a regular license will be issued. Usually, a learner's permit is obtainable at age fifteen. The period of time that a learner's permit is necessary before full driving privileges may be obtained varies from state to state. In many states, the permit is only necessary for ten days. Four states grant full licenses at age fifteen, and South Dakota issues permits to minors at the age of fourteen, allowing them to drive alone during daylight hours. By contrast, New Jersey licenses teenagers only when they have attained seventeen years of age.

In the final years of the twentieth century, as concern mounts over statistics showing high rates of traffic fatalities involving young drivers, states are moving to restrict the rights of teenagers to drive—following the New Jersey model rather than the South Dakota model. Under these new legislative initiatives, learner's permits are issued to teenagers beginning at the age of sixteen. The beginning driver must then go through an "internship" period of six months or more, during which a number of restrictions apply. These restrictions often require the presence of an adult licensed driver in the front seat of the car at all times that the learner is behind the wheel, nighttime curfews on learner driving, and immediate suspensions for traffic violations or evidence of alcohol use. These restrictions are gradually lifted in a step-by-step process known as graduated licensing, as the teenager gains experience, provided he or she has had no traffic tickets and has not been involved in any accidents. As of 1996, more than ten states had adopted these tougher laws, including Connecticut, Florida, Michigan, and Virginia. More states are expected to follow suit.

In most states, a parent or guardian must give consent for a young person to acquire a permit to drive, and some require that the minor take and pass a course in driver's education. Usually, after the permit is issued, an adult licensed driver must accompany the minor in the front seat of the vehicle at all times when the minor is driving. In most cases, a minor is not permitted to drive a vehicle for hire, in other words, a taxi or other delivery vehicle, except for his or her personal use.

In most states, after a period of time with a learner's permit, a minor may "graduate" to a less restricted type of license, often called a provisional license. This usually occurs at the age of sixteen. The young driver is now permitted to operate the vehicle without the presence of a licensed adult. However, he or she must still obtain a parent's or guardian's consent to acquire a license. The hours during which the minor may operate the vehicle alone are also restricted in a number of states. In some states, a minor with a provisional license may be restricted to driving to and from school or employment. In most states, all age-related restrictions on minors in the operation of a motor vehicle fall away at the age of **majority.** However, a few states may still impose special restrictions on drivers up to the age of twenty-one. In some states, a parent may revoke consent to a minor's license, giving the parent more control over the child's driving habits.

In many states, a parent's act of consenting to his or her child's application for a driver's license renders the parent legally liable for damages or injuries the child might cause while operating the vehicle in a negligent or reckless manner. Even in states without such specific laws, parents can usually be held liable in such cases under various legal theories, such as the **family purpose doctrine,** or because the child could be considered the agent of the parent, or because the parent was negligent to entrust the car to the child. A parent may even be liable for accidents caused by someone else if his or her child gave that person permission to use the car. The liability of a parent for accidents caused by a minor's use of a motor vehicle may even extend past the age of majority in some states, for example, if the young person is in college and still dependent on his or her parents for financial support.

In some states, if a child drives against the wishes of his or her parents, the parents will not be liable for injuries that result from the child's negligent operation of the car. In addition, if a child purchases a car from his or her own resources, some states will exempt the parents from liability for accidents involving the child in that vehicle. A minor may also file a paper in some states showing proof of financial responsibility, which will exempt his or her parents from responsibility for the minor's vehicular accidents.

Most courts have held that driving is a privilege that the state can grant to its citizens with certain conditions attached. In the latter half of the 1990s, some states have attempted to influence other areas of citizens' behavior by withholding driving privileges. For example, in Alabama the driver's licenses of teenagers who drop out of high school may be revoked. The constitutionality of such provisions, particularly if the state's compulsory attendance laws do not require graduation from high school, remains to be determined.

DUE PROCESS OF LAW   Procedures that must be taken whenever the government acts to deprive a person of life, liberty, or property. The requirement of due process is found in the Fifth Amendment of the Constitution and is imposed on the governments of the states through the Fourteenth Amendment. Although the specific procedures required are not described, over the two centuries of the Constitution's existence, courts of law have gradually defined them.

Generally speaking, due process requires that the person whose life, liberty, or property is at stake be notified of the reason for the government's action before it takes place. Most often the context is that of a criminal trial, in which the government seeks to take the action in order to punish the wrongdoer. However, the government frequently takes actions that affect people's liberty or property for other reasons. For example, a state may need to build a new road and may require certain property that is privately owned. The state may take the property, provided it follows due process of law—which includes compensating the owner fairly.

Following notice, due process requires the person whose interests are at stake to be given an opportunity to tell his or her side of the story and present arguments as to why the action should not be taken. The presentation must be before an impartial decision maker. Usually, the affected person must have an opportunity to call witnesses who will testify in his or her behalf as well as to confront any persons testifying against him or her and cross-examine them in an effort to discredit their stories.

Over the years, the definition of what constitutes a person's liberty and property has expanded. Most fundamentally, of course, liberty involves the ability to move about freely—an interest that is hurt whenever a person is arrested, jailed, or sent to prison. Liberty interests are broader than this, however. A person may have a liberty interest in choosing a profession, practicing a trade, attending school, driving a car, choosing a mate, or in any number of other things. Similarly, the definition of "property" has expanded. For example, one may claim a property interest in benefits associated with a job—even welfare benefits. Any time the government acts to limit any of these interests, the need to invoke some sort of due process procedures arises.

The definition of "government action" has also expanded. Today, the official acts of virtually any person employed with public funds may be found to be the actions of government if they affect citizens. Thus, the activities of the public schools are usually considered government action and must conform to due process requirements. In addition, the activities of private entities that receive government funding may also qualify as government action.

The concept of due process of law is flexible. It varies depending on the importance of the interest affected. The greatest number of protective procedures are required when an individual faces loss of life or incarceration for long periods. Fewer protective procedures are required when the interest involved is less important. Although juveniles are entitled to some due process procedures when they are accused of infractions of school rules, the interests at risk (e.g., getting a good education, protecting one's reputation), although important, are not as crucial as the interest in staying out of jail. Therefore, the types of procedures that must be afforded schoolchildren are usually minimal.

The 1967 ruling in *In re Gault* and numerous other cases since have made clear that juveniles accused of acts that would be criminal if committed by an adult must be given due process of law. However, it has also been established that due process for a juvenile tried in **juvenile court** need not be exactly the same as due process for an adult. Courts have reasoned that all the protections given to adults are not necessary for children, because the focus (at least theoretically) of the juvenile justice system is on rehabilitating errant children, rather than punishing misbehavior.

EARLY AND PERIODIC SCREENING, DIAGNOSIS, AND TREATMENT SERVICES (EPSDT)

Organized under the auspices of the federal Medicaid insurance institution, the Early and Periodic Screening, Diagnosis, and Treatment Services (EPSDT) program is designed to see that needy children have access to health care prior to the manifestation of a medical problem. Unlike the regular Medicaid benefits, which only "kick in" after a recipient becomes ill, the EPSDT program requires that eligible children receive regular screening and diagnostic services free of charge. This is important to prevent disease and to treat diseases and conditions in their early, often most curable, stages. It is also important to identify hearing and vision deficiencies early in children to prevent developmental delays in other aspects of their lives.

The EPSDT program requires each participating state to aggressively identify poor children who are eligible for the program, to set up the actual screening procedures for them, and to see that children receive follow-up treatment if health problems are detected. In addition to normal physical examinations, the program requires vision and hearing testing and dental services to be provided to children at regular intervals. The program also requires the states to disseminate information to minors and their parents about medical assistance that is available to them and information about immunizations that are necessary or advisable.

Poor children who are diagnosed through the EPSDT program as needing organ transplants may be eligible to receive them, even though the same transplant would not be covered by Medicaid if the patient were an adult.

EDUCATIONAL MALPRACTICE

From time to time students attempt to sue their teachers or schools for failure to provide them an adequate education. Basically, the students claim that the teachers are incompetent or negligent in performing their professional duties and that they, the students, have suffered harm because of this. To date, no court in the United States has recognized this claim as one justiciable under the law.

Courts that have considered the issue have noted that it is virtually impossible to define what makes a teacher "incompetent." It is also virtually impossible to measure the harm to the student occasioned by having a bad teacher, in order to set some amount of compensation for the student's loss. Finally, it would be very problematic, to say the least, to prove that it was the teacher's inability to teach, and not the student's unwillingness to work, that resulted in the student's failure to learn. Some courts have simply refused to hear educational malpractice cases out of reluctance to become entangled in school administration issues. They merely cite "public policy" reasons as a justification for dismissing such lawsuits.

Critics of the courts on this issue argue that setting standards for competence and measuring losses from incompetence are really no more difficult for the teaching profession than they are for law or medicine, where suits for malpractice are common. These critics argue that the schools and teaching personnel should bear the burden of failing to teach, rather than innocent students who suffer thereby.

EDUCATIONAL RIGHTS   The U.S. Constitution contains no provision regarding education of the country's citizens. Traditionally, the education of children was left to parents, who could either provide it themselves or contract with a private or religious institution to teach their children. However, very early in the existence of the United States, a belief arose that universal, free public education and public schools were essential to the functioning of a democratic society. The exposure of children to mainstream cultural values is viewed by many to supply the cohesion for a heterogeneous nation to exist in peace and prosperity.

Although no federal law requires it, the governments of all fifty states have established public school systems. Having chosen to do so, the states are then obliged by the Constitution to offer these educational benefits equally to all who reside within their borders. Moreover, all states today have some form of **compulsory attendance laws,** requiring children of certain ages to go to school. These laws also, by corollary, create not only a duty but also a right of children to attend school.

Typically, state legislatures delegate authority to administer public schools to local school districts. These, in turn, establish "boards" that conduct the day-to-day business of running the schools. Public schools are funded primarily by state tax dollars. In recent years, however, grants of federal money have assumed greater importance in financing public school programs. This federal money usually is conditioned on state compliance with federal regulations. And, of course, by virtue of the Fourteenth Amendment, which imposes the provisions of the Bill of Rights (the first ten amendments to the Constitution) on the states, public school programs must pass constitutional muster with regard to nondiscrimination and **due process of law** requirements.

Although the federal government looms large in public education today, both federal and state authorities operate on the principal that education is a matter of local interest. Hence, provided the broad mandates of the Constitution are met, the important features of a public school education, including the choice of curriculum, textbooks, personnel, and teaching methods are left to local administrators.

The right of children to attend school is generally broader than the obligation to attend. In other words, if a compulsory attendance law requires attendance up to age sixteen, but the school offers classes to the age of eighteen, a student has a right to attend until the age of eighteen, not just sixteen. Within certain limits, parents have the right to choose a school for their children. Provided a school meets state-established academic standards, the state will not interfere with the choice of a family to send a child to that school. Thus, private and parochial schools, as well as **home schools** in states that allow them, are all viable choices for children's education. The right to choose among accredited schools is not absolute, however. School districts may require public school students to attend specific public schools depending on where they live. This requirement may be pursuant to districting plans designed to keep the ratio of students to teachers constant or pursuant to court-ordered **desegregation.**

Schools may also limit attendance based on academic credentials. Public schools, for example, may require that students demonstrate a certain level of achievement before they will be allowed to advance to higher classes and ultimately graduation. However, except in very limited circumstances, public schools may not exclude students on the basis of supposed lack of intellectual capacity. Public schools must take all students who apply, unless it can be shown that the presence of the student would be disruptive to the educational process for others. Even in cases in which a student is so handicapped as to be unable to function in a public school setting, federal laws and the courts have held that the right to a public education requires a school district to provide alternative learning opportunities for such students.

By contrast, private schools may restrict their enrollment based on a variety of factors, including academic achievement, talent, ability to pay, and other factors. Generally, however, if a private school receives any sort of public funding, or even public privileges such as tax breaks or nonprofit status, the school may not discriminate against applicants on the basis of race, gender, religion, or national origin. A private school may, of course, charge tuition as it chooses.

Once enrolled in a school, there is no absolute right for any particular student to continue to attend if he or she breaks school rules to an extent that the educational process is substantially disrupted. All schools may expel students for inappropriate behavior.

EDWARDS V. AGUILLARD   In this 1987 case, the U.S. Supreme Court struck down a Louisiana law requiring public schools to teach something styled "creation science," or creationism. It is the latest attempt by the high Court to reconcile the recognized freedom of states to set public school curricula with the First Amendment's prohibition on the "establishment" of a religion.

"Creation science" was defined by its proponents as "origin through abrupt appearance in complex form" by the agency of a supernatural being. Despite the fact that numerous scientists, theologians, and educators contended that this viewpoint constituted a true "scientific" theory, the Court was unconvinced.

Instead, the Court ruled that disguising religious beliefs as alternative scientific theories of explaining the origin of life would not serve to circumvent the establishment clause of the First Amendment. The statute at issue in *Edwards* forbade the teaching of the theory of evolution in public schools unless it was accompanied by instruction in the theory of creation science. A school could choose not to offer any instruction in the origin of life, but if it chose to do so, it could not instruct in evolution without creation science. However, it appeared that a school could choose to instruct in creation science without also teaching evolution.

Applying its usual test to the statute, the Court explained that the statute would be unconstitutional if it lacked a clear secular purpose. The statute's alleged purpose was to "further academic freedom." Although this appeared secular on paper, the statute itself revealed that—rather than advance academic freedom—it restricted it. Requiring teachers to include creation science with evolution restricted flexibility. Other provisions of the law evidenced a discriminatory purpose against the theory of evolution and in favor of creation science. The act required that curriculum guides be developed and resource services supplied for teaching creationism but not for teaching evolution, it limited membership on something called the Resource Services Panel to "creation scientists," and forbade school boards to discriminate against anyone who "chooses to be a creation-scientist" or to teach creationism, while failing to protect those who choose to teach other theories or who refuse to teach creation science. A law intended to maximize the comprehensiveness and effectiveness of science instruction would encourage the teaching of all scientific theories about human origins. Clearly this law had a distinctly different purpose of discrediting evolution by counterbalancing its teaching at every turn with the teaching of creationism.

The Court concluded that "the Act is designed either to promote the theory of creation science that embodies a particular religious tenet or to prohibit the teaching of a scientific theory disfavored by certain religious sects. In either case, the Act violates the First Amendment." [482 U.S. at 589–594]

EMANCIPATION A procedure by which a minor may become independent of his or her parents before reaching the age of **majority.** A parent no longer has any right to control an emancipated child's life or to receive the emancipated child's earnings or services. On the other hand, the child no longer is entitled to parental support. Also, parents are relieved of liability for the actions of an emancipated child, except in some states that specifically hold parents liable for automobile accidents caused by their children.

Under the traditional common law, emancipation changes the rights and duties of parents and children in relationship to each other, but it does not affect the child's rights and duties with respect to third parties. The child's legal status with regard to third parties remains unchanged. For example, an emancipated minor may still disaffirm contracts [see **contract rights**], must observe school attendance laws, and may not drink alcohol, vote, or engage in any other activities forbidden to minors. Moreover, an emancipated minor is not considered an adult for purposes of criminal prosecution and is still subject to **status offense** laws. However, emancipated children generally are permitted to give consent for their own **medical treatment.**

For most intents and purposes, a child is automatically emancipated upon reaching the age of **majority,** which is eighteen in most states. However, some states' laws hold that attaining the age of majority only raises a presumption that the minor is emancipated. In other words, a young person over the age of majority may remain unemancipated in some circumstances: for example, when he or she suffers from a physical, mental, or emotional disability that prevents independent living. In some states, a young person over the age of eighteen remains unemancipated during the time he or she is attending college and depends on the financial support of parents.

Theoretically, at least, emancipation takes place only if the parent and child agree that the child is now independent. This agreement can be evidenced by the parent and child expressly stating that the child is independent, or it can be implied by their conduct. For emancipation to occur, a child's parents must at least acquiesce in his or her living independently. For example, a child who has run away from home and eluded detection for a period of time during which he or she has lived independently is not emancipated under the law if his or her parents continued to look for their child during the child's absence and continued to assert their parental rights to control him or her. However, if the parents ceased actively looking for their child and acquiesced in his or her disappearance, emancipation may have taken place.

By the same token, a child also does not become emancipated without his or her desire to do so. A child whose parents have kicked him or her out of the family home does not forfeit a claim for financial support merely because the child now lives apart from the parents.

Regardless of whether the parents and the child agree expressly or through conduct alone that the child should now be emancipated, certain circumstances must exist for the law to recognize the emancipation. Generally, the child must demonstrate financial independence from the parent and have established a residence away from the parental home. The source of the child's independent income is usually not significant, provided that it is legal. The conduct of the parents and child must indicate that the independent living arrangement is at least intended to be permanent. For example, if a youth takes a summer job and moves into an apartment that he intends to give up once school starts in the fall, he is not emancipated.

Most courts also recognize that a child may be emancipated although still living at home. If the minor pays his or her parents rent for room and board and contributes to household expenses, emancipation may have occurred. It is also significant if a parent allows the child to keep earnings from a job. In addition, if the parents continue to claim the child as a dependent on their income tax returns, it is likely that there has been no emancipation.

A few major life events generally are considered sufficient to emancipate a young person under the age of majority. For example, if the minor gets married or joins the armed forces, emancipation is presumed.

Generally, the issue of whether a child is emancipated only arises as part of another dispute. For example, a noncustodial parent may claim that child support payments should be terminated because the child is emancipated. A doctor who has treated a minor and seeks payment for the treatment from the minor's parents may be expected to argue that the minor is not emancipated and that the parents owe the cost of the treatment. Or, a child who wishes to sue his or her parents for a wrongful act may argue that emancipation has occurred in order to get around the **family immunity doctrine,** which prohibits minor children from suing their parents. A parent demanding that his or her child's employer pay the child's wages to the parent as an assertion of parental rights may be restricted by the child arguing that emancipation has occurred. Usually, courts hold that the party who is claiming emancipation has the burden of proving it.

Many states have statutes that govern the procedure for emancipating a minor. Some of them provide for partial emancipation. This means that the child would have some of the rights of adulthood, but not others. A typical problem with all emancipation statutes, however, concerns their scope. It is not clear whether they are meant to override all of the customary, or common law, criteria for emancipation or only to supplement them. Many state emancipation statutes provide a way for a minor child to file a petition with a court for a hearing and judgment as to whether he or she is officially emancipated. Usually, a child must be at least sixteen years of age to file such a petition.

EMOTIONAL ABUSE A type of **child abuse** characterized by a pattern of verbal assault, belittlement, threat, or rejection that damages a child's psychological development. Although most state laws against child abuse include emotional, or psychological, abuse among the forbidden acts, a precise definition of behavior that is emotionally abusive to a child is not forthcoming. Some examples include constant screaming at a child, calling the child foul names or belittling him or her as worthless or worse than worthless, comparing the child negatively to other children, or, in some cases, totally ignoring the child's emotional needs.

In most states, a charge of emotional abuse alone will not justify intervention by a child welfare agency or prosecution of the perpetrator. There must usually be some other sort of maltreatment alleged at the same time: for example, **neglect** of the child's physical needs or **physical abuse** of some sort. In the few states that do allow a separate and independent charge of emotional abuse, there must be proof that the child suffered an identifiable mental or emotional injury caused by the abuser's conduct. The mental injury must be diagnosed by a qualified medical professional, such as a doctor or psychiatrist. Emotional injuries may consist of diminished intellectual functioning, failure to thrive, inability to control aggressive or self-destructive impulses, severe anxiety, depression, withdrawal, or gross misbehavior.

Because the causes of mental illness are so complex, it is frequently very difficult to prove that the actions of the child's caregiver in constantly subjecting him or her to verbal assaults and belittlement caused the child's emotional problems. Moreover, because judicial intervention in a family's affairs also can cause mental and emotional turmoil for the child, child welfare agencies are reluctant to act to curb emotional abuse unless there is evidence that the child's health is endangered in some other way as well.

EMPLOYMENT REGULATIONS   One of the first areas of governmental intervention in family affairs was the regulation of child employment. Oddly, however, it was also one of the least effective—at least for the first century such laws existed. The first child labor laws were passed in the nineteenth century in response to the widespread practice of employing small children in factories. There they were often forced to toil in dangerous conditions for low wages, sometimes up to twelve hours per day, six days per week. Needless to say, these children were often injured and were precluded from attending school, rendering them even less able to escape their lowly station in life.

The first child labor laws were passed by the individual states. They were weak, inconsistent between states, and filled with exceptions. Competition among states to attract new businesses often meant that what child labor laws existed were laxly enforced or ignored altogether.

On a federal level, Congress passed the first attempt to restrict child labor in 1916, known simply as the Child Labor Act. This law forbade the sale in interstate commerce of products made with child labor. The Supreme Court struck it down two years later, finding that it represented overreaching by Congress in regulating interstate commerce. Congress attempted to circumvent this ruling with passage of the Child Labor Tax Act in 1918. That law imposed a 10 percent tax on products produced by child labor. Again the Supreme Court struck it down for infringing on interstate commerce. Frustrated, reformers introduced a constitutional amendment in 1924, known as the Child Labor Amendment, that specifically granted Congress the power to legislate restrictions on child labor. However, in the succeeding eight years, only six states ratified it. Fourteen more states ratified the amendment in the mid-1930s, spurred by the fear that children might be taking adult employment opportunities during the Great Depression. Despite this, the amendment remained short of the required number of ratifications until, in 1938, it became irrelevant with the passage of the **Fair Labor Standards Act** (FLSA). This federal law specifically addressed child labor in the United States with a series of regulations. This time the law was upheld by the Supreme Court in 1941. [*United States v. Darby* (1991)]

The fact that it took so long for any real restrictions on the exploitation of children in the workforce suggests a disturbing indifference to the welfare of children if economic interests are involved. So long as legislation involving children was restricted to protecting them from bodily abuse or providing them an education, the public was vastly in favor of it. But, despite the lip service given to saving children from exploitation in factories and mines, real progress on that front was long in coming.

Today, the labor of minors is regulated mostly by the FLSA on the federal level and a plethora of state laws in every state in the Union. Where provisions of state laws conflict with the FLSA, the law that provides the most protection for children will apply.

These laws place restrictions on the ages at which minors may work in certain jobs, the hours they may work, and the minimum wages that must be paid. Generally, persons over the age of eighteen may work in any occupation. A few states restrict the employment of persons under age twenty-one from working in bars where alcohol is served. See **Fair Labor Standards Act** for more information on the guidelines for minors' work opportunities, which are followed by most states.

In the 1990s, views on labor restrictions on minors are coming full circle. Many critics believe there is no longer a need for the rigid regulations of the FLSA and many state laws. Many commentators call for the repeal of restrictions on the employment of youth over the age of sixteen. Suggested reforms are the phasing out of some classifications of hazardous work, because technology has made them safer, and simplifying the work certificate application process. The reasons cited for favoring these changes are an increase in teenage unemployment and the lack of apprenticeship programs to train youth prior to employing them.

EQUAL ACCESS ACT (EAA)   A federal law prohibiting public secondary schools from discriminating against religiously oriented extracurricular student groups. Under this federal law, passed in 1984, any public secondary school that allows student groups or clubs to meet on its property during noninstructional hours must also allow religiously oriented student groups to meet there. A school may choose to exclude all groups, but if it allows any, religious groups must also be given access under the same conditions as the other groups.

Religiously oriented groups for which access is required must not be sponsored by the school, must be organized entirely at the students' own initiative, and must be strictly voluntary. The meetings of these groups must not interfere in any way with the official educational activities of the school. In fact, one court has held that such meetings may not be held immediately after school hours, because of the risk that the group might be misinterpreted as being school-sponsored. That court required the religiously oriented meetings to be held in the evenings only. [*Quappe v. Endry* (1991)] In addition, school or government employees may attend the meetings only if they do not participate in them. No expenditure of public funds may be made to benefit these groups, beyond the incidental cost of providing space for their meetings.

The Equal Access Act has survived a challenge to its constitutionality in the Supreme Court. In the case of *Board of Education of Westside Community Schools v. Mergens*, 496 U.S. 226 (1990), the high Court held that the EAA did not violate the establishment clause of the First Amendment, which prohibits the government from establishing or promoting any particular religious beliefs. Rather, the act was designed to end discrimination against student-run religious groups and allow students to meet voluntarily and discuss religion during nonschool hours. However, a number of states' constitutions expressly forbid the use of public money or property by religious groups. It is as yet unclear whether a state may be compelled to violate its own constitution in order to comply with the federal EAA.

EQUAL PROTECTION   The Fourteenth Amendment of the U.S. Constitution guarantees citizens "equal protection" under the law. This means that the government must treat similarly situated people the same, or have a good reason for treating them differently. Usually, the government may justify a law that treats people differently by showing that it is reasonably related to a legitimate government purpose. For example, a zoning law that requires houses near a fault line to conform to certain safety codes while houses elsewhere do not have to comply discriminates against people depending on where they live. However, the law is rationally related to the legitimate government purpose of protecting citizens' lives and property and, hence, is constitutional.

If the government treats people differently on the basis of race, gender, religion, national origin, age, or disability, there must be more than just a "rational" reason for doing so. There must be a "compelling" reason or an "important" reason. Otherwise, equal protection of the laws is denied. These six criteria are special because they represent either "immutable" characteristics over which people have no control or characteristics for which people historically have been unfairly singled out for detrimental treatment. (Often both of these factors are involved.) The six categories are known as "suspect" categories, and laws that discriminate on the basis of any of them will be subjected to "strict scrutiny" by a court to determine whether the government's reason for the law is "compelling." (Discriminating on the basis of gender or age is subject to a level of scrutiny below "strict scrutiny" but above mere "rational relationship.") Usually, laws that discriminate on any of these bases are unconstitutional. However, occasionally there is a "compelling" reason for such discrimination. For example, a law that requires only the female applicant for a marriage license to be tested for immunity to rubella (German measles) makes sense because serious birth defects can affect a child whose mother contracts the disease during pregnancy. A state's interest in protecting future citizens from birth defects might be "compelling" enough to justify discrimination on the basis of gender in this case.

It is rare that a law or government regulation openly declares that it is treating people differently on the basis of one of the six suspect criteria. However, many laws distinguish between people on the basis of other characteristics that could be linked to one of the six criteria. For example, an employer might require applicants for a job to be able to lift a certain amount of weight, reach a certain height, or speak a certain language. Such laws are frequently challenged because—although they appear "neutral" on their face—they may result in impermissible discrimination when applied. For example, because women are generally shorter than men, a requirement that police officers be a certain minimum height might effectively screen out most women applicants for the job. With laws such as these, it must usually be shown that there is a real, job-related reason for the requirement.

Technically, the equal protection guarantee of the Fourteenth Amendment applies only to actions by the government: the federal government or the governments of the states. Of course, this includes actions by any governmental agency, institution, or office—from the U.S. Congress to the smallest municipal office, including the public schools. Theoretically, discrimination by purely private entities is not forbidden. In reality, however, the law and the courts have stretched the definition of "government action" to find it operating in all sorts of places that seem purely private. For example, the activities of a private entity that benefits from any government funding, government tax rebates, or government-provided services may be found to be "government action," such that discrimination by the entity will be illegal. In addition, the federal government and the states have passed laws that directly forbid private entities from engaging in discrimination.

Although "age" is one of the suspect categories for illegal discrimination, it generally is of concern only when the discriminatory treatment occurs against people over the age of forty who lose job opportunities because employers think they are "too old." Many challenges have been raised to laws that treat young people under the age of majority differently than adults. For the most part, however, these challenges are unsuccessful. Generally, the consensus is that young people need extra protection and treatment because of their immature judgment. While it is true that this different treatment burdens some young people who are exceptionally mature, the law justifies this by the fact that the burden of youth-oriented regulations is finite and will be lifted when the youth reaches majority. By contrast, discrimination based on "excessive" age is not automatically alleviated. Instead, the problem just gets worse.

Many equal protection challenges based on different treatment of juveniles concern the procedures of the juvenile justice system. In this realm, challenges are more successful. The reasoning is that, since adult penalties are increasingly imposed on youthful offenders in juvenile court, it is only just to give juveniles all the benefits of adult court procedures. The benevolent, informal process of the idealized juvenile system is even less in evidence today than in years past. Therefore, there is no "compelling," or even "rational," reason to treat youngsters differently in this arena. Despite much progress in this area toward equal treatment, the pronouncement of the Supreme Court on this issue continues to be that the Constitution does not require juveniles to be treated exactly the same way as adults when they are accused of criminal (or delinquent) acts.

At the same time that some advocate giving juveniles in juvenile court all the same procedural protections that adults receive, others decry the growing movement to try juvenile offenders as adults. Depending on the state's law and the seriousness of the offense, children as young as twelve or thirteen may be tried as adults at the discretion of the prosecuting authorities. Critics of this trend argue in reverse that children *are* different and *should* be handled in their own institutions. In short, these people are arguing that there is a *compelling* reason to treat children differently because of their age.

Regardless of how these issues involving juvenile court procedure may play out, it is settled that in other areas of their lives, minors—just like adults—are entitled to be free of discrimination based on any of the five other suspect categories: race, religion, gender, national origin, or disability.

EXPULSION   Although children have a right to a free public education in all states, that right may be revoked if necessary to maintain order and discipline within the school. Courts generally defer to school authorities on what misbehavior is so egregious as to justify a student's expulsion. Expulsion typically may be ordered for acts of violence or vandalism on school property, coming to school under the influence of alcohol or drugs, or engaging in illegal conduct on school grounds. In general, expulsion is the barring from school of a student for more than five days up to and including permanent dismissal from school.

Because the right to receive an education is so basic and important to a child's future, expulsion of a student can only occur after providing the child with **due process of law.** Thus, before any student can be expelled, he or she must be notified of the charges against him or her and have the opportunity to refute them. Due process procedures in the context of school expulsions do not have to measure up to the requirements that must be afforded juveniles when they are arrested for criminal acts. Nevertheless, basic fairness must be observed. This usually means that a hearing, albeit informal, must be held at which the child can confront the witnesses against him or her. However, a full-blown trial is not necessary. Once a student has been expelled, the state has no further obligation to educate him or her.

Despite general deference to school districts on expulsion, courts will review an expulsion if it appears that the punishment was much more severe than the child's infraction of the rules merited, if the decision appeared arbitrary, or if basic due process procedures were not met. Permanent expulsions are considered such a severe sanction that a court is more likely to hear a challenge in those cases than for temporary suspensions.

FAIR LABOR STANDARDS ACT (FLSA)

FAIR LABOR STANDARDS ACT (FLSA) The major federal law that regulates employment practices, including the labor of children under the age of **majority.** The act was passed in 1938. Its Section 212, which permitted the federal government to ban "oppressive child labor," represented the culmination of a fight to impose government regulation of the heretofore "anything goes" policies of employers regarding the labor of young children. The child labor provisions survived a constitutional challenge in 1941. [*United States v. Darby*] Since that time, the act has been amended numerous times, and regulations affecting minors are drafted by the secretary of labor.

The FLSA regulations promulgated under Section 212 specify the types of employment minors may engage in, the minimum wage they must receive for their efforts, and the maximum number of hours they may work. Most state laws governing child labor are patterned after the FLSA. There are some differences, however. When a state labor law has different provisions than the FLSA, the law with the greatest protection for children will apply.

Ages of Employment

The FLSA and most state laws operate on a so-called rule of sixteen, which prohibits the employment of anyone under the age of sixteen, unless certain exceptions apply.

Minimum Wages

Employers must pay all their employees, including minors, at least an amount equaling the federal minimum wage. Since 1996, that amount has been set at $5.15 per hour. If a state law has a higher minimum wage than this, employers in that state must pay minors the higher amount. However, there are a number of exceptions to this rule that allow employers to pay less than the minimum wage to young persons doing particular types of work. These exceptions include baby-sitting, house cleaning, newspaper delivery, work done at recreational camps or amusement parks, agricultural labor, fishing, and independent sales representative jobs. The secretary of labor is authorized to add other types of employment to this list of exceptions. The exceptions are designed to prevent curtailment of opportunities for the employment of young persons that might occur in certain fields if employers are required to pay the minimum wage.

Maximum Hours

Generally, no employee, regardless of age, may be required to work more than forty hours in one week, without receiving an overtime wage equal to at least one and one-half times the employee's normal hourly wage. There are numerous more restrictive regulations for minors, however. Many state laws restrict the number of hours children may work to twenty during times when school is in session. Other regulations prohibit minors from working past a certain hour at night. Because these laws are more protective of children, they apply over contrary federal regulations. There are some exceptions to the hours restrictions of both state and federal laws, including exceptions for children in the entertainment industry and theater, or students workings as "learners" or "apprentices" in various trades.

Types of Employment

Under the FLSA, between the ages of sixteen and eighteen, a young person may work in any job that is not "hazardous." The secretary of labor has developed a list of jobs that are considered too hazardous for young people to perform. Generally, these include any jobs requiring the operation or servicing of heavy machinery, power-driven machines, or cutting devices, or any work in environments that are inherently unsafe, such as mines and laboratories using hazardous materials. More specifically, jobs in which minors under the age of eighteen may not engage include the manufacturing of explosives; mining; driving a motor vehicle; logging; woodworking with power-driven machinery; operating hoists or forklifts; metal forming of any type; slaughtering or butchering animals; operating bakery machines; operating power-driven paper products machines; manufacturing brick, tile, and ceramics; operating power saws or cutting devices; wrecking or demolition work; roofing; or excavating. An exception is made for minors of any age to work on a farm owned by their parents, even if this involves operating heavy farm equipment.

Between the ages of fourteen and sixteen, children may be employed outside the home if they obtain a special permit and work in nonhazardous, nonmanufacturing jobs that do not interfere with their schooling or their health or welfare. Typical examples are fast-food servers, filling station attendants, retail clerks, office workers, grocery baggers, dishwashers, and waiters or waitresses. Although children may work in restaurants or other food establishments, they may not be required to operate power-driven slicers, to cook, to work in freezers, to load or unload merchandise, or to work on ladders or scaffolds.

Between the ages of twelve and fourteen, children may be employed as occasional baby-sitters, housecleaners, newspaper delivery persons, or laborers in seasonal agricultural occupations, provided their jobs do not injure their welfare.

Under age twelve, children generally may not be employed outside their own homes. A few states allow such children to work on farms in the summer months so long as they are not exposed to hazardous chemicals.

Children of any age may work as actors or performers in motion pictures, theater, television, or radio, provided certain measures are taken to ensure their welfare.

Family Educational Rights and Privacy Act (FERPA)

Passed in 1974, this act requires all educational institutions that receive federal funding to allow parents to inspect and review all official education records regarding their children. Parents may challenge the accuracy of such records and request changes. After a child reaches the age of eighteen, this right passes to the young person himself or herself.

Any record directly related to a student and kept by a school receiving federal funding is an "education record" subject to the provisions of FERPA. All records, not just those from the specific programs within a school that receive federal funds, are covered. Nevertheless, there is some disagreement about which records are, in fact, "educational." Records relating to evaluations of a child by teachers, medical practitioners (including psychiatrists), and administrators are usually covered. However, records relating to athletic performance and crime reports involving students are not. Also, while records pertaining to evaluations of a child are covered, not all aspects of the records are subject to challenge. For example, a parent usually may not object to the grading process used by a specific teacher, although the parent could question the accuracy of the grade under the teacher's method.

Under FERPA, the parents of minor children are entitled to review requested records no later than forty-five days after the request. In addition to receiving the records (or copies of them) to examine, a parent may request an explanation or interpretation of the records. If, after review, the parent believes the records are inaccurate, misleading, or compromise the child's or family's privacy, the parent may petition the school to have the records changed. If the school denies the request for a record change, the parent is entitled to a hearing on the matter. This hearing must be conducted by a disinterested party, which may include school officials, if they were not directly involved in making the record. The parent must have an opportunity to present evidence as to why the record should be changed. The parent may be represented at the hearing by an attorney. Within a reasonable time the party hearing the case must present a written decision on the matter. The act does not provide for an appeal following this decision.

If a request for a record change is decided in favor of the parent, the school must make the desired change. Even if the decision is that the record is accurate, the parent must be given the opportunity to place a statement of his or her opinion about the record into the record. This may be a statement setting forth the reasons the parent disagrees with the school's decision not to change the records. It must be kept as long as the record itself is kept and must be released along with the record any time the record is released or disclosed.

FERPA also provides for the privacy of matters contained in educational records. Educational records are routinely requested by all sorts of parties. Under FERPA, unless the request comes from within the same school or a local education agency with a legitimate educational interest, the records may not be released without the parents' (or the student's if over eighteen) permission. There are certain narrow exceptions to this rule. Information about a student may be disclosed to a criminal defendant if necessary for a claim in defense. Routine "directory" information, such as names and addresses of students may be disclosed without permission.

FERPA requires that parents (or students over eighteen) receive notification of any requests for information from education records made by third parties, as well as records of the information disclosed. In addition, any disclosures of personally identifiable information about a student may be made only on the stipulation that the recipient of the information will not disclose it to anyone else.

FAMILY IMMUNITY DOCTRINE   A legal doctrine that bars unemancipated minors from suing their parents for compensation for injuries caused to them by the parents' wrongful acts. In many states, the doctrine protects any immediate family member from suits by other members. For example, in these states a sibling may not sue another sibling.

Before the late nineteenth century, there was no such rule—probably because there was never a perceived "need" for one. Children were viewed as mere property without any rights at all, so that a lawsuit initiated by a child against his or her parents was an idea so preposterous as not to have occurred to anyone. However, in the late 1800s a reform movement had taken hold that sought to improve the lot of children in abusive or neglectful family situations.

The 1891 case in which the family immunity doctrine first appeared was probably one of the very first lawsuits ever brought by a child against a parent. Hence, the court was anxious to nip the development in the bud. In that case, *Hewllette v. Georgia* (1891), a boy was barred from suing his mother for false imprisonment stemming from her committal of him to a mental hospital against his will. The court found that the need for the "peace of society" and the "repose of families" outweighed any rights of the boy. This holding was soon seized by other courts, which developed further justifications for it. Accordingly, the traditional justifications for the family immunity doctrine are the preservation of family harmony, the fear of collusion between family members in bringing lawsuits, and the fear that judgments against parents could impoverish the family and take resources away from other children in the family. Additionally, courts fear interfering in parents' child-rearing decisions.

Beginning in the 1930s, the family immunity doctrine began to erode. Today, most states have considerably narrowed its scope, either through the decisions of state courts or laws passed by state legislatures. Some states have abolished it altogether, except in very limited circumstances. Critics have charged that the doctrine serves arbitrarily to dispossess a whole class of injured children from recovering any compensation. They point out that the goal of fostering family harmony is little served by not allowing children to sue their parents since the need for a lawsuit indicates that harmony already does not exist. Moreover, children have always been allowed to sue their parents on contractual and property matters, also potentially causing disharmony. Also, collusion is no more likely in a suit brought by a minor child against his or her parents, which is barred by the doctrine, than a suit brought by an adult child, which is not barred. Furthermore, the widespread availability of liability insurance means that the parents' resources will not be depleted by an adverse judgment.

The first crack in the family immunity doctrine was an exception for lawsuits based on intentionally or maliciously caused injuries by a parent to his or her child. Thus, any injury caused by behavior fitting the definition of **"child abuse"** is probably not within the family immunity doctrine, and a child may sue to recover.

Opening parents up to lawsuits by their children for negligently caused harm has been more problematic. In this situation, courts fear interfering in parents' rights to determine how to raise their children. Nevertheless, a widespread exception to the family immunity rule is made for parental negligence in the operation of a motor vehicle that injures a child. In some states the child's recovery is limited to the amount of the parents' automobile insurance policy. When the parent is killed in the same automobile accident that injures the child, most states allow the child to sue the parent's estate for compensation.

In addition, most states allow children to sue their parents for injuries negligently caused by the parents while the children work in their parents' business or trade. In this situation, courts believe the relationship between the parties is more like that of an employer to an employee than a parent to a child.

In other situations involving a parent's negligent conduct that injures his or her child, the states are divided on whether the child may sue the parent. In some states, such suits are allowed if the family unit is already broken and the child seeks recovery from the noncustodial parent. If one parent causes the death of the other, some states allow the child to sue the remaining parent for the wrongful death of the other. Courts are careful, however, to disallow claims if it appears that the parent's conduct that caused the death was not unreasonable.

Some laws that narrow the family immunity doctrine carefully retain the rule in cases where "parental discretion" in child-rearing issues is involved. Determining when a parent's decision involves "parental discretion" and when it does not is, of course, a very thorny issue. Some courts have resolved it by testing whether the duty breached by the parent's negligent conduct was a duty owed to society at large, or to the parent's child only. If the latter, the issue is one of "parental discretion" and a child may not sue if the parent's conduct resulted in injury. For example, the duty to refrain from smoking in bed lest a fire be started is a duty owed to society at large, not just to one's child. After all, the fire could cause widespread injury and damage. A child injured by a fire caused by his or her parent's smoking in bed would be allowed to sue the parent. By contrast, a duty to determine whether it is safe for one's seven-year-old child to fly an airplane is arguably a duty owed to the child alone. A child injured by flying a plane could not sue the parent who negligently allowed him or her to do so.

Other states' laws do allow a child to sue his or her parents for negligent supervision that injures the child. Presently, however, no state has recognized a lawsuit by a child against a parent for parenting malpractice. Unless they have suffered a physical injury, children may not sue their parents simply because they believe the parents' parenting skills were inadequate and left them with psychological problems, maladjustments, or emotional harm.

FAMILY PURPOSE DOCTRINE A rule of law in some states that holds parents liable for injuries caused by their children's negligent driving. In some states, other members of the family, such as spouses or elderly parents, may be included in the class of persons whose negligence will be vicariously "imputed" to the car's owner. In some cases, children who are legally adults but continue to live in the same household are also covered.

The family purpose doctrine is a variation of the old "master-servant" theory that makes an employer liable for injuries caused by an employee acting within the scope of employment. The purpose of the doctrine is to ensure that innocent victims of negligent teenage drivers have recourse to someone with financial means to pay compensation. Most minors, although they could be sued, have no money to pay a judgment.

In order for the family purpose doctrine to be applicable, the owner of the car must usually be in the position of the "head of the household." However, in some states the car's owner may be any adult in the family. The owner must have given family members blanket permission to use the automobile for their convenience or pleasure. The doctrine does not apply if the driver of the automobile did not have permission to use it at the time his or her negligence caused an accident. In that case, a third person injured in the accident may recover compensation from the negligent driver only.

FEDERAL CHILD SUPPORT ENFORCEMENT PROGRAM

The major federal legislation governing the enforcement of child **support obligation**s is the Federal Child Support Enforcement Program [42 U.S.C. §§ 651–669], sometimes simply known as Title IV-D. Traditionally, laws dealing with the welfare of children have been left to the states. However, the federal government's interest in child support issues has grown over the last decades of the twentieth century—largely because of the drain on the federal treasury caused by an increase in federal welfare payments under the **Aid to Families with Dependent Children** (AFDC) program. In 1950, Congress passed the first federal child support legislation, by amending the Social Security Act to require states to notify law enforcement officials when parents of families on AFDC deserted them. By the mid-1970s, studies had shown that the burgeoning cost of the AFDC program could be attributed in large part to the failure of noncustodial parents to pay child support following a divorce. The law was passed in 1974 in an effort to help states collect child support payments from absent parents and simultaneously lower the demands on federal funding to support single-parent households from public revenues.

Title IV-D, with its 1984 amendments known as the Child Support Enforcement Amendments, achieves this goal by demanding that states take a more proactive approach to collecting child support payments as a condition to receiving federal money under the AFDC program. Specifically, states are required to:

- Institute procedures to determine the paternity of children born out of wedlock. [See **paternity action.**] The state must establish the paternity of at least 50 percent of out-of-wedlock births each year in order to qualify for federal funds.

- Set up their own child welfare agencies designed to establish paternity, locate absent parents through state **parent locator services**, obtain support orders, and collect support payments due.

- Institute mandatory wage withholding from parents who fall one month or more behind in child support payments. All child support orders issued by a court must contain an authorization for employers to withhold support payments from wages if the owing parent falls behind.

- Intercept state income tax refunds addressed to defaulting parents and use them to make up for missing child support payments.

- Establish procedures to place liens on the property of defaulting parents and require them to post bonds or give other collateral to guarantee that they will make up the payments.

- Establish procedures by which information about overdue child support payments may be shared with credit reporting agencies to consider in their evaluation of prospective borrowers.

- Establish procedures for expediting determinations of child support obligations and the enforcement of ensuing court-ordered child support.

- Establish guidelines, usually following a formula based on income, for determining child support amounts due.

Title IV-D also authorizes the interception of federal income tax refunds sent to parents who are behind in child support and authorizes their payment to the custodial parent. Under the act, the federal government may also place a lien on an owing parent's property as security for the debt. The act allows states to garnish the wages of federal workers and withhold money from federally funded benefits to be paid to the unsupported child. The amount withheld may reach 65 percent of the nonpaying parent's income, if he or she has no other dependents and is more than twelve weeks behind on child support payments. The act set up the Federal Office of Child Support Enforcement (OCSE) to oversee the state programs and ensure their compliance. The OCSE also maintains a federal parent locator service to gather information about the whereabouts of parents owing child support from other federal agencies and share this information with states seeking to enforce child support orders.

FIREARMS   Persons under the age of twenty-one are prohibited by federal law from purchasing handguns or handgun ammunition. Rifles and shotguns may not be purchased by anyone under the age of eighteen. Children under these ages may possess these types of weapons if they received them as a gift from an adult.

State laws and municipal ordinances may further restrict the rights of minors to carry firearms. Moreover, weapons may be banned entirely from some public places, such as auditoriums, stores, and schools. Possession of a gun by *anyone* on such property is illegal.

Adults who negligently furnish weapons to children may be sued for injuries caused by the child in using the weapon. In such a case, a court must decide whether the adult's action in allowing a minor to possess or use a gun created such an unreasonable risk of harm to others as to justify holding the adult responsible for the harm. Such factors as the child's age, temperament, and mental health will be important considerations, as well as other circumstances, such as where, when, and for what purpose the gun was furnished and whether the child had adult supervision when using it.

FOSTER CARE Temporary care of a child by an adult who is not the child's parent or legal guardian, which is arranged through a government child welfare organization. The purpose of foster care is to provide the child with the stable, nurturing environment that his or her parents are temporarily unable to provide. Because the intention in foster care is to return the child to his or her **biological parent**s, or to find suitable **adoptive parent**s, the formation of strong emotional ties between **foster parent**s and their charges is not encouraged. Rather, the arrangement is viewed by the law as an officially sanctioned, long-term baby-sitting assignment. Generally, foster parents volunteer for the job, are paid a reasonable amount to defray the costs of the care they provide, and are free to resign at any time.

Foster care most frequently is ordered by a court after it has removed a child from the parents' custody. This removal usually occurs because the child is not receiving adequate care there, either because of **abandonment, child abuse,** or **neglect.** In extreme cases, the problem may be so intractable that the **parental rights** of the child's parents are terminated entirely. In any case, the court then vests custody of the child in a state or local child welfare agency. This agency, in turn, places the child with willing foster parents to provide for his or her day-to-day care until a permanent situation is found.

State laws differ as to how much authority over a foster child is delegated when custody is taken away from the parents. Typically, unless parental rights have been terminated, the child's biological parents retain some control over their child even though he or she is no longer officially living with them. The biological parents retain the right to determine the child's religious upbringing, to give consent for the child to marry or join the armed forces, and to consent to major medical treatments. The consent of the biological parents is also still necessary if a child in foster care is to be adopted by someone else. State laws differ with regard to whether biological parents retain a right to visit their children in foster care. Today, the trend is toward allowing, even encouraging, such visits because they may help to strengthen the biological family's emotional bonds. At least one federal court has held that a parent whose child is in foster care has a constitutionally recognized "liberty interest" in continued contact and visitation with his or her child that cannot be abridged absent compelling circumstances. [*Winston v. Children and Youth Services of Delaware City* (1990)] However, if the reason for the child's removal from the parents was some sort of abuse that is likely to be repeated, visitation may be denied.

The child welfare agency that has been given official custody of a child also has a certain scope of authority over him or her. This agency may control into which home the child is placed, what school he or she will attend, what type of education he or she will receive, and how the child is to be disciplined. The agency may also make some medical decisions for the child, including giving consent for psychiatric treatment.

Traditionally, foster parents were expected merely to carry out the details of decisions for the child's care that were made by the child welfare agency or the biological parents. Although the child lived with the foster parents, the welfare agency theoretically was expected to closely supervise all aspects of the care the child received from them. Decisions delegated to the foster parents usually were concerned with only routine matters: what the child would have for dinner, when the child would bathe, go to bed, watch television, play outdoors, etc. However, in recent years, the role of foster parents has expanded. Gradually, the law has recognized that the reality of foster care is often little like its theoretical purpose. Instead of making a quick return to loving biological parents who have remedied whatever problems led to removal of the child from their custody, a foster child is more likely to drift for years in and out of many different foster homes and never reunite with his or her parents. Recognizing the extreme need children have for stability and predictability, the law is now allowing more long-term placements with foster families. Some states encourage the participation of the foster parents in major child care decisions. And more states are allowing foster parents to adopt the children in their care if all parties agree.

Another way a child may be placed in foster care is through a voluntary relinquishment of custody by parents who realize on their own that they are unable to adequately care for their children. In these cases, the parents voluntarily apply to a child welfare agency for help. Sometimes they have chosen the individuals they wish to be foster parents for their children. In others, they ask for the recommendation of the agency. In this case, participation of a court is not involved. Usually, the parents and the welfare agency sign a standard form that details exactly what powers over the child have been delegated to the agency and, through the agency, to the foster parents. Unlike **adoption,** the relinquishment of a child to foster care usually requires only the consent of the custodial parent. Sometimes, the parents and the agency will create a customized agreement to meet the unique needs and desires of the parties. However, biological parents may not voluntarily agree to transfer all legal custody of their children. The law does not allow custody of a child to be determined by contract. This rule is to prevent the "sale" of children. Therefore, some degree of authority will always remain with biological parents who voluntarily place their child in foster care. Generally, parents who voluntarily place their children have the right to revoke their consent to the arrangement at any time. However, a few states restrict the parents' rights to change their minds. The reasoning in such jurisdictions is that once an agency has taken responsibility for a child's welfare, it must continue to look out for the child's best interests, including determining whether a return home is the best course of action.

Children who are placed in foster care have certain rights with regard to their situation. The trend in the late twentieth century is toward increased recognition of rights for foster children. Ironically, however, children who are voluntarily placed in foster care by their parents may have fewer of these rights than children whose placement was pursuant to a court order, even though both types of placement occur through child welfare agencies.

Generally, a foster child may not merely be "warehoused" in foster homes and forgotten. Federal law requires child welfare agencies to develop "case plans" for any child in foster care in order to make a permanent decision regarding his or her custody within a reasonable period of time. Usually this means that the agency must decide whether to return the child to his or her biological parents, to seek adoptive parents for the child, or to make a more permanent placement with a foster family within eighteen months of the child's initial placement in foster care. The **Adoption and Safe Families Act of 1997** mandates swift permanent placement of children in foster care, with more emphasis on finding a loving family than on reuniting the child with his or her biological parents.

A number of federal courts have held that children in foster care enjoy basic due process rights in any proceeding involving their status or placement. These include the right to representation by an attorney [see *guardian ad litem*], the right to be heard, the right to present evidence and to subpoena witnesses, and the right to cross-examine witnesses presented by other parties. In all states, foster children have the right to be protected from abuse and neglect by their foster parents. Laws authorizing foster placement, including the federal Adoption and Safe Families Act of 1997, usually include special procedures to investigate reports of abuse of foster children. The obligation to investigate and report suspected maltreatment is often greater for foster children than for children in other settings. A child who has been subjected to abuse or neglect while in foster care may be entitled to compensation if the child welfare agency was negligent in supervising his or her placement.

A foster child has the right to receive adequate food, clothing, shelter, education, and medical treatment at state expense. If the child has special medical or psychiatric needs, the state must provide those as well. Some state laws include rehabilitation and vocational training for foster children who have been in trouble with the law as part of the services to which they are entitled. Counseling services with the foster child and his or her biological parents are often mandated to speed the child's return to their custody.

FOSTER PARENT An adult who temporarily assumes the day-to-day, routine care of a child through a delegation of authority from a state child welfare agency having legal custody of the child. Custody of the child may have been given to the agency as a result of a court order or a voluntary agreement with the child's parents. See also **foster care.**

Typically, adults wishing to serve as foster parents apply with a state child welfare agency. The agency screens applicants for suitability as child care providers and places those who possess the requirements on a roster of available foster parents. Prospective foster parents may be evaluated on the basis of age, health, income, and how many children are already in the family, as well as other factors. The federal **Adoption and Safe Families Act of 1997** requires that a background check of any potential foster parent be conducted to disqualify those with criminal records.

When placement of a child to foster care is made, the foster parents sign a contract with the agency that defines each party's rights and duties with respect to the child. Traditionally, foster parents were expected merely to carry out the details of major care decisions that were already made for the child by the agency. Thus, the welfare agency would determine what type of education the child was to have, how he or she was to be disciplined, what kind of medical treatment would be administered, etc. The foster parents merely provided shelter, food, and clothing and made day-to-day decisions within the bounds of the welfare agency's dictates.

Today, the role of foster parents is changing. Foster parents are increasingly being delegated more authority over the major issues in a child's upbringing. Moreover, in some states, the foster parents assume an active role as part of a team working to devise a permanent solution for the child's placement. This may mean that the foster parent will work with the agency to create a "case plan" for the child, or maybe even work with the child's **biological parent**s in an effort to solve family problems and facilitate the child's return home. Also, in recognition of a child's need for stability, more states are making long-term assignments of a child to a particular foster home, instead of constantly moving the child from home to home, as frequently happened in the past.

As a result of passage of the Adoption and Safe Families Act of 1997, return to their biological parents is no longer the primary goal for children placed in foster care. Today, the best interest of the child is paramount. This means that an adoptive home may be considered the best solution. Formerly, foster parents were forbidden to adopt their foster children, partly as a way of discouraging strong emotional ties between people whose association with each other was designed to be temporary. However, many states now allow foster parents to adopt their foster children. In some states, foster parents also have standing to initiate a lawsuit to terminate the parental rights of their foster child's biological parents.

Foster parents receive a stipend from the state to cover the costs of caring for the children placed in their homes. Foster parents may terminate their tenure at any time. However, they generally may not object if a child is removed from their care and placed elsewhere. Nevertheless, some states' laws provide a mechanism by which foster parents can block the decision of a child welfare agency to remove a foster child from their home. The Supreme Court has also ruled that, under certain circumstances, a foster parent may have a constitutional right to due process procedures in challenging the removal of their foster child. [*Smith v. Organization of Foster*

Families for Equality and Reform (1977)] However, no court has yet found those circumstances to exist.

Occasionally, the issue arises as to who is legally liable for injuries to a foster child caused by the negligence of the foster parents. Generally, the law views the foster parents as responsible, and not the state welfare agency supervising the foster care. However, courts in a few cases have held that the state was responsible for the harm, because the foster parents were merely acting as agents of the state in providing care to the child.

FREEDOM OF CHOICE PLANS Popularly seen as a remedy for deteriorating educational standards, freedom of choice plans allow students to choose to transfer to other schools within their same school system. Ostensibly, students will transfer into the schools having the best reputation for teachers and facilities. While seemingly sound in concept, such plans can be fraught with problems. First, popular schools cannot take all the students who want to go to them. Some limit of occupancy must be imposed in order to keep educational standards high. Second, flight from unpopular schools can leave them without resources and even less likely to attract entrants. Finally, freedom of choice plans can mask a subterfuge to evade **desegregation** orders. For example, in the late 1960s, schools in Virginia maintained that they had complied with federal orders to desegregate by creating a plan whereby students of any race could choose the schools they wished to attend. In reality, no white students chose to attend any of the formerly segregated all-black schools. Because students who wished to attend schools outside their own districts were required to provide their own transportation, many minority students—who could not afford this luxury—were precluded from attending all-white schools. This downside of freedom of choice plans persists today. Therefore, where such a plan exists, courts may be called upon to ensure that it is not a means of perpetuating segregation. Transfers of students that serve to create student bodies of virtually the same race are disapproved. However, if the majority of transfers serve to help the "mix" in area schools, they will be approved.

FRIENDLY PARENT PROVISION A provision in some states' laws dealing with **child custody** awards that gives a preference for sole custody to the parent who agrees to allow the noncustodial parent greater visitation privileges with the child [see **visitation rights**]. Detractors of these types of provisions point out that some divorcing parents may feel forced into de facto **joint custody** agreements as each vies to be found the most "friendly" parent and hence to be awarded sole custody.

FUNDING EQUALITY   At least since the 1954 Supreme Court decision in *Brown v. Board of Education,* it has been considered a fundamental right for all children to receive equal educational opportunities. It has been considered almost equally important to leave the design, running, and administration of public schools up to state and local governments. These two tenets have come into conflict in recent years.

In most states, schools are at least partially financed by taxes on residents in local school districts. As a result, schools located in affluent districts can draw on more resources and, hence, are typically better equipped and staffed than schools in poor districts. In addition, the costs of running schools in poor districts are often higher due to higher costs of basic services, such as police and fire protection. As a result, schools in poor neighborhoods are often understaffed and underequipped. Most states have some sort of grant program whereby state tax monies are shifted to poorer school districts in an effort to bring them closer to the level of quality of schools in richer districts. Despite these efforts, some critics believe that not enough has been done. The practice of allowing more affluent schools to exist has been challenged on constitutional grounds. The allegation has been that failure to equalize funding to all school districts has resulted in a violation of the right to **equal protection** under the law.

In 1973, this issue was decided on the federal level by the Supreme Court in a case involving a school district in Texas. In *San Antonio Independent School District v. Rodriguez,* the Court held that public school children do not have a constitutional entitlement to any particular level of education. Thus, the state's funding program did not violate the equal protection clause of the Constitution. The Court instead placed the duty to guarantee roughly equal educational opportunities for children on the legislatures of the various states. Challenges to inequitable school finance schemes have therefore shifted to state courts, where they are based on alleged violations of state antidiscrimination laws. These lawsuits have met with varying degrees of success.

GANG BOOK A collection of photographs of known or suspected gang members that is used by police to investigate crimes believed to be perpetrated by gangs. Typically, the book is shown to witnesses of criminal acts to aid in making an identification of the perpetrators. At least one court has held certain uses of gang books to be a violation of the Fourth Amendment rights of people whose photographs appear in them, including juveniles. [*People v. Rodriguez* (1993)]

The *Rodriguez* case involved a youth who was identified by use of a gang book as the person who shot a man. The youth, Arnold Rodriguez, was later convicted of second-degree murder. Rodriguez challenged the constitutionality of his conviction. The appellate court allowed the conviction to stand because other evidence also led to Rodriguez's arrest and he was ultimately identified as the perpetrator of the crime through use of a different photograph taken of him after his arrest. However, the court ruled that taking pictures of people for inclusion in a gang book to be used exclusively for criminal investigations and presented as evidence in a court of law was unconstitutional. Noting that mere membership in a gang is not a crime, the court explained that gang books contradict the presumption of innocence so important to the functioning of the American system of criminal justice. Moreover, taking photographs of citizens who have committed no crime merely because they are suspected of associating with a certain group of people whose members may be involved in crime is a violation of the privacy rights of those citizens.

GIFTED AND TALENTED STUDENTS EDUCATION ACT OF 1988 This federal law is designed to provide states funding to develop programs that meet the educational needs of academically gifted children. The law recognizes that identifying children who are exceptionally endowed as early as possible is important in helping them achieve their potential, because some of these students are likely to become bored and unmotivated in regular classroom settings.

Gifted and talented programs in public schools have, however, generated their share of challenges, mostly from parents who believe that their children have been unfairly excluded. Thus, an important part of any such program is to ensure that fair and accurate measurements of children's relative gifts can be achieved. They must also provide some means of reevaluating students periodically so that "late bloomers" can be accommodated.

GINSBERG V. NEW YORK   A 1968 case decided by the Supreme Court that reinforced the power of state governments to restrict the activities of children more stringently than the activities of adults—even when the regulation impinges on one of the most important rights of the American citizen: the right to free speech embodied in the First Amendment of the Constitution.

Ginsberg was a store owner who was convicted of violating a state statute making it illegal to sell "indecent" material to minors under the age of seventeen, even though the same material could lawfully be sold to adults. Ginsberg challenged the constitutionality of the statute on the grounds that it infringed on his First Amendment rights to free speech.

The Court rejected the appeal, saying that the state had important interests in regulating the type of material that impressionable young people might read, even though it might restrict access to material otherwise deemed harmless for adults. As Justice Stewart put it in his concurring opinion, "a child is not possessed of that full capacity for individual choice which is the presupposition of first amendment guarantees." [at 649–650]

The Court came to the conclusion that the statute was necessary to protect children from harmful influences, even though the plentiful expert testimony in the case was inconclusive as to whether there was a causal link between pornography and juvenile delinquency or impaired morals among youth. The Court found the mere possibility of such harmful consequences sufficient to justify the state's intervention under the **parens patriae doctrine.** Moreover, the statute served to strengthen parents' unquestioned authority to censor the materials to which their minor children are exposed. The Court noted that if parents wished their children to have such material, they could provide it to them themselves.

On the other side of the balance, the store owner's right to sell material not considered obscene for adults to minors—although important—was not viewed as of the same rank in significance as competing interests in other cases involving restrictions on the activity of children, notably **parental rights** to raise their children without governmental interference. See *Meyer v. Nebraska; Pierce v. Society of Sisters; Prince v. Massachusetts;* and other early cases.

Although *Ginsberg* was technically about the rights of a store owner to sell material to children—and not the children's right to buy it—the case marks an important milestone in striking a balance regarding how children's First Amendment rights may be defined.

GOSS V. LOPEZ   This 1975 Supreme Court case determined that school authorities must give students notice of charges of mis conduct made against them and a hearing on the merits of the charges before suspending them from school. The plaintiffs in the case were students at several Columbus, Ohio, middle and high schools. During a period of student unrest in February and March 1971, Dwight Lopez and Betty Crome were suspended from school for ten days following unruly demonstrations on school property. They received no notice of the charges against them and were given no chance to defend themselves at a hearing. Both Lopez and Crome contended that they had not taken part in any demonstrations and were mere innocent bystanders of the fray.

In hearing their appeal, the high Court noted that the state of Ohio had created an entitlement to a free public education for children between five and twenty-one years of age. Having created such an entitlement, the state could not then deprive citizens of it without **due process of law.** The Court noted that the plaintiffs lost significant educational benefits during the days of their suspension, disagreeing with the state's argument that ten days of lost classes was a "negligible" punishment. Moreover, the Court recognized that the children's reputations had also been injured by the school district's action.

Having determined that notice and a hearing must be given to students before suspension, the Court went on to make clear that the type of notice and hearing could be very minimal. Basically, oral charges and an immediate chance to present one's own side of the story are sufficient. The hearing may occur almost immediately following the charges. However, the hearing must be conducted before the student is suspended and removed from school. Counsel is not necessary. If a student disputes the facts upon which the disciplinary action is based, the school might be obliged to present the accuser for cross-examination and allow the student to present witnesses. The Court noted that long suspensions, lasting weeks or months, or permanent expulsions may require more formal procedures.

This case was decided by a narrow margin. The dissenting justices worried that the ruling would open up schools to micro-management by the courts.

GOVERNMENT AID TO PRIVATE RELIGIOUS SCHOOLS

State and local governments occasionally extend services or give equipment to private religious schools as a general welfare measure to help school-age children. These efforts may result in fostering "an excessive government entanglement with religion" in violation of the First Amendment to the U.S. Constitution. For example, giving public funds to pay parochial schools' teachers' salaries or to buy equipment for and maintain the physical plants of religious schools is forbidden. Even money to aid parochial schools in testing children for visual, hearing, or speech deficiencies has been ruled off limits by courts hearing constitutional challenges to such practices. Direct subsidies to parents to help them pay for their children's tuition at religious schools is also forbidden.

Nevertheless, state aid to religious schools that can be shown to have a purely secular purpose and effect that does not either inhibit or foster any of the religious teachings of the schools may be permissible. In *Zobrest v. Catalina Foothills School District*, 113 S. Ct. 2462 (1993), the Supreme Court ruled that it was permissible for an Arizona public school district to provide an interpreter for a deaf student at a Roman Catholic high school. Likewise, it has been ruled permissible for a state to loan strictly secular textbooks to religious schools. Also, a law that allows parents to deduct certain expenses for their children's education from their taxes is not unconstitutional, so long as it gives the same tax benefits to parents of children in all types of schools.

GRANDPARENT VISITATION STATUTE

A law that permits a family court to order parents or **guardians** to allow a child's grandparents to visit him or her when it is in the best interests of the child. See **best interests of the child rule.**

Grandparents have no automatic legal right to visit with their grandchildren. The right of parents to raise their children as they see fit includes the right to determine with whom they will associate. This may mean cutting off the access of grandparents to their grandchildren, if the parents of the children so desire. Traditionally, the law has viewed parents' obligations to allow grandparents to visit their children as a moral issue and not a legal one. In spite of this customary rule of law, forty-eight states now have grandparent visitation statutes.

Grandparents who wish to invoke the protection of a grandparent visitation statute in order to be allowed visits with their grandchildren must petition a court for an order granting access to the children. Generally, they must be prepared to show why visitation is in the best interests of the child. This is consistent with the view that the right to be protected is the child's right to know his or her grandparents, and not the grandparents' right to the society of the child. Based on the evidence presented, the court may then choose to grant visitation or reject the petition.

Usually, grandparents may seek visitation rights only if the custodial parent or guardian of their grandchild is not their own biological child. This reflects the law's reluctance to get involved in disputes within intact, biologically related families. Thus, most grandparent visitation statutes only apply when the child's parents are divorced, or one parent has died, and the remaining custodial parent is not the grandparents' own child. A few states' laws allow grandparent visitation to be ordered against the wishes of parents who are the grandparents' biological children. Other statutes flatly forbid courts to grant visitation if both biological parents object.

Grandparent visitation is most likely to be granted where the grandparents have already forged a strong relationship with the child. For example, grandparents who have served as the child's guardian are usually granted visitation rights after the child returns to his or her parents. Where no meaningful relationship between the grandparents and the child has ever existed, it is unlikely that visitation will be granted. Likewise, animosity toward the grandparents on the part of the child is likely to defeat a petition for visitation. Grandparents are also more likely to be granted visitation if the child's parents are proven unfit. See **unfit parent.**

Grandparents of children who have been adopted by strangers generally have no rights to even petition for visitation. This is in keeping with the philosophy of cutting off all contact of an adopted child with his or her biological family. [See also **adoption.**] However, if the child has been adopted by a stepparent, visitation by the child's biological grandparents (the parents of the noncustodial parent) may sometimes be allowed. The rationale in this situation is that visits by the grandparents will not disrupt a family relationship already in existence. Great-grandparents generally have no rights to petition for visitation at all.

Grandparents who have been granted visitation rights must usually make do with considerably less time with the children than noncustodial parents—sometimes a matter of no more than a few weeks per year.

GUARDIAN An individual or organization that has authority over certain aspects of a child's life by virtue of a court order. Generally, a guardian is appointed where a child's **biological parent**s are absent or for some other reason unable to perform their parental duties. The scope of a guardian's authority is spelled out in special guardianship statutes in all states, or in the court decree that appoints the guardian. The authority of a guardian is similar to, but somewhat more limited than, full parental authority.

There are two types of guardians. A *guardian of the person* is usually an individual to whom legal custody of a child is awarded, and who has the right to make decisions regarding the child's upbringing, discipline, education, and physical care, including a choice of residence and medical treatment. The child is obligated to obey the guardian within the scope of his or her appointed powers. The guardian of the person does not have full discretion in all matters relating to the child's upbringing, however. Guardianship statutes frequently require the child to be brought up in the religious faith of his or her biological parents. And, unless parental rights have been terminated, the child's biological parents usually retain the right to visit and have contact with him or her.

Usually, a guardian will not have a duty to support the child, or *ward,* as one under a guardianship is called. That duty usually remains with the child's parents if they are still alive. Otherwise, the state may provide the funds necessary for the child's care. In some cases, however, a guardian may voluntarily assume support obligations for the child.

A *guardian of the estate* is a person or an organization, such as a bank, that is given the obligation of managing property owned by a child. Children may own property, but they are generally considered to be incapable of managing it wisely for their own benefit. Therefore, when a child comes into property, usually through a gift or inheritance, the appointment of a guardian of the estate is necessary. [See **property rights.**] A guardian of a child's estate manages the child's property and assets for the child's benefit. Rules regarding such management are strict and the appointing court monitors the guardian's actions. A guardian of the estate may make investments with the child's assets or may sell the child's property and invest the proceeds, provided such actions are reasonably designed to preserve the value of the estate for the child when he or she reaches the age of **majority.** Investments are usually restricted to relatively "safe" buys that bear little risk of losing value. Usually, a court must approve any sale or investment made by the guardian. A guardian of the estate is required to make a periodic report, or accounting, to the court that shows the status of the child's property.

Frequently, the guardian of a child's property will be the child's parents. However, there is no automatic right for a parent to assume the guardianship of his or her child's property. Sometimes a guardian of the person and a guardian of the estate will be the same entity. In this case, the guardian is known as a *general guardian.*

In order for a guardian to be appointed, a petition must be filed with a court. It may be filed by the person seeking to be appointed guardian or by someone else with an interest in the child's welfare. Generally, the person petitioning must prove that there is a need for the guardian: usually that the child has been abandoned, that his or her parents are dead, that the parents' parental rights have been terminated, or that parental rights should be terminated because the parents are unfit. See **abandonment; unfit parent.**

Sometimes parents designate a person to serve as their children's guardian in the event that they die or become incapacitated. Although the appointing court will give deference to this wish, the court is not bound by it. The child may also nominate a guardian if he or she is of sufficient age— usually fourteen. However, a child's wishes regarding with whom he or she will live are not binding on a court until the child reaches the age of sixteen. If no one steps forward to request the guardianship of a child in need, the state may nominate itself to be the child's guardian through the **parens patriae doctrine.** If the state is appointed guardian, the child is known as a ward of the state. The actual custody of a child who is a ward of the state will be placed with the state's child welfare agency.

A guardian is usually compensated for his or her services, although guardians may agree to serve without pay. The expenses for the maintenance of the child are normally paid from the child's property, from the child's parents, or from state funds if the parents and the child lack funds. A guardian of a child's estate is usually paid from the assets in the estate. However, the fees must be reasonable, and a court usually must approve them.

A guardian generally will be removed when the child's parents are again able to resume care, when the child reaches the age of **majority,** or if cause can be shown why the guardianship should not continue. This usually involves proof that the guardian is incompetent or dishonest. It should be noted that guardianships are not just for children. Anyone who is unable to care for himself or herself due to a handicap, an illness, or the infirmities of old age may require a guardian.

GUARDIAN AD LITEM   An adult who represents the legal interests of a child or other person lacking the ability to represent himself or herself. Presumed to be too immature to conduct legal affairs, children are said to lack "legal capacity" and may not be parties to a lawsuit or any other legal procedure in their own names. Therefore, an adult must step in to represent the child's legal interests on the child's behalf. This disability continues until the child reaches the age of **majority.**

Traditionally, the term *guardian ad litem* referred only to an adult representing a child as a defendant in a lawsuit, while an adult representing a child as a plaintiff was known as the child's next friend. Today, the term *guardian ad litem* is commonly used in all circumstances. The Latin words *ad litem* mean "for the proceeding." In court papers, the child's name will usually appear first, followed by the name of the guardian ad litem. For example: "Mary Jones, a minor, by and through John Jones, next friend (or guardian ad litem)." A guardian ad litem is also sometimes referred to as the child's "duly appointed representative."

Usually, a guardian ad litem will be the child's parent, legal **guardian,** or close relative. If a relative is not available, most states allow any person "having an interest in the welfare of the child" to serve as a guardian ad litem. In most cases, a guardian ad litem who is not an attorney must hire an attorney to do the actual legal work and stand up in court, although a growing number of states allow guardians ad litem who are not attorneys for particular types of child welfare procedures. A guardian ad litem may not be necessary in all cases in which a child is involved. However, the court hearing the case must make a determination that the child's interests are being adequately represented without the benefit of a guardian ad litem. If the court decides that the child's interests are not being represented, the court will appoint a guardian ad litem. The guardian ad litem will initiate any lawsuit or answer in defense to a lawsuit, and will control and direct any litigation. However, a child who is fourteen years of age or older must usually give consent to have a lawsuit brought on his or her behalf.

The most important aspect of a guardian ad litem is that he or she represents the separate interests of the child. If the child's interests in a legal matter differ from those of his or her parents, or any other person, the parent or other person may not serve as the child's guardian ad litem. If there is a possible conflict of interest, the court will appoint another, neutral party to represent the child.

The clearest example of a conflict between a child's interests and those of the parents occurs when the child sues the parents. [See also **family immunity doctrine.**] However, there are many other situations in which children's interests are enough different from those of their parents that a separate guardian ad litem must be appointed for them. For example, it would be inappropriate to name a parent as the guardian ad litem of a minor who is seeking an abortion or other medical treatment without parental consent. Similarly, a child being sued for beating up the neighborhood bully could not be represented by his parents if the child's defense is that his parents encouraged him to "stand up for himself." This would tend to incriminate the parents, who might then be sued for negligent supervision. See **tort responsibility.**

In any proceeding in which **child abuse** or **neglect** of a child is alleged, a separate guardian ad litem, who is not the child's parent, is required by the federal **Child Abuse Prevention and Treatment Act.** In many states, a separate guardian ad litem is also required for any child who is the subject of a **paternity action,** custody dispute, litigation over child support payments, visitation rights, **adoption,** or commitment to **foster care** or to a mental institution. Disputes involving a child's medical treatment also normally require a guardian ad litem. In these cases, it is likely that the parents' interests differ from those of the child.

A guardian ad litem is also frequently appointed in situations in which a child is only peripherally affected. Legal proceedings involving wills, trust funds, insurance policies, workers' compensation claims, or other entitlements to benefits may require a guardian ad litem to safeguard the interests of a child who might be affected by the disposition of the proceeds—even though the child was not a named beneficiary, or even mentioned, in the document at issue. In fact, courts may appoint a guardian ad litem for a child that has not yet been born, if his or her interests will be affected by a court's order.

A guardian ad litem is considered to be an officer of the court that appoints him or her. This means that a judge will supervise the guardian ad litem's actions to ensure that the best interests of the child are represented. If the guardian ad litem is a third party (not the child's parent, close relative, or guardian), he or she is entitled to be paid for representing the child. These fees can include the costs of litigation—for example, attorneys' fees and court costs—and a reasonable fee for the guardian ad litem's own services. In some states, the child's parents must pay these fees if they are able. Otherwise, the state will defray the costs of a guardian ad litem. In some states, the government pays regardless of the financial means of the child's family. Generally, a guardian ad litem is immune from legal liability for mistakes made in representing the child. However, a guardian ad litem may be removed for incompetence, bad faith, or other malfeasance. Unless terminated by a court, however, the guardian ad litem may not usually resign as the child's representative.

In recent years, the role of guardian ad litem for children has expanded. Instead of a mostly passive spectator, today's guardian ad litem is considered a critical participant in all phases of proceedings that might affect the child's welfare. The guardian ad litem can initiate contempt of court proceedings on behalf of a child if custody, visitation, or support orders have not been obeyed. The guardian ad litem is also frequently present to ensure the proper treatment of any child who has been called as a witness in a variety of legal procedures.

An unresolved issue concerning guardians ad litem who are also attorneys involves a conflict between the traditional missions of each. Technically, an attorney is obliged to represent his or her client's expressed wishes. A guardian ad litem is obliged to represent the client's best interests—even if they are at odds with the client's expressed wishes. For example, a child represented by a guardian ad litem may express a wish to return to an abusive home, even though this is not in his or her best interest. If the guardian ad litem is an attorney, he or she will be torn as to whether to represent the child's wishes or the child's best interests. One way in which this conflict may be resolved is by determining whether the child is capable of forming reasoned judgments about his or her own welfare. Teenagers are frequently considered capable of reasoned judgments, while younger children are not. Thus, an attorney representing a teenager as a guardian ad litem may ethically decide to advocate the teenager's wishes, even though it might conflict with the attorney's own idea of the teen's best interests.

HAZELWOOD SCHOOL DISTRICT V. KUHLMEIER   An

important Supreme Court decision in 1988 that further defines the limits of students' rights of expression in the public schools. Three former students of Hazelwood East High School in St. Louis County, Missouri, sued the school district and school officials for infringement of their First Amendment rights, which allegedly occurred when the school's principal censored certain articles from a school paper that the students edited.

The school newspaper, *Spectrum,* was the class project of a regularly scheduled journalism course taught during school hours. Pursuant to normal practice, the teacher of the course submitted the proof pages for the 13 May 1983 issue to the principal for his approval two days prior to publication. The principal objected to two articles, one about the experiences of pregnant students, and the other about the effect of divorce on children. Although the names of pregnant students interviewed for the pregnancy story were changed, the principal believed there was enough other information about them contained in the article that they could be readily identified. This unfairly compromised not only the pregnant students' privacy but the privacy of the girls' boyfriends and parents, the principal believed. In addition, certain frank talk about sexual practices and contraceptive use was—in the principal's opinion—inappropriate for school freshmen, who were fourteen years old. In the divorce story, one student, who was identified by name, had harsh criticism of her father. The principal believed that it was improper not to give the man an opportunity to respond in print to his daughter's charges. Because the principal believed that there was no time to rewrite the objectionable articles before publication, he decided that the two pages on which the material was to appear would be excised from the issue. Some other articles that happened to appear on the same pages and which the principal did not find offensive were also dropped.

The former students' case reached the Supreme Court in 1988. The high Court found that the students' First Amendment rights were not violated by the principal's actions. For the six justices voting in the majority, the issue turned on whether *Spectrum* could be characterized as a "public forum" in which anyone was invited to express an opinion. Because the paper was produced as part of the normal high school curriculum and was ostensibly founded for the purpose of teaching students about the profession of journalism, the Court answered this question in the negative: *Spectrum* was not a public forum. Therefore, school officials could impose reasonable restrictions on student speech that occurred through this school-sponsored medium. "The First Amendment rights of students in public schools are not automatically coextensive with the rights of adults in other settings and must be applied in light of the special characteristics of the school environment," Justice White wrote. Moreover, in the opinion of the Court, the principal's concerns about privacy, propriety, and fairness reasonably justified removing the two pages on which the offending material appeared. The Court noted that, at trial, an editor of a large, respected city newspaper testified that the student articles in question did not meet journalistic standards of fairness and balance.

The Court took pains to distinguish the situation in *Hazelwood* with that in *Tinker v. Des Moines Independent Community School District*. In *Tinker*, decided nearly two decades earlier, the Court found a violation of students' First Amendment rights when the school suspended them for wearing black armbands in protest of the war in Vietnam. *Hazelwood* was different, said the Court, because it involved a publication sponsored by the school. By contrast, the students in *Tinker* were clearly expressing purely personal points of view that no one could mistake for an official school policy. "The standard for determining when a school may punish student expression that happens to occur on school premises [*Tinker*] is not the standard for determining when a school may refuse to lend its name and resources to the dissemination of student expression [*Hazelwood*]."

Three justices dissented from the holding in *Hazelwood*. Justices Brennan, Marshall, and Blackmun believed that the standard set forth in *Tinker* should also apply in *Hazelwood*. The Court in *Tinker* found that school authorities could restrict student speech only if it "materially and substantially" interfered with legitimate objectives of the school. The articles involved in *Hazelwood* did not reach the level of material or substantial interference, these justices believed. By allowing the school to censor this type of speech, the majority of the Court frustrated the goal of "teaching children to respect the diversity of ideas that is fundamental to the American system," argued the dissent. Moreover, if the school was concerned about appearing to sponsor the opinions expressed in the two articles at issue, it could have remedied this situation in a far less drastic way. It could, for example, have required the publication of a disclaimer in the same issue, explaining that the opinions expressed therein were not "official" school policy. While the majority would teach the students of Hazelwood a lesson in civics, raged the dissenters, it was not the one they expected.

HEAD START   An educational program funded by the federal government aimed at stimulating the intellectual development of preschool children living in poverty so that they do not lag behind their more affluent peers when they reach school age.

The Head Start program was inaugurated in 1965, during the heyday of President Johnson's War on Poverty campaign. The program has enjoyed broad bipartisan support in Congress and survived several rounds of federal budget cutting fervor in the decades since. The reasons for Head Start's popularity can be attributed to its effectiveness: Numerous studies have shown that poor children who attend Head Start programs are, in fact, better able to compete academically when they start school. (A few studies have shown that this advantage is lost if the children do not receive ongoing special academic attention and support.)

Unlike other programs aimed at the poor in the United States, Head Start is not an entitlement program. The program operates under a set budget and is therefore able to accommodate only a percentage of those needing its services. As of 1994, it was estimated that Head Start had served approximately 14 million children over a period of nearly thirty years. This seems like a large number; however, it represents only about one-half of the children who were eligible during that time. In 1990, approximately 500,000 children nationwide were attending Head Start programs, only about one-fifth of eligible children at the time.

Funding for Head Start is distributed as grants by the federal Health and Human Services Department to public and nonprofit agencies that typically set up "shop" in grade schools or churches in poor communities. Although children from ages three through five are eligible, the typical Head Start program offers a half-day of preschool instruction for four-year-olds, five days a week. Many Head Start programs have adjunct services for the families of the children. In some programs, parents are encouraged to accompany their children and take part in teaching them. In others, the parents may attend a separate class held at the same time in which they receive instruction in basic child care and the learn the necessity of interacting intellectually with their offspring.

The presence of a Head Start program in a community may have an influence greater than just improving the academic achievement of its participants. Parents whose children attend may be able to take part in job-training courses or hold down part-time jobs during the hours their children are cared for in the Head Start school. Head Start programs have been known to act as magnets for other programs for the disadvantaged to open in the same communities. The fact that federal money has been earmarked for a neighborhood in the form of a Head Start school seems to lend a degree of stability to the area upon which other enterprises can build. This in turn opens up opportunities for children and their parents who are not eligible to attend Head Start, provides jobs, and in general fosters a spirit of beneficial community involvement.

In spite of this rosy assessment, Head Start programs are increasingly called on to counter other devastating effects of poverty in the lives of children. Beyond trying to reverse stunted intellectual development in their young charges, Head Start personnel may be faced with intervening to prevent child abuse and neglect, to arrange needed medical care, and to motivate parents to deal with their own debilitating addictions, diseases, and habits. Stretched to the limit of its ability, Head Start is not a panacea for the ills of America's underclasses as the twenty-first century dawns.

HEARSAY STATEMENTS A statement attributed to someone other than the person who relates it. For example, A's statement, "B said he wanted to kill C," is a hearsay statement, because it relays what A heard B say. Hearsay statements usually may not be used as evidence in a court of law, unless the person who allegedly made the statement is available to testify. In the above example, A's statement may be entered into evidence only if B can be called to testify about whether he actually said what A said she heard him say. If B is unavailable, A's statement will not be admissible in court. The reason for this rule is the inherent unreliability of reported speech. Anyone who has ever played the game "telephone," in which a statement is relayed down a chain of recipients, knows how garbled the message becomes at the end. Moreover, the potential for fabricating another's motives is increased if a witness can blithely report what the other supposedly said.

Because children often make unreliable witnesses in court [see also **testimonial competency**], the rule against hearsay evidence has been relaxed when the statements of children are involved. In other words, a witness may testify about what a child told him or her, without the child himself or herself being available to testify. This exception to the normal rule excluding hearsay statements is viewed as particularly necessary in cases of alleged **child abuse.** In those cases, the child victim is usually the only witness to the crime. Moreover, the trauma of the event itself and the possibility that the child has been threatened with retaliation if he or she tells anyone about it combine to make eliciting the child's testimony particularly difficult.

Some states have passed statutes specifically allowing certain types of hearsay evidence from children into trials. Many states adhere to a so-called first statement, or outcry statement, rule. Under this variation, the first statement a child makes to an adult about the incident that is the subject of the testimony is admissible into evidence. Such statements are believed to be more likely to be truthful, because the child will not have had time to "make something up" and is spontaneously moved to cry out about the bad thing that has happened. Most courts make allowances for a delay between the incident and the outcry in cases in which the child has been threatened with retaliation if he or she tells about it.

In states without specific hearsay statutes, it is up to the judge in a trial to determine whether reported statements made by a child are admissible into evidence. The judge will assess the character of the proposed hearsay evidence to determine its reliability. Usually, statements made by a child to a parent, another trusted adult, a friend, or a medical doctor are considered more likely to be truthful than statements made to others. Statements made spontaneously by a child in his or her own words are more reliable than statements made under repeated questioning by an adult who might unwittingly suggest answers. Emotional statements are considered more reliable than statements made with indifference. In addition, the judge will consider the child's general reputation for truthfulness, and whether he or she had any motive for lying—as for example, whether a parent embittered by divorce had a hand in coaching the child's allegations. In a case decided by the U.S. Supreme Court, it was held that the admission of hearsay statements about an assault made by a four-year-old girl to her baby-sitter, her mother, a police officer, an emergency room nurse, and the examining doctor did not violate the criminal defendant's constitutional rights to a fair trial. All five adults were allowed to testify as to what the girl told them. The girl herself was too traumatized to testify. [*White v. Illinois* (1992)]

The exception for hearsay statements made by children usually applies only to young children, typically only those under the ages of ten or twelve.

There are several reasons for this. First, children over those ages are usually able to testify in court reliably, so there is no need to rely on statements they allegedly made to others. Second, a child's capacity to concoct a story increases with age. At or about ten or twelve years of age, most children know enough to make up a pretty good yarn. It is important to subject them to cross-examination to ensure that their stories hold up.

HOME SCHOOL   In the last decade of the twentieth century, the education of children at home is gaining popularity, partly as a palliative for real or perceived deficiencies in public school programs, and partly as a further statement of identity with an ideological background.

Not all states allow home schooling. In those that do, laws may require that the educational program for the home-schooled child meets the same minimum standards as public schools. Many laws require that the education a child receives in a home school environment be "substantially equivalent" in time and quality to that provided in public schools. To this end, parents may be required to submit lesson plans, along with textbooks and other materials, to a state board for approval. Some states' laws allow home schooling only with a qualified teacher. Thus, parents who wish their children to be educated in their homes must either prove that they possess the credentials to teach in the state or hire a teacher who does. Usually, it is not necessary for the home in which a child attends school to meet the building requirements of bona fide schools, or to have the same amenities and equipment as other schools.

Even with approval for lesson plans and qualifications for teachers, states may also resort to standardized achievement tests to be given to home-schooled children. If a child falls behind in academic achievements relative to children the same age in public schools, many states reserve the right to revoke permission for the child to remain in home school. The child must then either return to the public school system or attend some sort of alternative school that meets state academic standards.

While state requirements for home schooling must be reasonable and allow a certain amount of flexibility, some situations have been held clearly not acceptable. For example, a parent who set aside only one and one-half hours per day to school her youngsters, allowed the children to choose what subjects would be taught, and herself had only a high school education was found not to be in compliance with the compulsory attendance laws of her state.

Critics of home schooling contend that, no matter how academically advanced the instruction a child receives at home is, the child is still not receiving one of the most important lessons from school attendance, that is, how to relate to other people in the world outside one's own family. Some states have embraced this argument, finding that home school is not "substantially equivalent" to the school experience of other children and, therefore, is not allowed. In these states, children must attend some school, whether public, private, or parochial.

HOUSING DISCRIMINATION

Currently, it is a violation of federal law (and of the laws of many states) to refuse to rent or sell a dwelling to a person on the basis of his or her "familial status." This is the result of amendments made to the federal Fair Housing Act in 1988, which were designed to put an end to housing discrimination against families with children. Prior to the passage of these amendments, many rental properties were designated "for adults only," as a result of landlords' fears that children would damage their property or disturb tenants who desired peace and quiet.

Today, it is rare that rental property managers blatantly proclaim "adults only" policies. However, some policies that seem neutral on their face can have the effect of excluding children and may be challenged under the Fair Housing Act. For example, one apartment complex that had a "one person per bedroom" policy was found to have violated the act when it refused to rent a one-bedroom apartment to a single mother with a five-year-old child. The complex justified the rule by the fact that one-bedroom apartments at the complex had only one parking space each. The court found this rationale insufficient in light of the fact that a five-year-old would hardly be driving.

The prohibition on discrimination in housing against families with children applies to single-parent families, to pregnant women, to any parent who is attempting to secure custody of his or her children, or a couple that is seeking a foster or adoptive child.

ILLEGITIMACY The state of having been born to parents who are not married. Under the traditional common law and until relatively recently, being illegitimate had severe consequences for a child's welfare. For example, although the father of an illegitimate child had a duty to see that the child did not become so poverty-stricken that the state had to provide support, an illegitimate child had no right to receive the same type and degree of support that the father provided to his legitimate children. Moreover, an illegitimate child had no right to inherit from his or her father, or to receive other benefits—such as to recover damages in a lawsuit for the wrongful death of the father, to share in workers' compensation benefits paid for the father's injury, or to receive other welfare benefits.

Beginning in 1968, however, the Supreme Court has consistently held that distinguishing between children on the basis of their parents' marital status when they were born is a violation of the constitutional right of equal protection under the law, guaranteed by the Fourteenth Amendment to the U.S. Constitution. This means that an illegitimate child is not only entitled to all the types of support to which a legitimate child is entitled, but is entitled to inherit an equal share with legitimate children, and to share in any other benefits to which legitimate children are entitled.

This change in the law has mirrored society's relative destigmatizing of out-of-wedlock birth. Today, in most states, the major legal consequence of having been born a "bastard" is that the child might have to establish the identity of his or her biological father before the full panoply of filial entitlements from the father are available. The identity of a man as a child's biological father, or the man's paternity, may be established various ways: by the man's voluntary acknowledgment of a child as his [see **acknowledgment statute**], by actions of the man tending to show that he considers himself to be the child's father (including marriage to the child's mother), or through a civil lawsuit in which both scientific and circumstantial evidence of fatherhood are presented. See **paternity action.**

The law assumes that children who are born to a married mother are the legitimate children of the mother's husband, whether or not this is truly the case. In most states, this presumption can be rebutted only by the strongest evidence, such as the husband's nonaccess to the mother at the time of conception of the child or proof of impotence or sterility of the husband. Scientific evidence, through blood or DNA testing, may also be sufficient to rebut the presumption of legitimacy of a child born in wedlock and to establish that another man fathered the child. However, many states restrict who may bring a paternity action when the mother of the child at issue is married. These states believe that the interest in protecting an established family unit is so strong that it outweighs the right of someone outside the marriage to claim, and to attempt to prove, that someone else is really the father of the married couple's child.

Traditionally, many states have required a determination of paternity to be made during the lifetime of the putative father in order for a child to be able to claim an inheritance from him. However, the constitutionality of this rule is questionable in light of rulings by the Supreme Court that a state may not erect insurmountable barriers to an illegitimate child's access to rights and benefits enjoyed by legitimate children. [*Gomez v. Perez* (1973)] A flat rule that a child may not prove that a deceased man was his or her father would probably be such an impermissible insurmountable barrier. Moreover, with the increased accuracy and use of DNA testing, the feasibility of proving paternity posthumously is increasing. Indeed, in a few cases, courts have approved the disinterment of a putative father's body in order to make DNA tests and determine parentage.

The Supreme Court has ruled that a state may place some restrictions on an illegitimate child's right to inherit from a man. [*Lalli v. Lalli* (1978)] First, it is absolutely necessary to prove paternity, since one has no right to inherit from someone to whom one is not related. Some states hold that a court order establishing paternity is the only acceptable proof to enable an illegitimate child to inherit. Other states will allow an illegitimate child to inherit if there are indications of paternity, such as the man's voluntary acceptance or formal acknowledgment of the child, or the man's marriage to the child's mother. Second, it is permissible to put some time limit on claims to inherit from a deceased man on the grounds that the man was the biological father of the claimant. [*Reed v. Campbell* (1986)] A state's interest in winding up the affairs of deceased citizens and distributing their property in an orderly and permanent fashion justifies setting a time period within which an illegitimate child may claim an inheritance. See also **inheritance rights.**

In Loco Parentis   A Latin phrase meaning "in the place of a parent." People or organizations are in loco parentis when they have assumed some of the duties and have been granted some of the rights of parents with respect to children left in their care. For example, the teachers and administration of a school are in loco parentis to the children who are attending. The school has the right to set certain rules of behavior for the children while they are present. At the same time, the school has the obligation to protect and provide certain necessities for the children in much the same way as a parent. Similarly, a baby-sitter is acting in loco parentis to children left in his or her care until the parents return. The state may also be in loco parentis when it enforces child support or abuse statutes and when it takes children into custody for their own protection. See also **parens patriae doctrine.**

Generally, one who is not a parent can only be in loco parentis by voluntarily accepting temporary authority over a child that has been delegated by the parent or **guardian** of the child. An adult who sees unsupervised children playing with matches but does nothing to stop them may be morally responsible if they accidentally start a fire, but cannot be legally to blame unless he or she actually accepted the responsibility of caring for them.

Acting in loco parentis is not the same as having legal custody of a child. Although one having custody is also in loco parentis to the child, he or she has a far greater range of duties and rights with respect to controlling and caring for the child. See **child custody.**

In re Gault   A landmark Supreme Court case (1967) that helped shift American juvenile justice from an arbitrary, unregulated system dependent on the supposed benevolent wisdom of public officials to a system based on the same type of automatic constitutional rights enjoyed by adults.

Prior to *Gault*, the general philosophy was that, unlike adults, children had no right to liberty at all. Instead, they had only a right to "custody," that is, a right to be protected and provided for by their parents or guardians. If the parent or guardian failed at this task, and the child became delinquent as a result, the state could take over the custodial duties under the **parens patriae doctrine.** This policy, which was begun around the turn of the twentieth century, was intended to reform the ills of an older system in which children over the age of seven were tried for crimes in adult courts, under adult standards, and sentenced to prison with adult offenders. While the new "reformed" policy recognized that children could not be held to adult standards and should not be housed with adult offenders, it also led to situations in which children could be incarcerated for years (albeit in separate facilities) without advance notice of the specific charges against them, without an opportunity to confront their accusers, without the right to an attorney, and without any protection against self-incrimination.

Such were the circumstances in *Gault*. A fifteen-year-old Arizona boy, Gerald Gault, was arrested along with a friend on the accusation of a neighbor woman that the boys had made obscene remarks to her over the phone. No one informed Gerald's parents, who were at work, that their son had been arrested. They first found out his whereabouts when they set out to look for him that evening and were told by the other boy's family that Gerald was in custody. When Gerald's parents went to the juvenile detention center at which he was held, they were told only that a hearing would take place the following day in juvenile court.

At that hearing, which was held in the judge's chambers, the neighbor woman who made the complaint was not even present. Neither was Gerald's father. The arresting officer simply presented a petition alleging that Gerald was a "delinquent" and was in need of the protection of the court, without stating the specific details of what Gerald was alleged to have done. No one was compelled to swear to their testimony, and no transcript or record of any kind was made. Six days later, another hearing was held at which Gerald's father, the other boy's parents, and the two arresting police officers were present. The complaining witness was still not there. Her accusation that Gerald had made the obscene phone call to her was relayed secondhand by one of the arresting officers, who apparently had talked to her only once about the case. The arresting officer also stated that Gerald had admitted to making the lewd remarks after questioning. However, it appeared that this interrogation took place out of the presence of the boy's parents, without counsel, and without Gerald being advised of his right to silence. Neither the boy nor his parents were notified of the boy's right to be represented by counsel and of the right to appointed counsel if they could not afford a lawyer. At the conclusion of this second hearing, the judge ordered Gerald to be committed as a juvenile delinquent to a detention center until he was twenty-one years old—a period of six long years. No appeal of this decision was permitted under Arizona law.

In a protracted series of attacks on this judgment, Gerald's case finally came before the U.S. Supreme Court. The Court decided that Gerald's constitutional rights had indeed been violated. The high Court held for the first time that the Bill of Rights in the Constitution was not for adults only. The so-called due process protections of the Constitution must be observed for children as well as adults. The Court held the following:

- A minor charged in juvenile court must be given sufficient notice in advance of any hearing as to the substance of the charges against him or her. Notice must also be given to the child's parents. The notice must be the same as that given to accused adult offenders.

- If punishment for the charged offense includes a possible incarceration, the child and his or her parents must be told that the child is entitled to be represented by a lawyer, and to have a lawyer appointed if they are unable to afford one.

- The privilege against self-incrimination applies to juvenile proceedings. The child must be informed of the right to remain silent before any interrogation begins.

- Confessions may not be obtained through threats or coercion.

- Absent a valid confession, no adjudication of delinquency may be made without the sworn testimony of witnesses and the accused's opportunity to cross-examine them.

- A record of juvenile proceedings must be kept and appeals of such adjudications must be allowed.

The Court rejected the state's arguments that the Fifth Amendment protection against self-incrimination applied only to criminal trials and that, since juvenile proceedings were termed "civil" in nature, the amendment did not apply to them. At the same time, the Court reaffirmed that the Constitution allows for a separate juvenile justice system with different procedures and standards than adult courts. A juvenile proceeding need not conform to all the requirements of an adult criminal trial. It need only provide the basic protections of constitutional "due process." The kindly, benevolent, and informal guidance that the old system envisioned for dealing with juvenile offenders did not need to be sacrificed merely because the law now recognized the child's right to certain standard procedures and protections.

INCOME TAX Depending on how much they earn and whether they are claimed as dependents on their parents' income tax returns, minors may be required to pay federal and state income taxes. Generally, if a juvenile earns less per year than the amount of the standard deduction plus the exemption amount for that year, he or she is not required to file an income tax return. However, if money was withheld from his or her paycheck as taxes, even a child who made less than this amount should file a return in order to have the withholding returned as a refund.

A child who is claimed as a dependent on a parent's income and who makes more than a minimal amount ($1,200 in 1994) of *unearned* income must file a tax return. Unearned income is that derived from investments (dividends, interest) or from the rental or sale of properties. See also **kiddie tax.**

INDECENT MATERIALS Laws may restrict young people's access to materials that are not considered "obscene" by adult standards without violating the minors' First Amendment rights. [See *Ginsberg v. New York.*] Although sexually explicit materials are the main targets of this type of legislation, concerns are mounting that ubiquitous and constant depictions of violence in the media also have deleterious effects on children and should be restricted.

Restrictions on children's access to material deemed "indecent" usually take one of two forms: (1) forbidding the sale of the targeted material to minors or (2) requiring sellers to give adults the means to block their children's access to the material. The first of these approaches has been used by many communities to forbid the sale of sexually explicit printed or pictorial materials to minors. Typically, these laws make it a crime to sell the materials to persons under the age of eighteen. Giving minors the material may also be forbidden, unless the giver is a parent or guardian. This exception reflects the law's deference to parents to determine the material to which their children may have access. The possession of indecent materials by a minor is not usually a crime. To prevent minors from seeing the material accidentally or perusing it without buying, many jurisdictions require retail stores to hide the covers of sexually explicit magazines for sale on their newsstands, or to place such materials in separate rooms accessible only to adults.

While laws prohibiting sales to minors work well when the seller is a store or movie theater into which customers must come, they work less well when the material is disseminated through some other medium, such as the telephone, or via broadcast or electronic media. It is difficult to enforce laws restricting sale to minors in these cases, not to mention that there may be no practical way for sellers of the material to determine the age of their "customers" even if they wish to comply with the law.

One modest measure has been instituted with respect to the broadcast media: so-called safe haven regulations require broadcasters to program material with adult content at times when statistics show relatively few children are tuned in, such as during late night hours. Safe haven regulations are usually considered constitutional unless the hours during which programs with adult content may be shown are so restrictive as to impinge on adults' access to the material. In addition, under the Children's Television Act of 1990 [47 U.S.C. §§ 303a, b, 394 (Supp. IV 1992)] the Federal Communications Commission (FCC) is required to evaluate broadcasters for the amount of sex and violence they depict in their programming as part of the process of determining whether to grant a renewal license. (The act also limits the amount of advertising that may appear during children's programming.)

Efforts to regulate the electronic media that go beyond these measures are problematic, however. In 1997, the Supreme Court invalidated a federal law, the Communications Decency Act (CDA), that attempted to stem the flow of indecent material on the Internet by making it a crime to transmit the material to children. The Court found the Internet as a medium to be more like printed materials than like the broadcast media. Traditionally, printed information has been given the broadest freedom of expression because there is no shortage of paper on which to disseminate it. The broadcast media are different: there are only a finite number of broadcast frequencies upon which to send information. Because of this inherent limitation, not everyone can have access to a wavelength in order to broadcast his or her expression. The high Court pointed out that the Internet, if anything, is even more unlimited in capacity to carry the expressions of myriad voices than print media. And, unlike broadcast material, people are rarely subjected to unwanted communication on the Internet "by accident." This ruling set a precedent for the twenty-first century suggesting that the Internet will enjoy the most unrestricted flow of information possible. However, the Court did allow one provision of the CDA to stand—the one prohibiting patently "obscene" material, such as child pornography, from dissemination over the Internet. "Obscene" material, regardless of in what medium it is presented, is afforded no First Amendment protection.

(This is distinguished from material that is "indecent" for consumption by children but not adults.) [*Reno v. ACLU*]

Any law attempting to restrict the dissemination of certain information to minors must define with sufficient clarity the targeted material. If the law is worded too broadly, providers will not know which material to keep from minors and may end up preventing their access to important informative or literary works. For example, a law that forbade selling minors material "catering to a morbid interest in violence" was found by a court to be too broad and vague, as it was impossible for a reasonable adult to know what material met this criteria. Likewise, another law that prohibited the sale to children of information "unsuitable for persons under the age of 17" was also constitutionally defective. This law seems particularly puzzling: after all, if the law's drafters could not define what material was unsuitable for those under seventeen, how could they expect a seller to know either?

Because it is difficult to define "indecent" clearly and, in any case, people may reasonably differ in their opinions regarding such definitions, many laws designed to protect children from harmful exposure to adult information take the second approach to regulation: they require information providers to give parents a means to turn off the flow of objectionable material into their homes. In many ways, this approach seems the simplest solution, because it leaves the choice up to each individual parent to grant or deny their children access to information. Practical methods of turning away or blocking information in all media, including print, telephone, broadcast, or electronic media, are currently available. So long as the evaluation of the content of the material is left up to each parent or responsible adult, laws requiring a "turn off" option present few constitutional problems. After all, a corollary to the right of freedom of speech is the right to choose the speech one will hear.

Laws that require that a "rating" of the content of any information be done by anyone other than the end consumer, or parent, raise constitutional red flags. Of course, merely rating the content of various materials does not mean that the materials are "censored." However, if a government agency does the rating, it may be seen as an ominous first step in direct government control of speech. Moreover, government rating of content is an incentive for "self-censorship." A speaker, fearful of losing a favorable rating that will allow broader dissemination of his or her ideas, chooses instead to leave some important, but uncomfortable, topic unexplored. This is a way of "chilling" speech that is inimical to the free play of ideas guaranteed by the First Amendment.

Laws that require the speaker, or the originator of the material, to rate the content of the material seem more innocuous. However, another corollary to the First Amendment's freedom of speech is that no one will be compelled to speak. To require speakers to "rate" their own utterances is a form of compelled speech. This is why, to date, all rating systems, including those on motion pictures, video and audio recordings, and—most recently—television programming, are voluntarily undertaken by the producers of the material. Purveyors of entertainment, believing their customers want a rating system and prodded by the federal government, have so far acquiesced. However, it is unlikely that laws requiring self-rating would withstand constitutional challenges.

Such a constitutional challenge may come before the end of the millennium. In 1996, Congress passed into law the Telecommunications Act of 1996. This law requires all television sets with screens over thirteen inches wide to have the so-called V-chip, a device that allows the set owner to screen out certain programming. In itself this does not create a problem. However, the V-chip works by picking up a code that is broadcast in the signal carrying the program. The chip is then programmed to screen out transmissions that contain certain codes. Under the 1996 act, these codes would represent ratings of the content of the program for sexual explicitness, bad language, violence, or graphic images. For example, a show may be rated from one to seven, with one representing benign family content, and seven representing extreme violence, indecency, or sexual depictions. Thus, in order for the V-chip to work at all, the producer of a television program must rate the program and include the applicable rating "code" in the signal broadcasting the show. In this way, the broadcaster is compelled to speak by rating its own shows. So far, the government has stated that rating would be "voluntary." This means that certain broadcasters may opt not to rate their shows at all. The value of the device could be seriously undercut. Of course, viewers could choose to block out all programming without a coded signal, but this may result in many desirable programs being excluded.

It has also been suggested that the rating of the content of broadcast programs be left to private organizations that could apply their own criteria to the rating process. Parents could then choose which rating system to follow in order to make their choices of programming to allow into their homes. However, in order to work with the current V-chip technology, the "rating code" must be incorporated into the signal broadcasting the program at its source. It might be difficult for a broadcast station to incorporate a large number of codes corresponding to the ratings given to a particular program by various rating organizations. Moreover, requiring this coding would also raise the "compelled" speech problem, because the broadcaster may not agree with any of the ratings given to a particular show.

Even assuming the rating by diverse private organizations is feasible and not unconstitutional, it may not be desirable. A society of individuals reliant on others to choose acceptable programming abdicates more individual responsibility and faces further fragmentization, as each family chooses to tune in only to sources of information with which they agree. The broad "watering" of the citizenry with ideas of all sorts that was envisioned by the founding fathers would dry up. Society would lack reference to a common "culture" that—regardless of whether an individual agreed with it—would provide a starting point for understanding and accommodating different views.

INDIAN CHILD WELFARE ACT OF 1978 (ICWA) A federal law that gives more authority to Native American tribes to determine the placement of their children in adoptive or foster homes. The purpose of the law is to stabilize and preserve Indian cultures by preventing the breakup of Indian families through the placement of children needing a change of custody with other members of their own tribes. A child is considered to belong to a Native American tribe if one of his or her parents is a member of that tribe. Thus, a child who is only one-half Indian is still subject to the will of the tribe in determining custody. The ICWA gives exclusive jurisdiction to Indian tribes to determine custody of a child only if the child is living on a reservation or his or her legal domicile is on the reservation (although he or she is presently living elsewhere). For Indian children who live off a reservation, both the courts in the state where the child is located and the child's Indian tribe have concurrent jurisdiction over custody matters involving him or her.

The ICWA has been challenged on constitutional grounds because it classifies children on the basis of their race and treats them differently for that reason. Critics point out that the preference for placing Indian children with families within their own tribe is essentially the same as requiring that African-American children be placed only with African American parents—a practice that has received a great deal of criticism as perpetuating racism. Challenges to the ICWA have so far been unsuccessful. It remains to be seen whether the 1996 amendments to the federal Multiethnic Placement Act (MEPA), which prohibit agencies receiving federal funds from considering race when placing children in adoptive homes, will apply to Native American children. Technically, Native American tribes on reservations are sovereign nations. Recognizing a sovereign nation's jurisdiction over its own citizens is simply axiomatic. Thus, treatment of Native American children is arguably premised on their citizenship with their tribes, rather than on their race.

INDIVIDUALS WITH DISABILITIES EDUCATION ACT OF **1990 (IDEA)** This federal law mandates that states provide a "free appropriate public education" to children with disabilities. The meaning of these terms has been the subject of much litigation in the years since the law's passage.

Generally, an "appropriate" education for a student with disabilities is determined through the drafting of an individualized education program (IEP) for each child. The IEP is developed jointly by the child's parents and teacher and a representative of the local school district, whose duty it is to supervise the implementation of the IDEA within the school. The IEP includes an assessment of the present educational achievement of the child and sets forth goals, both long- and short-term, for instructional objectives to be achieved in the class. The IEP lists the specific educational services that must be provided to the child in order for him or her to achieve the IEP goals. For example, a sign-language interpreter may be needed for a deaf child. The IEP also discusses the extent to which the child can be "mainstreamed," or placed in regular classes with nondisabled children. It is the avowed policy of the IDEA that disabled children be mainstreamed to the maximum extent possible, because of a belief that the presence of "normal" children will stimulate the child to learn, help erase the stigma of disability, and at the same time educate the normal children about the humanity of their disabled peers. Finally, the IEP discusses what criteria will be used to evaluate whether the child has achieved his or her educational goals. All services provided to a disabled child pursuant to the child's IEP must be free of charge to the child's parents.

Many challenges to the IDEA have involved the "mainstreaming" requirement. The parents of nondisabled children frequently complain that their children's education suffers because of inordinate attention that must be paid by the teacher, frequently already handling an overcrowded class, to the handicapped child. On the other hand, parents of disabled children frequently complain that the state is all too eager to park their youngster in a regular classroom, rather than provide the child with the special—and expensive—resources he or she may actually need to make progress.

Generally, courts have held that schools do not have to provide the "best" or "state of the art" resources and equipment to disabled children in order to comply with the IDEA. It is sufficient if the resources provided are reasonably likely to result in the child deriving educational benefits roughly equal to his or her IEP. Schools are also not required to refit their buildings to be accessible to handicapped children if the cost to the local school district greatly outweighs the possible benefit to the child. Disabled children may be bused outside their neighborhoods to schools that have been modified for their easy access, rather than requiring all schools to restructure their buildings. Courts have also held that children with disabilities may be removed from regular classrooms if their behavior is so disruptive as to impair the education of the other students. The exact boundaries of accommodation and services that must be provided free of charge to disabled students is likely to occupy much judicial concern in the coming century.

INFANCY DOCTRINE A rule developed in the common law that a minor, being considered incompetent and unable to act with wisdom in his or her best interests, is permitted to disaffirm, or back out of, a contract into which he or she has entered. See **contract rights.**

INGRAHAM V. WRIGHT In this 1977 case, the U.S. Supreme Court decided that reasonable corporal punishment of students in school does not violate the Constitution, even when it is administered without the benefit of notice or a hearing. The case was brought by two students in Charles R. Drew Junior High School in Dade County, Florida. James Ingraham and Roosevelt Andrews alleged that for misconduct in school they and other students had been subjected to paddling by teachers that amounted to cruel and unusual punishment barred by the Eighth Amendment to the Constitution.

They also claimed that the paddling violated their rights to **due process of law** because it was inflicted without notice of any charges or a hearing on their truthfulness. The Court responded with the following:

- While children do have a constitutionally protected right to be free from bodily restraint and punishment except in accordance with due process of law, corporal punishment that is not excessive does not violate this right. In order to determine whether corporal punishment is "excessive," it is necessary to view the seriousness of the child's offense, his or her attitude and past behavior, the nature and severity of the punishment, the age and strength of the child, and the availability of less severe corrective means that would be equally effective.

- The Eighth Amendment protection against cruel and unusual punishment does not apply to children in school. That amendment was intended to aid prisoners who are locked away from society, where their treatment may not be properly monitored and abuse may occur. By contrast, schoolchildren attend open institutions where any mistreatment is instantly observed by family and friends, as well as teachers and other pupils. If corporal punishment becomes excessive, the normal laws punishing battery and abuse may be used to redress the offense. The threat of such a lawsuit should be enough to ensure that spanking would not get out of hand.

- No notice or hearings are required for corporal punishment in schools. The administrative costs of providing these procedures would be excessive. Unlike suspension from school, where a child may lose out on important days of education, corporal punishment is meant to provide a quick corrective after which the child is swiftly sent back to class. The interest at stake in avoiding an unfair paddling is not so great as the interest in obtaining an uninterrupted education. Hence, the safeguards of notice and a hearing are not necessary.

The decision in *Ingraham* was very narrowly in favor of corporal punishment without notice or a hearing. Only five justices voted with the majority. The dissenting four justices disagreed that the Eighth Amendment did not apply to punishment in schools. However, they did not go so far as to suggest that corporal punishment could never be used in a school setting.

INHERITANCE RIGHTS The right to become the owner of property following the previous owner's death. When one becomes the owner of property in this fashion, one is said to succeed to ownership. Rights of inheritance do not depend on the age of the person claiming them. In other words, children's rights to inherit are the same as those of adults. However, there may be restrictions on a minor child's right to manage inherited property, until such time as he or she reaches **majority** or an age stipulated in the will. See **property rights.**

The important factor in determining inheritance rights is the relationship—biological or legal—that the one claiming to inherit had with the deceased person, or decedent. Of course, anyone may inherit from someone who left a will directing the disposition of his or her property to that person. A decedent who left a valid will is said to have died testate. Generally, the decedent's property will be distributed in accordance with the will, although, in unusual circumstances, state laws may override the will's provisions. Particularly if the amount of property is small, many states' laws require that the entire estate go to a surviving spouse who requests it or to any minor children regardless of the provisions of the will.

A person who dies without making a valid will is said to have died intestate. All states have laws regulating the disposal of the property of a person who died intestate. These are known as the laws of intestate succession. Because the law does not recognize as valid any will made by a person under the age of eighteen, the property of minors is divided according to the laws of intestate succession, whether or not they attempted to make a will. See also **testamentary rights.**

Generally, the surviving spouse of an intestate decedent will receive one-third to one-half of the property, or estate, left by the decedent. The remainder of the property is divided equally among the decedent's children. If there is no surviving spouse, all the property is divided equally among the surviving children.

If a child of an intestate decedent died before him or her, that child's children will get some share of the decedent's (their grandparent's) estate. In some states, these children of a previously deceased child will inherit their grandparent's property as if they were children of the decedent themselves. For example, if a man died intestate leaving four daughters, and one of those daughters died before him leaving four children of her own, each of those four grandchildren would be entitled to one seventh of the man's estate. Thus, equal portions would be given to the three remaining living daughters and each of the four children of the previously deceased daughter. Laws that give the children of previously deceased children an equal share of an intestate grandparent's estate with living children are said to distribute the property per capita. In other states, the children of a previously deceased child of an intestate decedent would have to split the amount their dead parent would have gotten if he or she were still alive. Thus, in the above example, the estate would have been divided into four equal sections. Three of the portions would go to the three living daughters. The last portion would go to the four children of the previously deceased daughter (the grandchildren of the man who died intestate). These children would then have to divide this quarter portion equally among themselves. Thus, each would receive only one-sixteenth of the entire estate. This type of distribution is known as per *stirpes* (by the stock) distribution. The grandchildren of an intestate decedent do not inherit anything if their parents are still alive.

If there are no children of one who died intestate, the property goes to the parents, then the siblings, and then the grandparents of the decedent. If there are no remaining relatives at all, the property is given to the state. In this case, the property is said to escheat to the state.

Adopted Children

Because family relationships have become more complex as more people divorce and remarry, and as more children are born out of wedlock, inheritance laws are complicated. One of the most complex issues involves the rights of adopted children to inheritance. See **adoption.**

Generally, the policy regarding adopted children is to sever all ties with the child's biological relatives and create new ties with the adoptive family, such that there is no difference between an adopted child and a biological child. To this end, most state laws cut off the rights of an adopted child to inherit from his or her biological parents if they die intestate. (Generally, if biological parents provide for a biological child who has been adopted by another family in their wills, the provisions of that document will prevail.) However, in a few states, children who have been adopted still retain their right to inherit from their biological parents.

Conversely, the law generally allows adopted children to inherit from their adoptive parents who die without leaving a valid will, exactly the same as if they had been biological children. However, it is unclear whether adopted children have rights to inherit property from collateral relatives in their adoptive families (i.e., adoptive siblings, grandparents, aunts, uncles, etc.).

Stepchildren

Inheritance laws involving the rights of stepchildren have not kept up with the growth in the number of stepchildren in the country. Hence, the law is rather uncertain in this area. Of course, a stepchild may inherit from a **stepparent** who left the child a bequest in a valid will. Generally, however, a stepchild has no automatic right to inherit from a stepparent who died without a will. Some states do allow stepchildren to inherit if the stepparent relationship began when the child was a minor and it appeared as though the stepparent intended to adopt the child. In some states, a stepchild will inherit from a stepparent who died intestate if there are no other biological relatives to whom the estate may be given.

Illegitimate Children

Under the traditional common law, an illegitimate child had no inheritance rights through his or her father, even if paternity was established. (An illegitimate child could always inherit from his or her mother, as well as from his or her father if provided for in a will.) As public opinion about illegitimacy has softened, the rights of illegitimate children to inherit have expanded. The Supreme Court has determined that it is unconstitutional for states to flatly deny an illegitimate child the right to inherit from an intestate father. [See *Gomez v. Perez*.] However, the Court would allow states to restrict the rights of illegitimate children to inherit by requiring some proof that the decedent really was his or her biological father and setting a time limit within which an inheritance must be claimed. See also **illegitimacy; paternity action.**

Once paternity has been established, an illegitimate child may inherit from his or her intestate father in exactly the same way as a legitimate child. Moreover, the child can also inherit from all of his or her biological relatives on the father's side exactly as though he or she were legitimate.

Disinheritance

In all states except Louisiana, a parent may disinherit a child, or refuse to allow the child to share in property left after the parent's death. However, because the law favors the disposition of property to one's relatives, especially to minors or those who cannot provide for themselves, one wishing to disinherit his or her children must follow special rules. First, persons who die intestate cannot disinherit anyone who has a natural right to inherit, such as a child. A valid will is necessary to accomplish disinheritance. Second, a mere declaration in a will that the testator, or person making the will, intends to disinherit a certain child may not be sufficient to prevent that child from inheriting. Any declaration of an intent to disinherit a child must usually be in strong and convincing language. Third, the will must actually dispose of *all* of the testator's property. That is, every asset in the estate must be specifically earmarked for someone. If this is not done, the child the testator intended to disinherit may inherit anyway—in an amount equal to the share he or she would have received if the parent died without a will.

Courts are usually very sympathetic to children whose parents have attempted to disinherit them. Therefore, they carefully scrutinize the circumstances surrounding the making of the will to be sure there was no fraud, undue influence, or mental infirmity of the testator.

Oddly, disinheritance of adopted children is easier. Courts have interpreted such language as "to the heirs of the body" and "natural children born of this marriage" in a will to exclude adopted children.

Omitted Heirs

A person making a will may neglect to mention a relative who would normally have a right to inherit something. Often, wills are made years in advance of death and not updated. Hence, they contain no mention of children born or adopted after the will was made. Sometimes a testator simply forgets to mention a person in his or her will. The old common law considered such children to be automatically disinherited. Today, most states have what is known as pretermitted heir statutes, which allow these inadvertently omitted relatives to inherit something from the testator. Under some states' laws only children who were born after the will was made may be considered pretermitted heirs. In other states, only children who were living at the time the will was made are pretermitted heirs. Children who do not fit the definition of "pretermitted heirs" may lose out on an inheritance, unless other evidence is introduced to show that the testator did not intend to disinherit them. Children who are protected by pretermitted heir statutes may expect to receive the share they would have gotten if no will had been written, or to share equally with other children who were not omitted, depending on the state's law.

Advances

In some states, a gift of money or other valuable property from a living parent to a child is considered to be an advance of property that the child would inherit on the parent's death. In these states, the child's inheritance upon the parent's death is decreased by the amount of the gift. The rationale for this rule is that parents generally want all their children to share equally in their wealth. Thus, if one child gets a gift during the parent's lifetime, it is presumed that the parent meant to make up the difference to the other children when the estate is settled. However, some states have abolished this rule and require that any gift intended to be an advance on inheritance be so designated unequivocally at the time the gift is made.

INSTITUTIONAL RIGHTS Children may be committed to various types of institutions against their will: reform schools, training schools, detention facilities, mental hospitals, and other forms of secure confinement. [See **custodial confinement; mental hospital commitment.**] Once inside such an institution, children have specific rights.

First, an institutionalized child has the right to treatment in an attempt to make him or her capable of life outside the institution. Children generally cannot simply be "warehoused" in such facilities with no effort made to prepare them to live in the broader community. (Of course, some medical disabilities will be so severe that treatment options are limited.) This is true for children confined because they have been found guilty of criminal acts as well as for mentally ill children. Juvenile delinquents must be offered "treatment" in the form of rehabilitative services.

Institutionalized children must also have the right to refuse treatment. Courts generally limit this right to refusal of intrusive types of treatment, such as drugs, psychosurgery, or electric shock treatments. In such instances, refusal of treatment must be honored if the child is sufficiently competent to express a desire not to be treated. In cases of extreme behavioral disorders that threaten the child's own safety, intrusive treatments may, in fact, be necessary. In any case, the use of drugs or restraints simply for control or disciplinary purposes are absolutely forbidden. When drugs are given for any purpose in an institution, they must be ordered upon the prescription of a physician, and only a physician or registered nurse may administer them.

Children within institutions have a right to be informed of their rights. They have the right to have contact with an attorney or other counsel. These communications must be kept confidential, although the institution can set reasonable rules on the time, place, and manner that the communications take place.

In general, children in institutions have broader rights to communicate with the outside world than do incarcerated adults. The reason for the expanded rights is the recognition that communication with their families outside the facility is an important therapy for reintegrating the children in the community—the purpose of institutionalization. Thus, children are entitled to mail privileges, telephone privileges, and in-person visits with their family. Unlike communications with their attorneys, these communications need not be confidential. However, one court has ruled that the fact that communications are monitored by institutional staff members must be noted. For the most part, courts frown on restrictive communications policies. Letters, calls, and visits between institutionalized children and their families can therefore be restricted only for very good reasons. Nevertheless, juvenile facilities may restrict the institutionalized child's contact with members of his or her peer group because this association is often what got the child "in trouble" in the first place and could hinder his or her rehabilitation.

A child in an institution has a right not to be subjected to unreasonable searches and must be accorded some privacy. Searches may be conducted when there is reasonable cause to believe that the child has stolen property, weapons, or drugs. Generally, the child must be present for any search of his or her property.

The use of isolation cells and physical restraints on institutionalized children is controversial. Basically, these practices must be used only when the child is so physically violent and out of control as to pose a danger to himself or others. The measures should be used for the shortest time necessary to calm the child.

While vocational opportunities for confined juveniles are desirable, and even mandated in most states, it has been held a violation of the Thirteenth Amendment (prohibiting slavery) to force children in institutions to work. Unless it can be shown to be an important part of the child's rehabilitative therapy, forced work is constitutionally suspect. Children may be required to perform normal chores of living, such as cleaning their rooms. Any other productive work done by juveniles must be compensated.

Children in institutions have a right to appropriate educational and training programs; to adequate and healthy food, housing, and clothing; and to medical and dental care. They also have the right to have their continued stay in the institution periodically reviewed and to be released when appropriate.

INTAKE The first stop for a minor after being taken into custody on suspicion of committing a delinquent act or status offense is "intake." This relatively informal procedure that takes place before any **preliminary hearing** in a juvenile delinquency action is unique to juvenile court. After arrest, the minor suspect is brought to the intake office at juvenile hall. There, an intake officer, in addition to probation officers, social workers, the suspect's parents or guardian, and the suspect himself or herself meet to discuss how the case will be handled. That is, they decide whether the minor should be charged with a delinquent act and undergo the formal adjudication of juvenile court, should be placed on informal probation, or should be ordered to counseling or some other **diversion,** or whether the charges should be dropped entirely.

Because the intake procedure is not judicial in nature (rather it is a way to handle juvenile misbehavior outside of the court system), lawyers usually do not participate in these discussions. Although the minor suspect is present, it is up to him or her to decide whether to speak at the meeting. The suspect always has the right to remain silent.

The intake officer has the authority under state law to handle the minor's case through "informal adjustment" or to send it through the formal procedure of juvenile court. If the intake officer decides the charges merit a formal procedure, he or she may also decide whether to release the minor to parents or guardians or to place him or her in another setting, such as a foster home, residential half-way house, or a secure detention hall pending the formal adjudication process. These decisions are later reviewed by a judge. In fact, if the child is sent to live anywhere but with parents or guardians, the youth is entitled to an immediate hearing before a judge. In most states, this hearing must take place within seventy-two hours. In some, the limit is twenty-four hours. The issues of where the juvenile will live pending trial is usually combined with the **preliminary hearing** determining whether there is probable cause to believe the juvenile is guilty. See also **preventive detention.**

🏛 **INTERROGATION** The nineteenth-century reform movement that resulted in the establishment of a separate juvenile justice system embraced theories of criminology that seem quite odd today. One of these was the idea that confession was an important part of a delinquent youth's rehabilitation. By confessing their wrongs and accepting "correction" from a benign paternal authority, children were supposed to experience a sort of therapeutic catharsis that would put them back on the path of virtue. Until the Supreme Court's 1967 ruling in *In re Gault,* authorities could use virtually any form of threats and coercion short of torture to induce a youngster to confess to delinquent acts—all ostensibly for the child's own good. Children had no constitutional right to remain silent, nor were they required to be warned that what they said could be used against them.

The Supreme Court in *Gault* rejected this view, noting that children, like normal people of any age, are less likely to be cooperative if they feel tricked into a confession that is followed by punishment. Moreover, the Court recognized that children are considerably more vulnerable to the intimidation that is inherent whenever the police question any citizen. Children are also more suggestible than adults, and more prone to fantasy and fatigue, as well as overawed panic, when confronted by authority figures. Thus, having recognized that children do have a constitutional right against incriminating themselves, the Supreme Court cautioned that states must take measures to ensure that statements made by minors to the police are not coerced in any way.

Today, many states require that minors who are subject to custodial interrogation be given the same so-called Miranda warnings prior to questioning that adults receive. "Custodial interrogation" occurs when a person is arrested before questioning, or when a person reasonably believes that he or she is not free to leave the place where the police are asking the questions. For example, a court found that a teenager reasonably believed himself to be in custody when a police officer asked him to sit in a squad car while he was questioned. Therefore, the teenager had the right to be given Miranda warnings. On the other hand, mere "investigative interrogation" does not merit any warnings. A child who answered police questions while sitting in the living room of his parents' house was not in custody, and no warnings were required. Similarly, a twelve-year-old who gave information to the police over the telephone was only subjected to investigative interrogation.

The Miranda warnings, so named after the Supreme Court case in which they were formulated [*Miranda v. Arizona* (1966)], require the police to warn any person who has been taken into custody that he or she (1) may refuse to answer any questions and remain silent, (2) may call a lawyer or be assigned one at public expense if he or she is without sufficient funds to hire one, and (3) may stop answering police questions at any time and wait until a lawyer arrives. Perhaps most importantly, a person in police custody must also be told that anything he or she says may be used against him or her in a court of law.

In addition to these basic warnings, most states have requirements to ensure that confessions obtained from minors while in police custody are truly voluntary. To be voluntary, a statement must be made by a youth who has understood both the right to remain silent when questioned by the police and the possible consequences of not doing so. It is up to the state to prove that a minor's confession was voluntary. This is different for adults; the adult must prove that a confession was not voluntary. In all states, a minor who has been arrested has the right to call his or her parents, a guardian or other trusted adult, or an attorney before answering any questions. However, not all states require that the child be told of this right. Moreover, if the parent or other adult refuses to come at the child's request, questioning may commence without him or her.

If an adult is called, most states require that the Miranda warnings be explained to the adult so that he or she may then explain them to the child. Some states also require that the adult and child then be allowed to confer in private in order for the adult to explain the meaning of the Miranda warnings further and to guide the child in deciding whether to answer questions. States that require this conference time differ as to whether the adult and child must be told of its purpose. Some states merely offer the time, and the adult and child may use it as they wish. In some states, the conference between the adult and the child is not guaranteed to be private. Oddly, courts have allowed the admission into evidence of statements made by children to their parents that were surreptitiously recorded by the police during such conference time.

Some states' laws require that a parent or other "interested adult" be present during police questioning of a minor who has been taken into custody. A parent or other adult who is antagonistic toward the child or who has interests in the matter that conflict with those of the child does not qualify as a person who can help the arrested youth during questioning. Therefore, statements or confessions made by the child after conferring with that adult or with that adult present during questioning may not be admissible at a trial. However, an adult who is genuinely motivated by the child's best interests does not need to give the child the best possible advice when viewed in hindsight or measured by legal standards.

Many states have other rules about how a minor may be questioned by police. Some laws prescribe the place where questioning may occur. In some, questioning of a youth must be done in juvenile hall rather than the police station. Other states specify that the room in which questioning takes place must not be overly intimidating. For example, it must not be dark or filthy, or too hot or cold, or resemble a jail cell. The person asking the questions may not be visibly armed in some states. Many states forbid police officers to use threats, promises, or trickery to induce a child to talk to them.

Even when all the rules about interrogating children have been followed, courts usually consider all the circumstances surrounding a child's confession to be sure that the child voluntarily waived the right to remain silent. Thus, the court considers the child's age, intelligence, maturity, education, experience, and social background when deciding whether to admit the child's statements into evidence in a proceeding in which a child is on trial, or in which the child's statements could lead to his or her arrest and subsequent trial.

A child's right to the presence of an adult at questioning does not extend to hearings that take place after charges against the child are adjudicated. For example, questioning of a child for purposes of making a mental health assessment of him or her after a finding of guilt for delinquent acts could lawfully take place without an adult or attorney present.

JOINT CUSTODY   A situation in which divorced parents share equally in the legal custody of a child. [See **child custody.**] This means that both parents together are responsible for the major decisions in the child's life, including religious training, domicile, education, medical care, and discipline issues. The minor decisions—such as house rules, food and clothing choices, etc.—may also be shared, depending on the living arrangements of the child.

Most states allow for some form of joint custody award when parents divorce. However, the advisability of joint custody is fraught with controversy, and it will not always be ordered, even when both parents desire it. Proponents of joint custody argue that it is the closest thing to an intact family and, therefore, less traumatic on the child. With joint custody, the child's connection with both parents is maintained in an actual and important way. Parents are equally involved in the child's affairs, and the child is freed of loyalty conflicts between the parents.

While this may be true in theory, opponents of joint custody point out that the type of cooperation necessary to make joint custody a success for the child is rare among divorcing couples. The constant communication between parents that is required is frequently beyond the capability of bitter, antagonistic divorcees. In fact, most courts will grant joint custody only if they are satisfied that the parents are mature, cooperative, and willing to work together for the benefit of the child.

Joint custody orders need not require that each parent have equal time housing the child. Often, one parent takes the majority of time having physical custody of the child. However, legal custody, with its right to be involved in the major decisions in bringing up the child will still reside in both parents. Sometimes, of course, both parents wish equal physical custody of the child. Creative orders, such as rotating the child from one parent to the other weekly, monthly, or even yearly have been entered in joint custody determinations. But opponents are skeptical as to whether the constant moving from parent to parent is healthy for the child. They point out that children need consistency, including a place to call home, to entertain friends, etc. The problem is exacerbated when the child is required to change schools. For this reason, joint custody may not be awarded unless the parents live close enough together that the child can continue to attend the same school.

Despite the problems with joint custody, some states' laws give preference to it, requiring judges to justify a denial of joint custody. Some prefer joint custody to such an extent that it must be granted if even one parent desires it, although most states require that both parents agree to it. Most states that allow joint custody leave it up to the discretion of the court to grant it only if the court finds that it is in the child's best interest. Where joint custody is awarded, the **support obligation** for the child will frequently be less in the form of monetary payment, because each parent is contributing more in kind (housing, food, clothing, etc.) to the upkeep of the child.

JURY TRIAL There is no constitutional right to a trial by jury for minors who are on trial in juvenile court. [*McKeiver v. Pennsylvania* (1971)] However, as of 1993, seven states offered juvenile defendants the right to be tried by a jury in juvenile court. Several other states give juvenile judges the discretion to grant a jury trial for a juvenile defendant if the judge feels it is necessary.

The right to a trial by jury has been overlooked in juvenile court because of the original purpose of that institution to rehabilitate, rather than punish, youthful offenders. Consistent with that goal, juvenile court was supposed to provide a nonadversarial setting in which the child's guilt or innocence of the conduct charged was not nearly so important as determining what was "wrong" with the child and what could be done to correct it. A benevolent judge was to determine how to gently guide the troubled youth to reform without the pesky interference of formal due process requirements. [See **due process of law.**] Juvenile courts were able to operate for years on the fiction that they did not deal with "crimes" or "criminal" proceedings at all, but only with "delinquent" behavior adjudicated in "civil" courts.

Nearly a century after the first juvenile courts were established, this idealized vision is all but shattered. Today, serious violent crime committed by young people under the age of majority is steeply on the rise. The public is disillusioned with the notion of rehabilitation, and in more and more states, punishment of the guilty appears to be the real purpose behind the juvenile justice system. In response to a public outcry for tougher sentencing, the penalties awaiting youth who commit delinquent acts are becoming more harsh, including the possibility of incarceration for prolonged periods.

Because the focus of the juvenile justice system has changed, many critics argue that it is time to recognize an inviolable right to a trial by jury for youthful offenders. They point to the ways in which a jury trial promotes fairness in adjudicating guilt or innocence in contrast to trials before judges alone. Many biases may affect the juvenile court judge, even when he or she tries scrupulously to avoid them. For example, the judge may have seen evidence against the youth in a preliminary hearing that would be inadmissible at the adjudication. The judge may know about the youth's prior record, or even have adjudicated the youth in the past. The fact that certain prosecutors are handling the youth's case may signal the judge that the youth is considered a "habitual" offender. The judge may know that the child was kept in pretrial detention—an indication that someone thought he or she was too dangerous or likely to flee to send home. Ultimately, all of these possibilities may contribute to the judge having a more "relaxed" view of what constitutes the "shadow of a doubt," beyond which the youth's guilt must be proved before punishment may be imposed. These concerns were the same ones that prompted the U.S. Supreme Court to acknowledge the right of adults to a trial by jury. [*Duncan v. Louisiana* (1968)]

By contrast, a jury will know nothing of the youth's prior history, whether he or she is considered a habitual offender or was held in pretrial detention. The jury will not have seen incriminating, but inadmissible, evidence that it will have to try to forget. The jury is less subject to political pressure to be "tough" on crime and convict at all costs. Finally, juries are traditionally more likely to give the defendant the benefit of a doubt when one exists.

The opponents of jury trials for juveniles often cite the huge administrative headaches and expense that they would entail as a reason to keep them out of juvenile court. However, these concerns can be addressed by providing jury trials to youth only when the possible punishments they face for conviction are severe. In addition, juries of six members are already utilized in some states, garnering a considerable savings and yet providing the same checks on judicial bias as twelve-member juries. Even if some additional expense and time is unavoidable when extending the right to a trial by jury to juveniles, many believe that fundamental rights to fairness should not be abridged merely because the cost of providing them is high.

JUVENILE COURT A court with the power to hear cases involving children and young adults. The first juvenile court was created in Illinois in 1899 in response to social reformers' theories that wayward youths should not be judged or punished like adults. Today, all states have some sort of juvenile court system, called "family courts" in some states. These courts may be permanent institutions with their own specialized personnel, or they may consist of facilities and personnel drawn from other courts on a regular, intermittent basis to hear juvenile matters. They differ from ordinary courts in following special procedures that are intended to offer minors protections not given to adults charged with crimes. However, since the mid-1960s and the Supreme Court's decision in *In re Gault*, a debate has raged over whether juvenile courts really offer young offenders the benign rehabilitative opportunities that were envisioned by the social reformers of the nineteenth century.

Juvenile courts typically have jurisdiction over both dependency and delinquency cases. Dependency cases involve allegations of parental abuse and neglect, and terminations of parental rights. Delinquency cases involve trying minors for conduct that would be considered a criminal offense if the perpetrator were an adult. [See **delinquency proceeding.**] **Status offense** cases are also heard by juvenile courts. Technically, these are neither dependency nor delinquency cases, but a special category of their own. Early juvenile court proponents believed it was important to intervene early in the lives of youngsters who were exhibiting antisocial, immoral, or shiftless behavior before it blossomed into a "life of crime." Thus, juvenile courts were empowered to adjudicate children who habitually disobeyed their parents or were truant from school, among other offenses. The goal of the juvenile justice system was at all times the rehabilitation, rather than punishment, of young offenders.

A juvenile court is presided over by a judge, or, depending on the type of case involved, a hearing officer, master, or commissioner whose actions are subject to review by the judge. In most states, the officers of a juvenile court must be licensed attorneys. In a few states, judicial officers must be attorneys only in cases in which a minor is on trial for an offense that could result in deprivation of liberty.

Because most issues involving children are local, most juvenile courts are state courts. However, under the federal Juvenile Delinquency Act, any federal district court may convene as a juvenile court to hear cases in which minors are involved in federal offenses.

JUVENILE DELINQUENT　A person under the age of **majority** who has been convicted in **juvenile court** of conduct that would be classified as a crime if the perpetrator were an adult. The common use of the word *delinquent* to indicate any minor who engages in rowdy, obnoxious, or unbecoming behavior is technically incorrect. Likewise, the word *delinquent* technically does not apply to minors who have committed **status offense**s. On the other hand, a minor who has been tried in an adult court for a criminal offense is also not a juvenile delinquent, but a criminal.

JUVENILE JURISDICTION　The statutorily determined authority of **juvenile court**s to adjudicate young people charged with offenses that would be classified as crimes if the perpetrator were an adult. Oddly, the age under which a young person is subject to juvenile jurisdiction does not always correspond to the age of **majority.** In most states, seventeen is the age over which a young offender will normally be tried as an adult in a criminal court. In some states, as well as the federal court system, the age of eighteen is the cutoff for juvenile proceedings. A few states have established nineteen as the crucial divide between youthful misbehavior and adult criminal responsibility.

In many states, children younger than the statutory cutoff age may be tried as adults if their offense was particularly serious or violent. The decision whether to seek trial in an adult court is almost always up to the discretion of the district attorney. In making this decision, the district attorney considers the minor's age, social background, prior offenses, past progress in correcting errant behavior, and intellectual and emotional maturity, as well as the availability of alternative programs to address the minor's problems and the nature of the offense charged. Usually, children younger than the age of fourteen are not tried as adults, regardless of their offense. There have been exceptions, however. With the growing fear of adolescent crime that characterizes American society at the end of the twentieth century, there are more frequent calls for youngsters to face adult penalties for violent crimes. Generally, it has been held that there is no constitutional right to be tried in a juvenile court, regardless of age. Many states also do not make a distinction between minors and adults for traffic offenses, apparently reasoning that a person who is old enough to operate a dangerous piece of machinery, such as a motor vehicle, should be held to adult standards of conduct.

A young person who is no longer a "juvenile" in the eyes of the criminal law may still be tried in a juvenile court in most states if the offense was committed when the perpetrator was under the statutory cutoff age. Moreover, once a juvenile court has taken jurisdiction of a case, it may retain its authority over the case throughout each step of adjudication, or until the young person charged reaches the age of twenty-one. This "continuing jurisdiction" is usually for the purpose of monitoring probation, supervising incarceration in a correctional or mental institution, or hearing an appeal of the original adjudication.

JUVENILE JUSTICE AND DELINQUENCY PREVENTION ACT This federal law defines the basic rights to **due** process of **law** that must be accorded to juveniles who are tried in federal courts. It also imposes the same requirements on state courts in any state that desires to receive federal funding for programs designed to rehabilitate delinquents.

Essentially, the act makes the decisions in important Supreme Court cases such as *In re Gault* part of the written law. Thus, juveniles are entitled by the act to notice of the charges against them, representation by an attorney, the privilege against self-incrimination, the right to confront and examine witnesses, the right to be proved guilty beyond a reasonable doubt, and the right to a formal hearing before their cases may be transferred to adult court. There are other procedural requirements as well, including very specific rules for magistrates, arresting officers, and attorneys to ensure that the accused juvenile understands all the rights to which he or she is entitled.

One important safeguard in the act is for juveniles who admit their guilt. Before an admission will be accepted by the court, the prosecutor must still present to the judge the evidence that the state believes will prove the child's guilt. Then, the accused youth must agree that the government's proof of guilt is correct and that he or she agrees with the prosecutor's version of events and voluntarily admits the misconduct. Throughout the proceeding, the judge must be convinced that the accused juvenile understands the consequences of admitting guilt and is mentally competent to do so.

Another important provision of the act absolutely forbids the housing of juveniles, before or after adjudication, with adult criminals. Also, institutionalized juveniles are entitled to receive recreational, counseling, education, and training services, in addition to adequate food, clothing, and sanitary facilities.

The confidentiality of juvenile delinquency proceedings is a high priority of the federal law. Charges are brought under special provisions designed to avoid publicity. In addition, the act forbids the fingerprinting or photographing of accused juveniles, unless pursuant to a court order, and forbids giving the names or photographs of arrested juveniles to the media.

KENT V. UNITED STATES

KENT V. UNITED STATES This 1966 decision by the U.S. Supreme Court in 1966 virtually started the system of American juvenile justice on its long road to recognition of the constitutional rights of minors. Morris Kent Jr., sixteen years old and already with a lengthy police record, was arrested for housebreaking, robbery, and rape in September 1961. At police headquarters, Kent was interrogated for hours on end over the course of two days. During this time, he admitted involvement in the crimes. Only on the second day of Kent's detention was his mother able to secure an attorney for him. At an informal meeting with state authorities, Kent's mother and attorney were told that the juvenile court intended to give up jurisdiction over the case and try Kent in adult court, where he would be subject to adult penalties. Kent's attorney promptly opposed any such transfer, moving instead for a hearing in juvenile court at which the attorney offered to prove that Kent suffered from mental illness but could be rehabilitated if treated within juvenile court programs. The attorney also requested Kent's social service file that had been compiled by the state as a result of Kent's earlier brushes with the law, contending that this file would provide added evidence of Kent's mental illness, which was a mitigating factor in the crime.

Kent was kept in detention for nearly a week while his attorney labored in his behalf. Then, without any arraignment [see **preliminary hearing**] or hearing of any sort, the juvenile court judge ordered Kent's case transferred to adult court. The judge's ruling stated only that, after "full investigation," he decided to transfer the case. The judge had never conferred with Kent, with his parents, or with his attorney. In his ruling, the judge gave no reason for his decision and made no mention of the many motions filed by Kent's attorney. Kent was tried in adult court and convicted on several counts. His appeal reached the Supreme Court in 1966.

In a five to four decision to overturn the conviction, the Court for the first time acknowledged the shortcomings in the juvenile court system. Not entitled to the procedural protections given to adults, the child accused of criminal acts is supposed to receive benevolent guidance and rehabilitation in an informal "paternal" atmosphere in juvenile court. But the Court noted: "There is evidence, in fact, that there may be grounds for concern that the child receives the worst of both worlds: that he gets neither the protections accorded to adults nor the solicitous care and regenerative treatment postulated for children." [at 556] Moreover, while the state is supposed to function as a "parent" with juveniles accused of crimes, this is "not an invitation to procedural arbitrariness."

The high Court then noted that the decision to transfer a case from juvenile court to adult court is "critically important" to the accused juvenile. In Kent's case, it meant the difference between the maximum sentence of five years' confinement that could be doled out in juvenile court and a death sentence, which was theoretically available to punish Kent's crimes in adult court. At the very least, a juvenile in this situation deserves a hearing before the juvenile court may transfer his or her case to an adult court. In rendering a decision on transfer, the juvenile judge must provide some reasons beyond a mere statement that a "full investigation" has been conducted. And the child's attorney must be afforded an opportunity to see any social records compiled on the child that the juvenile court has used in making its decision. In stern tones, the Court reproved the juvenile judge: "The right to representation by counsel is not a formality. It is not a grudging gesture to a ritualistic requirement. It is the essence of justice. Appointment of counsel without affording an opportunity for a hearing on a 'critically important' decision is tantamount to denial of counsel."

At the same time, however, the Court clarified that the hearing to be held need not conform with all of the requirements of a trial in adult court. Rather, it need only measure up to the "essentials of due process and fair treatment." The boundaries of such "fair treatment" in cases involving juveniles were left to the pondering of judges in later cases. See also **trial as adult.**

KIDDIE TAX A term referring to the rule that children under the age of fourteen must pay income taxes on their unearned income (that is, income from investments rather than wages) at the same marginal rates that apply to their parents. The rule was designed to prevent affluent parents from making investments in their children's names in order that income from the investments could be taxed in a lower tax bracket, for which their children would normally qualify. See also **income tax.**

LAU V. NICHOLS The U.S. Supreme Court ruled in this 1974 case that a state's failure to provide public school programs to aid children who speak little or no English is a violation of the **Civil Rights Act of 1964.** Specifically, the Court held that failure either to provide English training to these students or to teach them in their native languages amounted to discrimination on the basis of national origin, forbidden under the act. The Court did not reach the issue of whether the constitutional right to **equal protection** of the laws is also violated when such instruction is lacking.

The case arose through a class action brought by children of Chinese ancestry living in the San Francisco, California, school system to have their deficiency in English remedied. A federal court of appeals rejected their claim of unfair treatment, noting that "[e]very student brings to the starting line of his educational career different advantages and disadvantages caused in part by social, economic and cultural background, created and continued completely apart from any contribution by the school system." The Supreme Court did not agree that inability to speak the English language was such a minor "disadvantage" that it could effectively be ignored as an innate but harmless anomaly in a student's school career. Said the Court:

> Basic English skills are at the very core of what these public schools teach. Imposition of a requirement that, before a child can effectively participate in the educational program, he must already have acquired those basic skills is to make a mockery of public education. We know that those who do not understand English are certain to find their classroom experiences wholly incomprehensible and in no way meaningful. [at 566]

The Court then pointed to federal regulations, designed to implement the Civil Rights Act, that require public schools to eliminate discrimination, in particular those arising as a result of English language deficiencies, with "affirmative steps." The school system here contractually agreed to "comply with Title VI of the Civil Rights Act of 1964 . . . and all requirements imposed by or pursuant to the Regulation." Because it failed to do so, the Court ordered relief for the plaintiffs. The ruling in *Lau* led directly to federal regulations mandating bilingual education or English language training in all public schools when foreign-born students are present. The practice has been controversial. See also **bilingual education.**

MAJORITY

The term *majority* refers to the age at which a child becomes independent of his or her parents, or it refers to the state of being independent of one's parents by virtue of having attained a certain age. In most states, the age of majority is eighteen, although some have set nineteen and even twenty-one as the age of independence. At the age of majority, parental authority over the child terminates. At the same time, parental duties of support come to an end. Generally, at the age of majority, a person is permitted to enter into binding contracts of all sorts, and to be a party to a lawsuit in one's own name. See **contract rights; guardian ad litem; property rights.**

Although majority commonly is said to be the age at which the law recognizes a person as an adult, there are many rights and privileges that a person may claim even before reaching the age of majority, such as the privilege of driving an automobile, the right to work for wages, or the right to vote in states with ages of majority set over eighteen. Children may be tried as adults for certain crimes before the age of majority as well. Although children may take advantage of these rights before reaching majority, they are still under the authority of their parents or legal guardian, so that the opportunity to exercise these rights might be limited. For example, a parent may forbid a child to drive or to work outside the home, even though the law would allow it.

Some rights may be claimed before the age of majority even without parental consent. In some states, for example, it is permissible to marry without the consent of one's parents before the age of majority. [See **marriage rights.**] Laws in many states allow a minor to consent to his or her own medical treatment without the consent, or even the knowledge, of the child's parents. This includes treatment for drug and alcohol abuse, treatment for venereal disease, and abortions in some states. A minor may also refuse medical treatment in some states. See **medical treatment.**

On the other hand, states may restrict some rights to those who have attained an age higher than the age of majority. For example, in most states, the age at which a person may buy alcohol is twenty-one. Other rights that may only be activated beyond the age of majority are the rights to sit on a jury and to be elected to public office.

In special circumstances, parental authority over a person may extend beyond the age of majority. For example, a handicapped person may be entitled to the continued support of parents if he or she is unable to exercise the rights and duties of adulthood. Also, the terms of a divorce decree may stipulate that one or both parents are obliged to support a child through college, or to pay tuition for some higher education. See also **emancipation.**

MARRIAGE RIGHTS   In most states, a minor may marry without parental consent at the age of eighteen. Some states have set the age at nineteen, and Mississippi requires the parents of a young person under the age of twenty-one to be notified of their child's pending marriage even if the child is old enough (seventeen for males; fifteen for females) to marry without the parent's consent. The minimum age for marriage with parental consent is sixteen in most states, although a few allow for marriage at fourteen. In some states, a pregnant teen over sixteen can marry without her parents' consent. The consent of a judge will usually substitute for parental consent. The marriage of a young person under the age of **majority** automatically results in the minor's **emancipation.**

The ages stated above are for official or ceremonial marriages. Some states recognize what is known as common law marriage. A common law marriage arises when a man and woman live together and act in every way as if they were married. After a certain time has passed, the law will treat them as if they were officially spouses. In some states that recognize common law marriages, young people below the age of eighteen may enter a recognized common law marriage without their parents' consent.

In states that do not recognize common law marriages, a marriage between minors who have not attained the statutory age is either void or voidable. The law will treat a void marriage as if it never occurred. The participants will have neither the benefits nor the obligations of a real marriage. By contrast, a voidable marriage will be viewed as valid by the law, unless or until one of the parties opts to end it. In that case, the marriage will be annulled. A void or voidable marriage automatically becomes valid if the couple remains together until each spouse has reached the age of consent.

Laws restricting marriages by minors have survived constitutional challenges in the past. Courts generally hold that marriage by young people is not a fundamental right that cannot be abridged without a compelling state interest. Instead, the state may intervene under the **parens patriae doctrine** to ensure that unstable marriages resulting from immaturity will not occur among those least able to act with wisdom in their own interests in marital matters.

Because states differ in age requirements for marriage, confusion exists regarding how to treat marriages performed outside their borders. The general rule is that a marriage must be recognized as valid if it was valid in the state in which it was performed. Therefore, if young people who are underage in their own state get married in a state with a lower marriageable age, their home state should be bound to recognize their marriage. In fact, this is the case in most instances. However, a few states refuse to honor marriages between young people performed in other states that would be invalid within the home state's borders. Conversely, most states will consider valid a marriage that would have been proper within the home state's borders, but that was invalid in the state in which it was actually performed.

MATERNAL PREFERENCE RULE A legal doctrine under which mothers are preferred over fathers for taking custody of children following a divorce. The doctrine first appeared in the mid-nineteenth century, as judges attempted to soften the harsh common law rule that children were virtually the property of their fathers. At the time, the doctrine was useful to justify taking children away from abusive fathers. Gradually, states began to pass statutes enshrining the doctrine as a rule of law. By 1900, fourteen states had passed such statutes. Some of these statutes specifically provided that mothers were to get custody of the children in a divorce.

Today, the pendulum has swung back toward a neutral position. At least officially, there is no maternal preference rule in custody cases in the United States. Many states have specifically abolished any use of the maternal preference rule. In most states, a custody ruling based on the gender of the parent is considered illegal sex discrimination. Theoretically, therefore, fathers enjoy equal rights with mothers in all states to receive custody of their children following a divorce.

However, the reality in custody decisions still shows a marked preference for mothers. In states that require the best interests of the child to rule custody decisions, the practice seems to show a broad prejudice that mothers are more suited to caring for children than men, especially when the children are small. This result may be explained by the fact that following a preconception of this sort is administratively simple. Courts in divorce cases obviate the need to hear lengthy presentations of evidence as to which parent is the better caregiver of the children. [See also **tender years doctrine**.] The result is that, although fathers should have an equal chance to win custody of their children, frequently they do not. Rather, they face a difficult burden of proving their qualifications to raise children in the face of the prejudice that mothers are better. However, as the twentieth century draws to a close, there is evidence that more fathers are winning custody of their children—proof, perhaps, that old prejudices can be eradicated.

MEDICAL TREATMENT Parents generally have the right to direct the type of medical care their children will receive. Under the traditional common law, a parent's or guardian's consent is necessary before any medical treatment can be given to a child. This rule reflects not just a deference to parental wishes in determining all aspects of their children's lives but also the principle of contract law that holds that children are incapable of making binding agreements [see **contract rights**]. The relationship between a doctor and patient is considered to be a contractual one, which children are incompetent to enter. If the parents of a child needing medical treatment are divorced, the consent of the custodial parent is usually required. Moreover, the custodial parent's preferences prevail if the parents cannot agree on the proposed medical treatment of their child. However, even though only the custodial parent's consent is necessary, both parents are usually equally liable to pay the child's medical bills.

A few exceptions to the traditional rule that parental consent is required for medical treatment of a child have long been recognized. In a medical emergency, a doctor may dispense with the requirement of obtaining a parent's consent to crucial treatment. Generally, the treatment must be necessary to save the child from imminent death or disabling injuries. A few courts have held that emergency medical care may be given without parental consent in order to relieve a child's pain and suffering resulting from an accident, even though serious injury or death is not threatened. A doctor may also treat a child who is not in immediate peril if the parents have unreasonably refused to consent to treatment that is necessary to save the child from eventual death or permanent injury. In such a situation, a court order is usually necessary attesting to the need for the treatment in spite of the parents' opposition. Finally, a doctor may treat an emancipated minor for any condition without the consent of his or her parents.

Except in the case of emancipated minors, parents must be informed of the medical treatment given to their children as soon as possible, and consent must be obtained for its continuation.

As the twentieth century draws to a close, children are all too frequently forced into adult situations with medical consequences that they may be reluctant to admit to their parents. A recognition of this fact has led to special statutes in most states that abrogate the common law rule in some situations. For example, many states now allow mature teenagers to consent to their own treatment for sexually transmitted diseases, AIDS, pregnancy, drug and alcohol abuse, and mental illness. Contraceptives and family planning services are also available to teenagers in some states without parental consent, in some cases free of charge based on the minor's own low-income status. In some states, a minor may also have an abortion without the consent of her parents. [See **abortion rights.**] In some states, minors living away from their parents at college may be allowed to consent to other types of nonemergency treatment if it would be burdensome to obtain the parents' consent.

The states that have such laws usually justify them on the grounds that children may be afraid to seek desperately needed medical treatment if their parents must be involved in the situation. Moreover, many teenagers covertly engage in sexual activity against their parents' wishes and regardless of any legal strictures, so the medical community should at least make available to them the means of protecting themselves from pregnancy and venereal diseases. In addition, doctors usually welcome such laws as a way to protect themselves from liability for unauthorized treatment. Under the traditional common law, any treatment or even "touching" by a doctor to whom consent has not been given may be considered a battery that could subject the doctor to a lawsuit and large damage awards. Laws that allow mature teenagers to consent to certain medical procedures take the uncertainty out of a doctor's decision whether to accept a young person as a patient. Even so, some states' laws authorize treatment on the consent of "mature" minors only. Others require that the minor have sufficient intelligence to understand the consequences and risks of treatment versus no treatment. Thus, a doctor may still have to make a judgment about the relative maturity of a young person seeking treatment. The doctor may still be liable for unauthorized treatment if he or she decides the minor is "mature" enough to consent, but a court of law decides otherwise.

Generally, statutes that allow teenagers to consent to their own medical treatment for certain conditions state that the child is emancipated for the limited purpose of consenting to medical treatment. This does not mean that the minor is emancipated for other purposes. Thus, parents are still generally responsible to pay for their teenagers' medical treatment, even if they did not consent to it. In cases in which the minor is insured under a policy carried by the minor's parents, the doctor can usually collect directly from the insurance company, even if the parents objected to the treatment. However, if the treatment is "necessary" for the child's health or well-being, the child himself or herself may be required to pay for it, if the parents refuse. [See **necessaries.**] Some states require that parents continue to pay for their children's medical care to age twenty-one, even though the age of majority is eighteen. Usually, however, parents are not obliged to pay for the medical treatment of their adult children, unless the treatment is for a disability or illness the child acquired prior to becoming an adult, which prevents the child from earning a living.

Although state statutes now make it possible for minors to consent to their own medical treatment in some situations, an unresolved issue is whether minors have the same right to confidentiality of their medical histories as do adults. Normally, any communication between a doctor and patient, or medical records generated by the doctor during the course of treatment, are confidential and cannot be disclosed without the patient's consent. Some states' laws address the confidentiality issue as it relates to minors. Some of these states require that a physician who treats a minor inform the minor's parents of the treatment sought and given. Other states leave the decision whether to inform the parents up to the discretion of the individual doctor. Most states stipulate that the physician/patient privilege of confidentiality does extend to minors who seek treatment without their parents' consent.

Even in states in which treatment rendered to minors is to be kept confidential, parental notification may be necessary if the minor is not emancipated and payment is to be made by the parents, or by the parents' insurance company.

Most states' laws address the issue of whether a minor may consent to treatment over the wishes of his or her parents. A few states' laws also address whether a minor may refuse medical treatment against his or her parents' wishes. In Louisiana, anyone over the age of eighteen can refuse medical treatment. In other states, minors have a limited right to refuse medical treatment over the objections of their parents. First, the minor must have the requisite degree of maturity to understand the consequences of refusing treatment. If so, treatment may be withdrawn or not commenced. However, this right to refuse is not absolute. A court will determine whether the state's interest in preserving life, preventing suicides, and upholding the ethical values of the medical profession outweighs the minor's right to refuse useful medical treatment.

MENTAL HOSPITAL COMMITMENT As in many areas of the law, the legal procedures required to commit a minor to a mental hospital are not so strictly prescribed as for adults. Although a child's unwilling commitment to a mental hospital results in the same extreme deprivation of liberty and stigma of being labeled mentally ill, the U.S. Constitution does not afford minors a full-fledged civil commitment hearing in a court of law. In *Parham v. J. R.*, the Supreme Court ruled that, so long as a neutral fact finder decides that commitment is in the child's best interest, the voluntary request of a minor's parents that he or she be committed is sufficient. No actual "hearing" need take place, provided the neutral fact finder has reviewed the facts relevant to the child's case.

The neutral fact finder chosen to review a child's condition prior to placement in a medical hospital does not require any particular training. He or she does not have to be a physician or a lawyer, or have any formal training in either field. However, the fact finder must have sufficient medical expertise to determine whether the child's condition meets the medical standards for admission to a mental hospital. The fact finder must review the child's case using all available resources, including school and medical records and interviews with the child's parents. The child must also be interviewed. Once committed, the child must be afforded a periodic independent review of the continuing need to keep him or her institutionalized.

Although the federal Constitution does not require hearings for minors whose parents request their commitment to mental hospitals, most states have laws providing a much greater degree of due process protection for children threatened with institutionalization. Most states do require a formal hearing, with the opportunity for the child to oppose the commitment, including the presentation and cross-examination of witnesses. Some states even require that a **guardian ad litem** or a separate attorney be appointed to represent the interests of any child whose parents request his or her commitment. Separate representation is necessary in the view of many experts because the motives of parents who request commitment for their children are not always purely concerned with the child's well-being. Other states reject mandatory separate representation for the child on the grounds that it creates dissension within families and could discourage parents from seeking needed hospitalization for troubled minors out of fear of lengthy and costly legal proceedings.

In most states, parents who request that their children be committed to mental institutions must pay for the costs of keeping their children there, as well as for any psychiatric treatments offered within the institution. In other states, the child's parents pay only what they can afford.

Juveniles who have been adjudicated delinquent in juvenile court may be ordered to a mental institution upon evidence that they are mentally ill and may pose a threat of harm to themselves or others.

MEYER V. NEBRASKA   One of the earliest Supreme Court cases dealing with traditionally family issues, *Meyer v. Nebraska* (1923) involved a teacher convicted under a state statute forbidding the teaching of any foreign language in public or private schools. The teacher contended that the law was unconstitutional, because it deprived him of the "liberty" of earning a living in his chosen trade. The Court agreed, and went further—holding that the law also infringed on the rights of parents to determine the type of education their children would have.

Although *Meyer* does not seem at first blush to be about children's rights at all, it was an important precedent for later cases involving children more directly. First, *Meyer* carefully set the groundwork for justifying state involvement in traditional family issues by stating, almost in passing, that no one questioned the state's power to do so: "The power of the state to compel attendance at some school and to make reasonable regulations for all schools . . . is not questioned." [at 402] Judicial statements, such as this, that do not touch the heart of the controversy in the case (here whether a law forbidding foreign language teaching infringed on the rights of teachers) are known as dicta. Although dicta is not authoritative guidance for judges in later cases, it is helpful in establishing a principle of law merely because it has already been stated, thus paving the way for public acceptance. Indeed, this passage from the *Meyer* case was to be relied on again and again in later cases justifying state educational requirements.

Second, *Meyer* was important because it came down squarely on the side of the rights of parents as opposed to the state in determining a proper education for the nation's youth. This represented the first balancing of state interests in maintaining the public welfare and the family's interests in determining their own destinies. In later cases, the Court would strike the balance elsewhere, sometimes favoring the state, and sometimes the individual parents or children. It has become a familiar mode of deciding issues involving children.

MISSING CHILDREN ACT Passed in 1982, this law places the resources of the Federal Bureau of Investigation's National Crime Information Center at the service of parents whose children have disappeared. The center's powerful computer is tapped to aid in the location of children who may have been taken across state lines. Parents who suspect their children have been kidnapped, by a noncustodial parent or anyone else, may initiate search procedures under the act by requesting that their local police department enter the data from the missing person report into the center's computer system. Confirmation that the data has been entered and is accessible to law enforcement agencies in other states should be forthcoming within a reasonable period.

Ⅲ NATIONAL SCHOOL LUNCH PROGRAM (NSLP)

The National School Lunch Program is the largest and oldest federal program concerned with the nutrition of the nation's children. Passed initially in 1946, and expanded frequently in the succeeding fifty years, the program ensures that children from low-income families receive a free or reduced price meal during the school day. The NSLP is administered jointly by the federal government and the government of states that choose to participate. States must match at least 30 percent of the federal subsidies for the program with their own funds in order to take part. The benefit of NSLP programs over the years is borne out by studies showing a direct relationship between good nutrition and children's capacity to learn.

In participating states, parents of eligible children fill out applications that specify the family's income. If the family income is less than 130 percent of the federal poverty level income for a family of the same size, the children in the applicant's family are entitled to a free lunch. If the family's income is more than 130 percent but less than 185 percent of the poverty level index for a similarly sized family, the children may receive lunches for a reduced price.

In order to minimize the stigma inevitably directed at poor children entitled to free lunches by their more affluent peers, the NSLP requires that the identities of the subsidized children be kept secret. Schools must issue the same cards or coupons for lunches to paying and nonpaying students.

In addition to school lunches, the NSLP operates similar services to bring children meals during the summer months when school is not in session. Another branch of the program provides breakfasts to poor children. The services of the NSLP also reach child care institutions of other types, such as recreational centers, day care centers, and Head Start operations.

In 1989, schools that offered "afterschool care" for children whose parents work beyond the hours that school is in session were entitled to receive additional meal supplements for the children in their care.

NECESSARIES   Goods or services that are indispensable, appropriate, or useful to a child's established way of life, and for which the child will be obligated to pay if he or she contracts to buy them. Contracts for the purchase of necessaries represent an exception to the rule that minors may back out of contracts at their option. [See **contract rights; infancy doctrine.**] The roots of the rule go back to the fifteenth century in England, and today the exception survives in the common law of all fifty American states.

Interestingly, the definition of a "necessary" is not firmly established, but is quite flexible. The definition will vary depending on the child's particular situation and station in life. Although food, clothing, shelter, medical care, and a proper education are frequently considered to be necessaries, they are not always so. Generally, if these items are being provided, or offered, to a child by the child's parents, they are not necessaries. The child is, therefore, not obligated to pay for them if the child contracts to buy them himself or herself. For example, a minor's agreement to lease an apartment is not a contract for a necessary if the minor's parents are willing to let him or her live at home. However, if the child's parents are not providing these items, they are necessaries and the child must pay for them. Items that are furnished to a child on another's credit are not necessaries. For example, if a parent agrees to pay for items, they are not necessaries, even though they are for use by the child.

Conversely, items usually considered to be luxuries may be necessaries under some conditions. For example, an automobile is usually considered a luxury for a minor, and a contract to purchase one is voidable at the minor's option. However, if the car is needed for the child's transportation to and from a job or school, it may be considered a necessary, especially if there is no reasonable alternative transportation. A college education, likewise, is usually a luxury. Nevertheless, at least one court has found that a minor's college tuition was a necessary because the child came from a family in which a college education was expected, if not taken for granted.

A more problematic case might be presented by a computer used simultaneously for homework and for video games. If preparing school work on a computer is expected and indispensable for learning to be a productive citizen in the modern world, the computer might well be considered a necessary. Likewise, a fancy prom dress or gown for a debutante ball is usually a luxury. However, if attending the prom is an absolute rite of passage in the minor's milieu, the dress may be considered a necessary for which the child is obligated to pay.

Courts are undecided about whether goods and services purchased by a minor in order to conduct a business are necessaries, even if they are indispensable to the operation of the business. Generally, if the minor must engage in the business to earn a living, the items will be considered necessaries. If the child has other means of support, these items, though necessary for the business, are luxuries.

Assuming that an item is determined to be a necessary, what are the consequences for the child? First, the minor cannot back out of the contract to buy the item. He or she must pay for it. However, most courts will give children a break even here and require only that the child pay the reasonable value of the goods, and not the actual purchase price. This is yet another protection to ensure that children are not taken advantage of when they naively agree to inflated prices. Of course, a child may not have the money to pay for the item, even if it is a necessary. In that situation, some states' laws require the child's parents to pay for the item. This is especially true in the case of goods or services that are truly indispensable to life, such as emergency medical care.

NEGLECT A form of **child abuse** that is characterized by a parental failure to provide a child basic necessities although the parent is able to do so. Necessities include not only adequate nutrition, clothing, and shelter, but education and health care as well. In addition, a failure to exercise proper supervision and control over a child may be considered neglect.

A parent need not intend to harm his or her children in order for a child protection agency to intervene on the grounds of neglect. Neglect frequently occurs as a result of a simple lack of caring about the welfare of the child without any particular animus or hostile feelings. Even parents who are concerned about their children's welfare, but are grossly ignorant about how to care for them properly, may be cited for child neglect.

In order to avoid punishing parents for merely being poor or having bad housekeeping habits, a finding must usually be made that the situation is hazardous to the child's health before a state agency may intervene in the family's affairs. For example, a child who is frequently seen in dirty clothing is not necessarily so neglected that the state will act to protect him or her. However, a child who is always filthy and whose body is covered with sores or whose hair is infested with lice may well be neglected in the sight of the law. If a child's family is so poor as not to be able to provide food, clothing, or shelter, an effort will be made to help the family with these necessities—either through welfare payments or in-kind contributions. Only if the parents refuse this help will a finding of neglect be made.

Neglect also may be found where children, otherwise adequately cared for, are left without proper supervision at too early an age. This type of neglect is becoming more frequent as thousands of "latch-key" children are left to fend for themselves after school because of the late hours of their working parents. If these children are very young, a welfare agency may decide that leaving them by themselves is likely to be hazardous to their health.

Older children who become involved in substance abuse, gang liaisons, or other illegal or dangerous activities may also be adjudged "neglected" in some states, even without proof that their parents have made inadequate attempts to control them.

Educational Neglect

Not only is an adequate education a right to which children are entitled [see **educational rights**], it is also mandatory under the laws of all states. Despite strong parental authority over the type of education children receive, the Supreme Court has repeatedly made it clear that parental autonomy is not absolute. The state has an important interest in assuring that all its citizens are, if not well educated, at least minimally so. Thus, the failure of parents to enroll their children in school and see to it that the children attend may make them liable for educational neglect.

Educational neglect generally takes one of two forms. In the first type, parents are simply unaware of, or do not care about, their children's failure to attend school. Sometimes the parents themselves remove the children from school for frivolous reasons. In the second type of neglect, the parents care about their children's education but have chosen a substandard method for achieving it. These cases frequently involve home schooling situations in which the state contends that the parents are failing to provide a minimally adequate education for their children. In other cases, parents may place their children in private schools that adhere to their religious beliefs but do not, in the state's view, provide adequate educational opportunities. Because of the constitutional protection given the practice of religious beliefs, the law gives much deference to these choices, intervening only if the school is clearly deficient in the basic skills that children need to lead minimally productive lives.

Medical Neglect

Normally, parents control the medical treatment their children receive. However, the Supreme Court has recognized that this right is not absolute. [*Parham v. J. R.* (1979)] Parents' failure to seek necessary, proper, or adequate health care for their children may result in the intervention of the state to care for the children and prosecute the parents for neglect.

"Medical neglect" is difficult to define because of the inherent uncertainty of medical science and the legitimate interests of parents in choosing medical care for their children. Usually, a child's medical condition must be immediately life-threatening before the state will intervene in this parental choice. In addition, there must be a well-recognized therapy for the child's condition that has a good chance of saving his or her life. A court will not generally intervene to require experimental therapies for a terminally ill child. Thus, the parents of babies born with unresolvable and severe birth defects are usually free to decline extraordinary medical efforts for their children that have limited chances of success and would in probability merely prolong the babies' agony. In borderline cases, however, a court may order a **guardian ad litem** for a severely defective or ill child to explore whether available treatments would have a good chance of saving the child's life at less than extreme cost in suffering. If the child also has a defect that is not life-threatening but may affect his or her quality of life—such as retardation or cerebral palsy—a special guardian for the child's interests is especially important to ensure that a decision not to seek extraordinary medical treatment for the life-threatening situation is not made merely because of the child's other disabilities.

If parents have simply ignored a child's medical emergency and done nothing, it is easy to justify the action of child welfare authorities to order medical treatment. However, frequently parents are aware of the emergency but fail to seek treatment or refuse to give consent to treatment because of religious beliefs or faith in nontraditional therapies. These cases are complex, because of the countervailing protection given to the parents' practice of a chosen religion. Nevertheless, the U.S. Supreme Court has held that parents may not carry their religious beliefs to the point of exposing their children to a risk of death. [See *Prince v. Massachusetts.*]

Sometimes, courts may investigate an older child's own religious beliefs with regard to the matter. If the child appears freely to adhere to the same religious beliefs with regard to the proposed medical treatment as his or her parents, the **medical treatment** may not be ordered.

Medical neglect may also arise in cases in which a child's medical condition is not serious, but the parents have ignored it. In other cases, the child appears to be in good health, but the parents have failed to provide the child with routine physical examinations or standard immunizations. Usually, these situations occur in the context of other types of neglect or abuse, so that a charge of medical neglect is only one of a number of things that justify the state to order treatment for the child and punish the parents. In the case of immunizations, the state's justification for intervention is enhanced because the failure of many individuals to be immunized over time can affect the entire community's resistance to disease.

Unless there are other types of child abuse occurring at the same time that medical neglect is found, a court will usually not remove the medically neglected child from his or her family. The court will merely order the needed medical treatment and authorize a child welfare agency to monitor that the treatment takes place. Also, many states' laws shield parents from criminal prosecution for medical neglect if they can show that their failure to seek the required treatment was based on a good faith religious belief. However, some of these same states do allow criminal prosecution for the same behavior under other statutes, such as child endangerment statutes, which do not allow a good faith defense.

NEW JERSEY V. T. L.O. The 1985 case in which the U.S. Supreme Court held that protection against "unreasonable searches and seizures" embodied in the Fourth Amendment to the Constitution applies to children in the public schools. The Court also clarified that the standard justifying a search of students in public schools is lower than the standard applied to a search of children or adults in other locations.

The case began when T. L.O., a fourteen-year-old freshman at Piscataway High School in Middlesex County, New Jersey, was caught smoking with another girl in a school rest room—a violation of school rules. At the principal's office T. L. O. denied she had been smoking, going so far as to say that she never smoked. The vice principal, Theodore Choplick, demanded to look in her purse. Upon opening it, he saw a pack of cigarettes and some rolling papers. Believing that rolling papers signaled possible drug use, Choplick made an extensive search of the purse. In it he found a small bag of marijuana, some empty plastic bags of the type commonly used to package marijuana for sale, a large amount of money in small bills, an index card with a list of names of other students that was entitled "People who owe me money," and two letters that implicated T. L. O. in drug dealing activities. Choplick notified the police and turned the incriminating evidence of drug use and sale over to them. T. L. O. was taken into custody and charged with delinquency. She admitted that she had been selling marijuana in school, but she challenged the legality of Vice Principal Choplick's search of her purse, claiming that it violated her constitutional rights.

The case reached the Supreme Court. All justices agreed that the Fourth Amendment applies to schoolchildren. As one justice pointed out, it would be odd, in light of numerous high Court rulings that the First Amendment applied to students, to find that the Fourth Amendment did not apply. At this point, the justices went their separate ways. A majority found that, while the Fourth Amendment applied in public schools, it did not require a finding of probable cause to conduct a search. Rather, a "reasonable suspicion"—something less than probable cause—was sufficient. This lesser standard was justified, in the view of the majority, in light of the special mission of the schools to maintain discipline and protect their students. A majority of the court also found that Choplick had reasonable suspicion to search T. L.O.'s purse: first in order to find evidence of her violation of a school rule, and then—after sighting the rolling papers—to find evidence of drug dealing.

Justices Stevens, Marshall, and Brennan dissented. They rejected the Court's fashioning of a lesser "reasonable suspicion" standard for school searches. Rather, they believed that the normal standard of "probable cause" should apply in schools as well as everywhere else. The dissenters also believed that the search in this case did not even meet the majority's newly minted "reasonable suspicion" standard. The dissent was persuaded by the argument that the contents of T. L.O.'s purse were not relevant to the initial charge that she had been smoking. After all, mere possession of cigarettes did not violate school rules, and the fact that they were in her purse did not prove that she had been smoking them in the rest room. In the dissent's view, the mere desire to show that T. L.O. was lying when she denied smoking was not enough justification to open her purse, a place where an expectation of privacy is very strong. Moreover, once inside T.L.O.'s purse, the vice principal did not have any reason to "rummage" through it and subject its contents to the minute scrutiny that he did, including opening and reading the contents of T. L.O.'s personal letters.

In response to these arguments, the majority noted that, although the possession of cigarettes did not prove that T. L.O. was smoking at school, "evidence, to be relevant, need not conclusively prove the ultimate fact at issue." It need only have a tendency to make the existence of a fact more or less probable. Here, there was clearly a "nexus" between alleged smoking in school and cigarettes in T. L O.'s purse. Moreover, the presence of rolling papers in plain view beside the cigarettes created a "reasonable suspicion" that further evidence of drug use would be found in the purse.

NOTICE OF CHARGES   Since the Supreme Court's ruling in *In re Gault,* a minor who has been arrested is entitled to be told specifically what delinquent acts he or she is accused of committing. The description of the allegedly offending activities must be sufficiently detailed so that the child will know against what he or she must defend. The notice must also give the date, time, and place of any hearing to be held on the matter. In most states, the notice must be in writing, usually a letter or a summons. The exact form for the notice is usually prescribed in each state's code of procedure for juvenile court. However, if there is no particular mention of notice requirements in that statute, the state's rules of criminal or civil procedure will apply. This is in keeping with the trend, in many states, that the type of notice given to a juvenile must satisfy the same requirements as notice given to an adult. If adequate notice is not given, any decision regarding the charges is likely to be found void.

Many states also require that a minor's parents be given notice of their child's arrest and any charges filed against him or her, including the time and place of any hearing. [See also **interrogation.**] Usually, the state must make an effort to notify both parents, even if they are divorced and the whereabouts of the noncustodial parent are unknown. If one parent cannot be found, notification of the custodial parent is sufficient in most cases. The purpose of notifying a child's parents of his or her arrest is usually seen as an added safeguard against violation of a minor's rights to **due process of law.**

A minor may waive, or voluntarily relinquish, the right to be notified of charges against him or her. But, as in most procedures involving children, such a waiver will be considered valid only upon the most compelling proof that the child understood his or her rights and deliberately gave them up. It has been held by courts that when a child, or his or her parent(s), makes an appearance in juvenile court, he or she has voluntarily agreed to the proceedings. Thus, the child cannot later complain that notice of the proceedings was not given. However, the appearance by one parent does not necessarily "waive" the right of the other parent to adequate notice of charges filed against his or her child. Therefore, the child may later appeal based on the lack of adequate notification to both parents.

PARENS PATRIAE DOCTRINE A legal doctrine that reflects the view that the state, through its various agencies, may intervene in the normally private spheres of its citizens' lives to act for the welfare of those who are unable, through some disability, to protect their own best interests. Literally meaning "the parent of the country" in Latin, the parens patriae doctrine may be looked on as recognizing for the state a sort of "parental" role over its citizens, especially children. This role of the state as a citizen's ultimate protector is not the creation of a statute, but is rather considered to be an inherent attribute of sovereign governmental power.

The idea of the state as a superparent arose in the nineteenth century. It was a justification for breaking the old notion that children were the mere property of their fathers and, at the same time, an excuse for experiments in social welfare. It came about during a time when the ugly side effects of industrialization and urbanization—poverty, overwork, and under-supervision—were leading increasing numbers of children into trouble with the law. A social reform movement was formed, the goal of which was to "save" and rehabilitate wayward youth, instead of punishing them in adult institutions. In this social climate, the doctrine of parens patriae was first espoused in a legal case in 1838. [*Ex parte Crouse*] Invoking the doctrine, the court in that case held that the state could keep a young girl alleged to be incorrigible in a so-called house of refuge against her father's wishes, because the institution was designed to rehabilitate, rather than punish, juveniles.

Over a century later, the U.S. Supreme Court first recognized the doctrine of parens patriae in the 1944 case of *Prince v. Massachusetts.* That case established the authority of a state to enact laws to restrict child labor. In many cases since that time, the Supreme Court and other courts have invoked the doctrine to justify many different types of interference in parental prerogatives regarding children's activities. Federal and state legislatures also rely on the doctrine when promulgating laws for the welfare of children. Today, parens patriae may be seen behind many government actions affecting children, such as:

- Mandatory school attendance laws.

- Child labor laws.

- Laws setting the ages at which persons may marry, buy alcohol, or drive.

- Laws authorizing a child welfare agency to remove abused or neglected children from the custody of their parents.

- Laws imposing **curfews** on youth in crime-ridden neighborhoods.

- Court orders directing life-saving medical treatment for children whose parents refuse, for religious reasons, to allow such treatment.

- Laws restricting the publication of the names of juvenile criminal offenders.

- Court-ordered termination of **parental rights.**

- Laws allowing children to rescind contracts they have made prior to reaching the age of **majority.** See also **contract rights.**

PARENT LOCATOR SERVICE (PLS) A service run by the federal government or a state **Title IV-D agency** that locates absent parents who owe child support, or who have taken a child of whom they do not have legal custody.

Requests for help locating a missing parent for child support purposes may come to a PLS from a resident parent (usually the custodial parent), a legal **guardian,** the child's **guardian ad litem,** or a court having jurisdiction over family matters. If the parent is receiving money under the Aid to Families with Dependent Children program, the search will be conducted for free. Otherwise, a fee for the service may be charged.

Typically, a PLS operates as a clearinghouse for information on the whereabouts of missing parents. After a request for help locating a parent has been made, the service searches through its own data for information on the person's whereabouts. If there is none, the service then searches local directories and the data banks of other organizations, such as telephone listings, welfare offices, motor vehicle bureaus, tax records, the U.S. Post Office, and union rolls. The absent parent's relatives, friends, and known employers are also contacted by the PLS, requesting information on his or her location. A state PLS may also contact the PLS agencies of other states and the federal government seeking information. Those agencies, in turn, share any information they have gathered on the individual in question.

The federal PLS also disseminates requests from state PLS agencies to other federal institutions, such as the Internal Revenue Service, the Social Security Administration, the Veterans Administration, and the Immigration and Naturalization Service, as well as others. Any information about the sought individual is then relayed back to the original requestor. Once the missing parent has been located, procedures for **support enforcement** may begin. See also **Parental Kidnapping Prevention Act; Uniform Interstate Family Support Act.**

PARENTAL CONSORTIUM   The association, guidance, affection, nurturance, comfort, services, and companionship that a child receives from a parent. Traditionally, children were not allowed to sue third parties for negligently causing injuries to their parents that deprived the children of these benefits. This was in contrast to injuries to other family relationships. For example, husbands and wives have always been permitted to sue for injuries to the marital relationship caused when a third party negligently hurts one spouse. The uninjured spouse may receive compensation for the loss of the affectionate companionship and services usually given by the spouse who was injured, as well as for the loss of sexual relations. Parents also traditionally have been allowed to sue to recover for the loss of an injured child's services and companionship. It seems odd, therefore, to deprive children of a reciprocal right.

The reasons for the traditional rule against parental consortium lawsuits seem lame today. Most centered around a fear of fostering frivolous lawsuits, and the difficulty of placing a monetary value on the various emotional components of the parent-child relationship. Proponents of parental consortium suits point out that, in most states, a child's lawsuit to recover for the wrongful death of a parent has been allowed for a long time. They see little sense in allowing children to recover if a parent has died, but not allowing recovery if a parent is only injured—since the difficulty of determining a fair amount of compensation is similar for both. Moreover, children who have lost the society of a parent have suffered a grave emotional injury. It seems unfair to deprive them of some attempt at compensation for that injury.

Fortunately, this harsh rule began to change in the late twentieth century. The state of Massachusetts was the first to recognize a child's lawsuit to recover for the loss of a parent's company and guidance in a case involving a father who was paralyzed because of his employer's negligence. [*Ferriter v. Daniel O'Connell's Sons*, (1980)] Since that time, a growing number of states have recognized lawsuits for the loss of parental consortium. One federal court has declared that children have a constitutional right to the companionship of a parent. [*Smith v. City of Fontana* (9th Cir. 1987)] However, some states, such as Nebraska, still do not recognize parental consortium lawsuits.

Compensation for lost parental consortium is usually only available when a parent has been so badly injured that the parent-child relationship is seriously impaired. The loss of an injured father's ability to play sports with his son, for example, was held not to be sufficiently serious to require compensation. The father was still able to give his son the important guidance, nurturance, support, and companionship expected from a parent. On the other hand, a parent who has suffered a head injury and memory loss and no longer recognizes his or her children is unlikely to have meaningful relations with them for some time into the future, if ever. Compensation could be recovered in that case.

Some states limit awards of compensation in parental consortium cases to cover only services that the parent is no longer able to perform for the child. For example, the value of transportation to and from school or other events may be an element of damages in such cases. By contrast, compensation for lost expressions of affection would not be allowed.

Most states' laws limit parental consortium lawsuits to minor children. Once the children are adults, they cannot sue to recover for loss of an injured parent's companionship.

PARENTAL KIDNAPPING PREVENTION ACT (PKPA)
A federal law passed in 1980 that is designed to deter parents involved in **child custody** disputes from taking their children from their homes across state lines as a tactic to gain custody. Before the law was passed, divorcing parents who faced a legal battle for custody of their children could take the children to another state where the laws may be more favorable to that parent's claim for custody. Such a parent would typically declare that the new state was the child's home state. Already divorced noncustodial parents frequently tried the same thing, and then applied for a modification of the original custody decree. Under the PKPA, once a state court takes proper jurisdiction of a child custody case, no court in another

state may adjudicate the same case. Moreover, once a decree has been properly entered in the state that initially takes jurisdiction, all other states' courts must give "full faith and credit" to that ruling. In other words, the other states' courts must respect the original court's ruling and abide by it as if it were their own.

Also, the PKPA forbids a state from modifying the custody decree of any other state, unless certain conditions are met. First, if none of the original participants in the custody battle (either parent or the child) still live in the state that originally issued the custody decree, and the new state is now the home of one of the participants, a court in the new state may modify the old decree. The state that originally issued the decree has no jurisdiction to modify it, once all of the participants in the original custody dispute have moved out of that state.

In order to make sure that parents are not stealing their children away from their homes to other states to apply for custody, the PKPA also makes available the services of the federal **Parent Locator Service** to parents whose children have been stolen by a noncustodial parent.

The PKPA is not self-executing. In other words, a contestant in a custody dispute who claims that a court may not exercise jurisdiction over the case because the matter has already been, or is already being, decided in another state's court must bring this information to the new court's attention as soon as possible.

PARENTAL RESPONSIBILITY STATUTE A state law that makes parents or **guardians** legally responsible for harm caused to others by their minor children. [See **tort responsibility.**] Under traditional common law rules, parents are not automatically bound to compensate others for harm caused by their children. They are liable to do so only if they were at fault in some way in failing to supervise their children adequately.

Parental responsibility statutes change the common law rule. They vary from state to state. Typically, these laws impose legal responsibility on the parents of children who cause harm, even if the parents were entirely blameless. Some statutes impose the liability only if the parent was negligent and failed to exercise reasonable supervision of the offending child. Usually, the statutes impose responsibility on the parents only for harm that was deliberate, malicious, or willfully caused by the child. Negligently caused harm does not trigger the parental responsibility statute. Some statutes are restricted to compensating for property damage only, while others also include compensation for personal injuries. Most have a statutory cap on the maximum amount the parent will be required to pay, ranging from $500 to $10,000 depending on the state's law.

Parental responsibility statutes are designed not only to help compensate for damage and injury caused maliciously by children but also to encourage parents to exercise greater supervision of their children's activities. Parental responsibility laws do not relieve the child of legal responsibility for the harm caused. Instead, they include the parents as responsible parties.

PARENTAL RIGHTS The scope of a parent's freedom to control the lives of his or her minor children. Parental rights have always been considered among the most fundamental and sacrosanct of freedoms in American law. Nevertheless, parental rights are not absolute. Their definition is fluid and changes with the evolution of societal mores.

Until the early nineteenth century, the relationship of parents to their children was considered virtually off-limits to any type of legal restraint. Children were mere chattels, or personal property, of their fathers. While religious teachings contained many dictates as to the proper treatment and training of children, the secular law was oblivious to the issue. A father could use or abuse his children as he wished, even to the point of causing their deaths—usually without any legal consequences. No legal duty to support children existed, except to the extent necessary to prevent them from becoming wards of the state.

By the mid-nineteenth century, industrialization led to cities crowded with the offspring of poor factory laborers, who could afford neither to supervise them properly nor to provide them an alternative to joining their parents in the mills. Altruistic societies became concerned with the plight of these children who labored long hours at early ages in the dangerous maws of factory machinery, and who could rely on little or no guidance from their exhausted parents—if they had parents at all. The idea that laws should be concerned with the welfare of children arose at this time.

The first laws designed to aid children included compulsory school attendance laws and laws restricting children's labor. At the same time, courts began to intervene in cases in which children were physically abused by their parents. Of course, as soon as law began to regulate the treatment of children, the freedom of parents to deal with them as they chose was correspondingly restricted. Nevertheless, by pressuring legislatures for laws regulating child labor and upholding court decisions taking away the freedom of parents to physically abuse their children, society let it be known that it approved of the government stepping in to protect its youngest members under the **parens patriae doctrine.**

From the mid-nineteenth century to the mid-twentieth century was an era of paternalistic governmental concern in the lives of the nation's children. State laws restricting child labor were strengthened, and federal legislation on family matters appeared for the first time. Juvenile courts were formed to deal with youthful offenders separately from adults. In these institutions, judges directed the care, custody, and control of delinquent minors without regard to legal rules but according to their own conceptions of discipline and rehabilitative treatment.

Yet it should be noted that restrictions on parental freedom in this era were effected by the government's acting under the parens patriae doctrine for the children's good. Children had no independent "rights" of their own. Rather, they had an entitlement to be treated in a certain way. In the 1960s, rights for children as persons were recognized for the first time. [See *In re Gault.*] Although these newly recognized rights also whittled away somewhat the concomitant rights of parents, they actually affected the parent-child relationship very little. Most of these so-called children's rights involve children's activities in school and do not pit minors against their parents.

Thus, the right of parents to control most aspects of their minor children's lives remain mostly intact today. Provided the parent's choices do not endanger the physical safety or well-being of the child, the parent generally has the final say in all important matters in the child's life, including religious training, educational choices, disciplinary rules, domicile, food, clothing, shelter, medical care, employment, and people with whom the child may associate. In addition, parents are entitled to the child's society and company, and the child's services—either chores performed by the child for the household or the money earned by the child when working for another. Of course, in each of the enumerated areas parental prerogatives are not absolute. Over time, they have been modified by laws and by the decisions of judges in court cases.

In the waning days of the twentieth century, a movement has been afoot to "return parental rights to parents." Numerous "parental rights" initiatives have been started at grassroots levels in many communities, partly as a reaction against the extremes of youth violence, dropping academic achievement, and rising out-of-wedlock births among teenagers. For the most part, these resolutions are hopelessly vague. Few would argue for the days when fathers had the power of life or death over their families: too many children have suffered pain, disfigurement, and even death at the hands of deranged parents. Few would suggest that parents be allowed to neglect basic skills and knowledge that a child will need to be a productive member of society in favor of "anything goes" home schooling by parents too ignorant to know the limitations of their own knowledge. Few would favor a return to sweatshops where children as young as six worked ten hours a day with the permission, even at the command, of their parents. Moreover, most would agree that the law's recognition that older minors are capable of independent thought and well-considered actions that are worthy of protection is a positive development. The respect the law accords to the developing adult in each adolescent American fosters a reciprocal respect for the rule of law and the protection of diverse viewpoints that are the touchstone of the American legal system.

Thus, nearly everyone agrees that some restrictions on parents' treatment of their children are necessary for the good of the children and society as a whole. So a call to return "parental rights" is meaningless unless it spells out precisely what those rights are. To some observers, parents' cries that they cannot control their children because "parental rights" have been usurped ring hollow. Instead, this breast-beating seems to be an attempt to mask the uncomfortable truth that many parents, preoccupied with the increasing challenges of life and chasing the material comforts that American society declares to be a mark of "success," have themselves ignored the needs of their children for guidance and support.

This points to the opposite side of the coin of parental rights: at the same time that parents have rights to control the lives of their children, they have duties as well. Parents must provide sufficient nourishment, clothing, and shelter to maintain the health and welfare of their children. They must provide educational opportunities and insist on their children taking advantage of them. They must also see to medical care. Yet, perhaps most important of all, parents are responsible for instilling the values in their children that will make up the values of society in the future. This latter responsibility is imposed more by the laws of nature than the laws passed by any legislature or defined by any court. What the parents value will be passed to the children, regardless of the law's dictates. The ways in which parents may rise to the challenge of this natural law are, unfortunately, beyond the scope of this book.

🏛 ***PARHAM V. J.R.***   Children may be admitted to mental hospitals by the voluntary decision of their parents, provided an investigation by a neutral party finds that hospitalization is in the child's best interest, according to this 1979 Supreme Court ruling. An unwilling adult, by contrast, may be committed to a mental institution only after a hearing in which the state proves by clear and convincing evidence that hospitalization is necessary. The Court reached its conclusion in *Parham* even though it recognized that children have privacy rights protecting them from unnecessary bodily restraint and from the emotional harm caused by a false diagnosis of mental illness.

Because parents share their children's interest in freedom and well-being, the Court believed that they would act only in the child's best interests in seeking hospitalization. Thus, extra safeguards for the child were not necessary. Parents could be trusted in these matters, according to the Court, because they "possess what a child lacks in maturity, experience, and capacity for judgment required for making life's difficult decisions." [at 602]

The *Parham* ruling evoked considerable controversy, with some critics terming it "child abuse" by the Supreme Court. It is important to note, however, that this ruling means only that it is not unconstitutional for a state to commit a child to a mental institution solely upon the parent's wishes and a cursory investigation by a neutral party. It is permissible for states to pass laws giving children more protection from involuntary commitment. Many states have done so and require either the child's consent to commitment or an evidentiary hearing similar to that guaranteed to adults.

🏛 ***PAROLE***   The release of a convicted **juvenile delinquent** from **custodial confinement** prior to the expiration of his or her sentence. Parole is similar to **probation** in that it is conditioned on the juvenile performing certain actions or refraining from certain behaviors. The juvenile's compliance is monitored by the court or an administrative agency in charge of the youth's rehabilitation, and parole may be revoked if the conditions of early release are not met. Like revocation of probation, any revocation of parole must come only after notice to the juvenile of the parole violation charges and a hearing at which violation is proved. Eligibility for parole is usually dependent on good behavior of the juvenile while in confinement. Parole is sometimes called "aftercare."

PATERNITY ACTION A lawsuit through which the status of a man as the biological father of a child is determined. [See **biological parent.**] Under traditional rules of common law, only a child's mother, or an interested third party, could initiate a paternity action. The child had no right to do so. The original purpose of the procedure was not to require that the father support the child, but only to force him to reimburse the state, or a church, for expenses it had already incurred in maintaining the unfortunate illegitimate. Today, most states recognize that it is in a child's best interest to know the identity of his or her father. Therefore, most states allow the child to initiate a paternity action, as well as the mother or another interested party. Although most paternity actions are brought to force a reluctant man to take on the obligations of fatherhood, increasingly, men are initiating such suits voluntarily in order to claim **parental rights** and assume responsibility toward their children. Most states' laws now also allow putative fathers to initiate paternity actions.

Before World War II, paternity cases were tried on circumstantial evidence, such as the locations of the mother and putative father during the period when conception could have taken place. Much hearsay testimony from friends and relatives and biased assertions from the parties themselves made up early paternity actions. Today, blood testing and DNA typing are indispensable and virtually conclusive evidence in paternity actions. In fact, the Supreme Court has recognized the importance of these scientific tests by finding unconstitutional the denial of a blood test to an indigent man in a paternity action. [*Little v. Streater* (1981)] Moreover, it is generally considered constitutional for a state to order that blood tests be taken from all the involved parties. This includes not only the putative father but also the mother and child in order to perform a proper analysis of the genetic likelihood that the man is the biological father. Results that show a 98 or 99 percent chance that a man is the biological father of a child raise a strong presumption that the man is the father. Usually, only evidence that the man is sterile or impotent or had no access to the mother of the child during the crucial period can overcome this presumption.

Despite the general recognition that it is in a child's best interest to know the identity of his or her father, all states recognize the competing interest of keeping established family relationships intact and avoiding rancorous charges that could destabilize them. Therefore, there are certain situations in which a paternity action will not be allowed. In general, if a man and the mother of a child have lived together as husband and wife during the gestation period and the subsequent birth of the child and the man has acted in a manner indicating that he is the child's father, neither the man nor the mother can initiate a paternity action. Under the law, they are said to be estopped, or blocked, from alleging that the child is not legitimate. Any time a man has reared a child as his own, he is estopped from denying that the child is his. This estoppel applies even though a blood test may show that the man is in fact not the child's father. Moreover, some states restrict the rights of putative fathers to prove paternity only of children born out of wedlock. These states consider it to be an impermissible intrusion on the peace of an established family unit to allow a man to claim to be the father of a child born to a woman who is married to someone else.

Most states have established a time period following a child's birth within which a paternity action must be commenced. These statutes of limitations can vary from a few years to as many as twenty-three years. Some states have no limitations at all, and a paternity action may be brought at any time after the child's birth. In light of the Supreme Court's suggestion that laws that discriminate against illegitimate children are unconstitutional [see *Gomez v. Perez*], it would seem that many of these statutes of limitations could be struck down. On the other hand, some statute of limitations would seem in order where a child is to be placed for **adoption.** If the putative father could assert paternity at any time during the child's life, the stability of adoptive families could be in jeopardy.

As the twentieth century comes to a close, technological advances in fertility treatments are posing difficult questions for laws concerning paternity. In Louisiana, the girlfriend of a man who died of cancer used his previously frozen sperm to become pregnant with his child. In this case, the child was conceived after the man had died. The dead man's relatives tried to stop the use of his sperm to father a child, arguing, essentially, that it would be an unfair surprise to allow children who come into being through the use of a dead parent's stray genetic material to then lay claims to the dead parent's estate—which could long since have been distributed. This case was settled before a court was asked to decide it. [Davis, Ann, "High-Tech Births Spawn Legal Riddles," *The Wall Street Journal*, January 26, 1998, B1.] See also **illegitimacy.**

PHYSICAL ABUSE A type of **child abuse** resulting from the use of physical violence against the body of a child by an adult with legal responsibility for the child's care.

Generally, statutes outlawing physical abuse of children take care to distinguish it from permissible **corporal punishment.** Physical violence becomes abuse, and not punishment, when it is excessive for the alleged misbehavior and where it is likely to cause actual injury to the child, rather than mere transitory pain. For example, the breaking of bones is always considered excessive force, as is burning, scalding, freezing, maiming, disfiguring, excessively bruising, or anything else that endangers the child's health. The degree of force used must be limited to that which would maintain discipline and prevent or punish misconduct. Anything more is likely to be considered physical abuse.

Another type of physical child abuse involves forcing the child to eat or drink harmful substances. This includes drugs or alcohol, or even poisons and caustic substances. An important question in the late twentieth century is whether a pregnant woman's abuse of drugs or alcohol can be considered physical abuse of her unborn child. Some states have laws specifically including this type of activity as child abuse and authorizing the state to intervene by taking the child away from its mother after it is born. It is not clear, however, whether it is constitutional for a state to force the mother to stop the use of drugs or alcohol during pregnancy.

PIERCE V. SOCIETY OF SISTERS In this 1925 Supreme Court case, the issue was whether the state of Oregon could compel children to go to public, rather than private, schools. A number of private schools challenged the constitutionality of a statute that required all Oregon children to attend public schools beyond the age of eight. Echoing the aggrieved teacher in *Meyer v. Nebraska,* the private schools alleged that this law would cause them to go out of business, thus interfering with their "liberty" under the Constitution to engage in a useful trade. They also alleged that the law interfered impermissibly with the rights of parents to choose their children's mode of education and—mentioned for the first time—the "right" of children to influence their parents' choice of a school.

The Court agreed. However, before announcing its decision, it referred again to its statement in *Meyer*, reiterating that the power of the state to set reasonable education requirements and to regulate schools was not questioned. Again, in this case the Court sided with **parental rights** to determine not only the mode of schooling for their children without state interference, but their entire upbringing as well:

> The child is not the mere creature of the state; those who nurture him and direct his destiny have the right, coupled with the high duty, to recognize and prepare him for additional obligations. [at 535]

PLANNED PARENTHOOD OF CENTRAL MISSOURI V. DANFORTH

PLANNED PARENTHOOD OF CENTRAL MISSOURI V. DANFORTH   In this important case, heard in 1976, the U.S. Supreme Court recognized that a mature adolescent girl's privacy regarding reproductive choices outweighs her parents' interest in controlling her pregnancy. This ruling was but one issue decided by the Court in a broader challenge to a Missouri law restricting abortion rights. The suit was brought by two Missouri licensed doctors who performed abortions within the state.

Among other things, the challenged law required any unmarried female under eighteen years of age to obtain the consent of a parent or guardian prior to undergoing an abortion within the first twelve weeks of pregnancy. The state argued that the law was consistent with the many other laws that place special restrictions on minors because of their relative inexperience and immature judgment. The law was necessary, in the state's view, in order to safeguard the family unit and parental authority.

The high Court rejected these arguments, noting the inconsistency of a law requiring parental consent for the single procedure of abortion, when Missouri law allows minors to consent to other medical procedures without their parents' consent, including procedures related to pregnancy, venereal disease, and substance abuse. The fact that the law singled out unmarried females was also unjustified, in the Court's view: a married woman under the age of eighteen did not need to get the consent of a parent before having an abortion. The Court also agreed with the argument that because the state clearly could not give parents the authority to order their daughter to have an abortion, it was inconsistent to give parents the authority to order their pregnant daughters to have the baby.

Most importantly, the Court rejected the argument that the law would strengthen the family unit:

> It is difficult . . . to conclude that providing a parent with absolute power to overrule a determination, made by the physician and his minor patient, to terminate the patient's pregnancy will serve to strengthen the family unity. Neither is it likely that such veto power will enhance parental authority or control where the minor and the nonconsenting parent are so fundamentally in conflict and the very existence of the pregnancy already has fractured the family structure. Any independent interest the parent may have in the termination of the minor daughter's pregnancy is no more weighty than the right of privacy of the competent minor mature enough to have become pregnant. [at 75]

Despite this, however, the Court went on to explain that their ruling did not mean that every minor, regardless of age or maturity, could give effective consent to an abortion. Rather, it is only "mature" minor females who must have the right to determine the course of a pregnancy.

PLEADING In juvenile court, a minor who is accused of delinquent acts may answer the charges by pleading "not guilty," "guilty," or *"nolo contendere"* (Latin for "no contest"). If the youth pleads not guilty, the case will move on to **adjudication,** or the trial part of the proceedings. A plea of "guilty" or "nolo contendere" will result in a waiver of the right to a trial. The court will instead move directly to the dispositional phase of the proceedings exactly as if the youth had been adjudged guilty.

A plea of guilty means that the minor admits committing the delinquent acts of which he or she is accused. A plea of nolo contendere means that the minor does not admit or deny the charges, but instead states an intention not to present any defense. Because either of these pleas may result in court-ordered restrictions on the child's liberty that can only be seen as punitive, the law provides special protections for children who make them. Children's general lack of experience and understanding requires courts to ensure that any minor's plea of guilty or nolo contendere is freely made with full understanding of the rights thereby relinquished and the consequences to follow.

States differ in their methods of ensuring voluntary and knowing pleas of guilt by minors. Some require that an attorney be present to advise the child on the pros and cons of a guilty or nolo contendere plea. In other states, a judge must explain to the child the consequences of these pleas and ascertain that the child is fully aware of all his or her rights and what the possible consequences are of pleading guilty. In most states, failure to follow the established procedures for determining an accused minor's understanding of, and motivation behind, a guilty or nolo contendere plea will give the accused the option of later withdrawing the plea, or will make the conviction vulnerable to reversal by a higher court.

PLYLER V. DOE In this important case, the U.S. Supreme Court in 1982 struck down a Texas law that withheld state funds from school districts that admitted the children of undocumented aliens and authorized school districts to refuse admittance into the public schools of such children. The statute was designed to discourage illegal immigration and preserve the state's limited financial resources for educating lawful citizens.

In an opinion by Justice Brennan, the Court first noted that the **equal protection** clause of the Fourteenth Amendment to the Constitution states that "no State shall deny to any person within its jurisdiction the equal protection of the laws." Clearly, said the Court, an alien is a "person." However, Texas argued that people illegally residing in the country are not "within the jurisdiction" of the state, hence, equal protection does not apply to them. The Court rejected this argument, noting that the high Court had already held that other amendments, such as the Fifth and Fourth Amendment applied universally. Why should the Fourteenth be different? Rather, the Fourteenth Amendment "extends to anyone, citizen or stranger, who is subject to laws of the State and reaches into every corner of the State's territory."

Finding that the Fourteenth Amendment applies to illegal aliens did not end the inquiry. It was then necessary for the Court to balance the competing interests involved. If the state had a very important reason for discriminating against illegal aliens and the aliens had a relatively minor interest in receiving a free education, the law might have been allowed to stand. This was not the case, according to the majority of justices. Education is not a "fundamental right," said the Court, but nevertheless it is not just a run-of-the-mill government benefit. Education has always been considered extremely important and deprivation of it entails severe handicaps. In the words of the Court:

> In addition to the pivotal role of education in sustaining our political and cultural heritage, denial of education to some isolated group of children poses an affront to one of the goals of the Equal Protection Clause: the abolition of governmental barriers presenting unreasonable obstacles to advancement on the basis of individual merit. Paradoxically, by depriving the children of any disfavored group of an education, we foreclose the means by which that group might raise the level of esteem in which it is held by the majority. . . . Illiteracy is an enduring disability. The inability to read and write will handicap the individual deprived of a basic education each and every day of his life. The inestimable toll of that deprivation on the social, economic, intellectual, and psychological well-being of the individual, and the obstacle it poses to individual achievement, make it most difficult to reconcile the cost or the principle of a status-based denial of basic education with the framework of equality embodied in the Equal Protection Clause. [at 222]

> The [Texas law] imposes a lifetime hardship on a discrete class of children not accountable for their disabling status. The stigma of illiteracy will mark them for the rest of their lives. By denying these children a basic education, we deny them the ability to live within the structure of our civic institutions, and foreclose any realistic possibility that they will contribute in even the smallest way to the progress of our Nation.

The Court noted that it made little sense to punish the innocent children of illegal aliens for their parents' unlawful act of coming to the United States, saying "[e]ven if the State found it expedient to control the conduct of adults by acting against their children, legislation directing the onus of a parent's misconduct against his children does not comport with fundamental conceptions of justice." Moreover, the majority rejected the argument that an education was not as important to illegal aliens as to others because they would not remain in the United States or, as aliens, would not be allowed to vote. There was no way of telling, said the Court, how many of these children would later become citizens.

Thus, said the Court, only a very important reason for the Texas law could outweigh the detriment to the undocumented children. What was the reason? Essentially, Texas sought to discourage illegal immigration and save money at the same time. The Court noted a paucity of real evidence that the law would discourage immigration. Furthermore, a mere desire to save money did not outweigh the children's right to be educated, especially since there was no real evidence that the quality of education offered by the public schools of Texas would suffer significantly by their addition.

Justices Burger, White, Rehnquist, and O'Connor dissented from the ruling. Their rationale was that it was the prerogative of state legislatures, and not the courts, to decide educational policies. The dissenters chastised the majority for "unabashedly result-oriented" analysis and for allegedly fashioning a standard of review for legislation somewhere between the very high standard applied to laws that discriminate on the basis of race and the very low standard applied to all other legislation. In effect, the new "middle" standard applied only to laws that denied illegal aliens a free public education. This was unworkable and not the way courts are to decide cases.

PREGNANCY The public schools may not discriminate against students who are pregnant by excluding them from classes or other school activities. A public school also may not segregate pregnant students by placing them in special programs, although the school may offer them special programs in which participation is voluntary. Schools must excuse absences related to pregnancy in the same way they would absences for any other medical reason.

The rule against pregnancy discrimination is part of **Title IX**'s general prohibition of gender discrimination. Thus, although discriminating against pregnant students (who, of course, are only female) is illegal, discriminating against pregnant students who are unmarried might be permitted. In at least one case, a school's dismissal of an unmarried pregnant student from the school's honor society was upheld because engaging in premarital sex was a violation of the society's standards. The standards were equally valid for males who engaged in premarital sex. Thus, a court concluded that expulsion from the society was not based on gender and was, therefore, permissible.

PRELIMINARY HEARING That phase of a juvenile delinquency proceeding during which charges are formally presented against the suspect in a court of law. Also called an "advisory hearing" or an "initial appearance," the preliminary hearing in juvenile court roughly corresponds to an "arraignment" on criminal charges in an adult court.

During the preliminary hearing, the juvenile suspected of committing a delinquent act is brought before a judge or magistrate in a courtroom. This usually takes place very shortly after **arrest** and **intake.** If the suspect has not been released to his or her parents or guardian, but has been sent to live in another setting or held in secure detention, the preliminary hearing normally must not be delayed more than a few days at most.

At the preliminary hearing, the juvenile judge first must decide whether a delinquent act is likely to have been committed. If the answer is "yes," the judge then briefly hears evidence for and against the proposition that the suspect committed the act. At this point, the judge is only interested in determining whether the evidence against the minor is sufficient to justify a full-blown trial. Therefore, the evidence received is limited. This evidence may consist entirely of the report of the intake officer as to the facts surrounding the juvenile's arrest. In some cases, the arresting officer may be present to explain why there was probable cause to suspect the juvenile defendant. If the juvenile has some alibi to prove that he or she was not present when the act was perpetrated, this would be the time to present it. In most states, the juvenile has the right to be represented by a lawyer at the preliminary hearing.

If the judge decides that the evidence against the arrested minor is sufficient to conduct a trial, the judge will formally read the charges against the minor into the juvenile court record. Then the judge will explain the charges to the suspect, inform him or her of the right to an attorney—at public expense, if necessary—and ask the suspect how he or she will plead to the charges, whether guilty or not guilty. If the juvenile pleads guilty, there will be no trial. The proceedings will skip directly to the **disposition.** If the minor pleads not guilty, the adjudicative, or trial, phase of the procedure will be scheduled.

If a trial is scheduled, the juvenile judge will also review the intake officer's recommendation for the child's living arrangements before trial. In most cases, the suspect will be released to parents, guardians, or other responsible relatives. In serious cases, however, a different living arrangement may be ordered. This can include **preventive detention.** See also **pleading.**

PREVENTIVE DETENTION   Keeping juveniles accused of delinquent acts in custody between the time they are charged with a delinquent act and the time the delinquency **adjudication** takes place.

Juveniles accused of delinquent acts have no constitutional right to **bail.** Nevertheless, a number of states do have laws providing juveniles with the right to be free on payment of a monetary sum to the court to ensure their appearance at trial. Regardless of a state's laws concerning bail for juveniles, there are circumstances in which a court will not release a juvenile accused of delinquent acts, even to his or her parents, prior to trial. In such cases, the court may order the accused youth to be locked up in a jail or other facility until trial.

The Supreme Court has upheld the use of preventive detention for juveniles. [See *Schall v. Martin.*] However, controversy still surrounds its use. Many critics believe that incarcerating young people before they are proved guilty of any wrongful act in facilities in which they may be in contact with hardened juvenile offenders—or even adults in some cases—is more damaging to the juveniles than the danger they pose if released. Even where a state takes pains to segregate accused children from adults, juveniles frequently suffer depression and commit suicide at high rates when kept isolated in jail facilities.

A court will order a child to remain in preventive detention only if the act of which he or she is accused is one that would be a crime if the perpetrator were an adult, and if there is a "serious risk" that the juvenile will commit another such act before the trial. The mere risk that the youth will flee the jurisdiction and not show up for trial is not usually sufficient to order him or her into preventive detention. Even if there is a serious risk that the juvenile will commit another criminal act in the meantime, preventive detention is not automatic. Courts almost always consider other factors, including the youth's prior criminal record, the seriousness of the charged offense, the seriousness of the injuries suffered by the victim of the act, the need to protect the public from similar acts, and the age and best interests of the accused minor. The court will also consider whether there is a less restrictive alternative to incarceration, such as release to a foster or group home, that will serve the youth and the community better.

When a child is ordered to preventive detention, the right to a **speedy trial** assumes even greater importance. In some states, if the child stays more than a reasonable time in preventive detention prior to trial, the charges against him or her must be dropped. This is an incentive for the juvenile justice system to process delinquency cases efficiently.

🏛 *Prince v. Massachusetts* The first express recognition by the U.S. Supreme Court of the **parens patriae doctrine,** which allows the state to intervene in the normally private matters of the family in order to protect the general welfare of children. The 1944 *Prince* case involved state statutes that prohibited children from selling magazines and newspapers in a public place, and prohibited adults from supplying children with literature to sell in such fashion. A woman convicted of violating the law by supplying her nieces and nephews with religious pamphlets for sale challenged its constitutionality. She claimed that the statute unduly interfered with her right as the children's **guardian** to control their activities. She also alleged that the statute violated her First Amendment right to practice her religion.

In earlier cases, such as *Meyer v. Nebraska* and *Pierce v. Society of Sisters,* the Court had struck a balance in favor of parental rights as opposed to state authority over children. Here, however, the Court weighed the competing rights of parents to control their children with the state's interest in fostering the general welfare of children and sided with the state. Announcing that a state may regulate the activities of children to a greater extent than those of adults, the Court held that the state had legitimate reasons to prohibit the employment of children in ways that were likely to harm them. Here, the Court was persuaded that selling religious literature on the street could expose children to unhealthy influences and cause "emotional excitement and psychological or physical injury." [at 170] In justifying the state's action in prohibiting children from selling on the street the Court noted:

> A democratic society rests, for its continuance, upon the healthy, well-rounded growth of young people into full maturity as citizens, with all that implies. [The state] may secure this against impending restraints and dangers, within a broad range of selection. Among evils most appropriate for such action are the crippling effects of child employment, more especially in public places. . . . [at 168]

Beyond the immediate holding, the *Prince* case is important for establishing the principle that parental authority is not absolute. Another interesting development can be found in a dissent from the majority opinion authored by Justice Murphy. Arguing that the state's interest in protecting children did not outweigh the important value in religious freedom, Justice Murphy referred for the first time to the "right" of children to practice religion. In later cases, the Supreme Court would begin a trend of recognizing the constitutional "rights" of children, including that of practicing one's religion.

▥ PROBATION   An alternative to sending a **juvenile delinquent** to a reform school or other institution is a release back into society on the condition that the minor conform to certain requirements tailored to furthering his or her rehabilitation. As the word itself suggests, probation is a "trial" period during which the convicted youth must behave. If the youth violates the terms of a probation order, probation may be rescinded and the minor may be institutionalized. Unlike adults, juveniles usually may not reject probation and request incarceration as a disposition for their delinquent acts.

A youth on probation for delinquent acts is normally subject to very tight supervision. Unlike probation for adults, which is considered a show of leniency in lieu of punishment, probation for minors is often the very heart of the rehabilitative effort. Therefore, probation orders for juveniles may impose a wide variety of conditions. Courts routinely uphold conditions for juvenile probationers that would violate the constitutional rights of adults on probation. For example, a youth on probation may be ordered to observe a strict curfew, not venturing out of his or her home between certain hours, or unless accompanied by a parent. Delinquents may be ordered to attend school and maintain a certain grade-point average, or participate in counseling or drug rehabilitation programs. A minor on probation may be required to submit to periodic random searches for weapons, or testing for drugs and alcohol. These searches, conducted without any probable cause to believe contraband will be found, would violate the Fourth Amendment if imposed on an adult. Youthful probationers' freedom of association may be curtailed. For example, they may be ordered not to associate with gang members, or not to be present at areas known to be gathering places for gangs. Delinquents may be ordered not to wear gang insignia or clothing. A court can order minors not to associate with anyone using or possessing alcohol or drugs, or persons who have weapons. A youth may even be ordered to obey all reasonable requests and demands of his or her parents, or face placement in **custodial confinement.** In one case, a probation order requiring a delinquent to attend a church youth program chosen by his mother was upheld as constitutional. The youth's argument that this violated his First Amendment rights to religious freedom was rejected by the Court. The Court pointed out that parents have a right to direct their minor children's religious training. A frequent condition of probation is that the delinquent give up his or her driver's license during probation. This, too, has been held constitutional.

While courts have wide discretion to fashion conditions of probation, the conditions must have some relationship to the offense for which the youth was convicted. For example, it is proper to order a youth convicted of possessing marijuana to participate in an educational program about the dangers of drugs. Such an order would not be appropriate for a youth caught shoplifting. In addition, any condition of probation must be one that the child can meet. Ordering a child of borderline intelligence to earn good grades is not permitted. Generally, when a court orders that a delinquent keep a certain grade-point average it is only within a range that the youth has already shown he or she can achieve. Similarly, ordering a youth to pay **restitution** as a condition for being released on parole is not permitted unless the court has determined that the youth is able to pay the required sum, or is given the opportunity to work off the amount in some sort of **community service** or by working directly for the victim of the delinquent act.

In most states, the term of probation cannot exceed two years. In some states, probation ends upon the juvenile reaching the age of majority, usually eighteen. Other states, however, allow periods of juvenile court probation to extend to the probationer's twenty-first birthday.

Typically, a legion of probation officers from juvenile court monitors delinquents' compliance with probation conditions. If a youth fails any condition, probation may be revoked. Prior to revocation, however, the juvenile court must conduct a hearing at which the delinquent may defend against charges that he or she failed to meet a condition. The juvenile has a right to be represented by a lawyer at this hearing. In most states, probation violations must be proved "beyond a reasonable doubt." Other states will revoke probation if the evidence merely shows it is more probable than not that a violation occurred. If the court decides that the youth did violate probation, the judge may sentence the minor to whatever disposition could have been imposed at the time of the original adjudication. In most cases, the youth will not get credit for the time he or she served on probation, but will have to serve the entire sentence anew.

PROPERTY RIGHTS Generally, children own any property given to them that was not extended by a parent or guardian for the child's maintenance, education, or general welfare. Personal items such as clothing, toys, books, computers, and other normal accoutrements of childhood technically belong to the parent or guardian who provided them. Parents also have a claim to any money earned by their children. This odd rule stems from the ancient tradition that parents have a right to services performed by their children. If the child performs services for someone else and receives money for it, the parents theoretically may claim this money to compensate for the loss of services to themselves because the child was working for that other person. See **employment regulations; parental rights.**

Other property, including land and real estate, may be owned by a child in his or her own right. However, the child's power to manage such property may be restricted if large sums are involved. Because children have traditionally been considered incapable of managing their financial affairs, a special **guardian** is usually appointed by a court for the purpose of managing real estate or large inheritance sums for a child's benefit until he or she attains the age of **majority.** Trust funds may be created for the same purpose. While courts frequently will appoint a child's own parents to be the guardians of the child's property, parents do not have an automatic right to be put in charge of such property. Nor do parents generally have any right to manage their children's property simply by virtue of their relationship to the child. Only a court order, a valid trust agreement, or other consensual arrangement will vest them with this right.

Even when a guardianship is in effect, a child may transfer his or her own property. This includes buying and selling, or giving and receiving. It applies to all types of property including real estate (land), personal property (generally any property that may be moved, including automobiles), and intangible property (such as stocks and bonds). However, the special rules regarding contracts made by children will apply to the transfer of such property. [See **contract rights.**] Basically, this means that an unemancipated [see **emancipation**] child who transfers property may change his or her mind and not be held to the contract in most situations. People are understandably reluctant to enter a contract with a minor, because the deal may be revoked at any time by the child before the age of majority, or for a reasonable time after the child comes of age. Nevertheless, sales or purchases of property that are made in the child's name by a guardian or custodian, pursuant to a trust agreement or with express approval by a court, are permanent and may not be avoided or revoked later. The transfer of small, inexpensive personal items, such as birthday presents and the like, is not subject to these rules. Money owned by a child and kept in a bank account, or in cash, is likewise available to him or her and may be transferred or spent in any way the child desires without restriction.

For the most part, all restrictions on a child's management of property disappear when the child reaches the age of majority, or is emancipated.

However, the freedom to manage funds in a trust account will generally depend on the document that created the trust. In some cases, restrictions on the trust beneficiary's (the person for whom the trust was set up) use of the money in the trust will extend far into adulthood, or even for life.

PROTECTIVE CUSTODY
Temporary custody of a child by a child welfare agency that is taken when there is reason to believe that the child is in imminent danger if he or she is not removed from home. Because protective custody is used only in emergencies, a prior court order or notice to the child's parents is not required. However, procedures to safeguard the parents' rights must be strictly observed in the days following the child's removal. A hearing must take place within a few days. The parents must receive notice of the hearing and have the opportunity to contest it. Usually, a **guardian ad litem** is appointed to represent the child.

Basically, protective custody statutes give police officers the authority to remove an endangered child from the parents and take him or her to a location where a child protective agency will provide care. Some statutes also allow hospitals to detain a child in their care if medical personnel believe that it would be dangerous for the child to return home.

While protective custody is sometimes necessary, it is not a step to be taken lightly. Critics of the procedure charge that, not only may it violate the family's constitutional rights, it also may cause profound and needless emotional distress for all involved.

A less disruptive alternative to protective custody for the child is a civil protection order, or CPO. Instead of removing the child from his or her home, a CPO requires the adult who is suspected of abuse to leave the home. Thus, the child's routine is less disrupted. The same procedural safeguards apply for the parents as in protective custody situations: speedy hearings and the chance to contest the action. In some cases, however, a CPO is not appropriate. For example, if there is reason to believe that the allegedly abusive parent will not obey the order to stay away from the child, protective custody is the only remedy.

PSYCHOLOGICAL PARENT DOCTRINE
A legal doctrine applied by some courts deciding **child custody** cases that is based on the theory that a child's best interests require his or her placement in the sole custody of the adult with whom the child feels the greatest emotional

attachment. This person need not be a **biological parent,** but could be another relative or an unrelated third party.

According to this theory, the psychological parent is the adult in a child's life who provides the most consistently available affection, comfort, and mental stimulation, as well as day-to-day physical care and nourishment. It is the adult with whom the child most closely identifies and respects. The proponents of the doctrine believe that children need the stability of an uninterrupted and consistent relationship with the psychological parent, such that the rights of other adults to the child's company, including those of biological parents, are greatly subordinated. These adherents particularly believe that **joint custody** is detrimental to children and serves the interests of the adults involved rather than the children.

The psychological parent doctrine is a relatively new legal theory and is accepted by only a small minority of courts. Courts that do accept it usually restrict its application to cases in which the custody dispute is between a biological parent and a third party. In cases in which two capable biological parents are vying for custody, courts will not usually consider the claims of other relatives or third parties, regardless of how much emotional attachment the child may have with them.

PUBLIC TRIAL   A basic tenet of American criminal law is that trials should be open to the public. The rights of adult criminal defendants to be tried in public were recognized by the Supreme Court in 1948. [*In re Oliver*] Public awareness and scrutiny of criminal prosecutions help keep these procedures fair. However, a competing interest in privacy is at stake in juvenile proceedings, where it is believed that publicizing the charges against juveniles prematurely stigmatizes them and interferes with the state's ability to help them reform. As the Supreme Court in *In re Gault* explained, it is necessary "to hide youthful errors from the full gaze of the public and bury them in the graveyard of the forgotten past." [*Gault* at 24]

The U.S. Constitution is silent on the issue of public trials for juveniles. In other words, it gives minors neither the right to a public trial nor the right to a private trial. It is up to the states, and sometimes to the discretion of individual judges, to decide whether to permit the public to observe juvenile adjudications. In general, practice has come down on the side of privacy for the accused youth. Thus, most juvenile delinquency proceedings are closed to the public. However, the accused minor, together with his or her attorney, has a constitutional right to be present. The parents or guardians of the youth are usually also in attendance. In addition, minor witnesses and their parents, as well as any other person who, in the court's opinion, has a direct interest in the case, may be permitted to observe as well. In certain cases, a juvenile judge may determine that it is in society's interest to open a delinquency proceeding to the public. This usually occurs if the charges against the youth are very serious.

In recent years, much criticism from extreme sides of the political spectrum has been leveled at the system of private trials for juveniles. Liberals rightly point out that the reality of juvenile court has shifted from emphasis on rehabilitation to emphasis on punishment—just as in adult court. If a child is exposed to the possibility of punishment for conduct, he or she should have the same safeguards operating to keep the adjudication procedure fair as do adults—namely, public scrutiny of the process. Conservatives, on the other hand, approve the new punitive purpose of juvenile court as more in tune with reality; rehabilitation is a pipe dream in their view. Thus, they argue that publicizing the charges against juveniles, including their names and addresses, serves two purposes: first, it warns the public about a danger in its midst and, second, the stigma and community disapproval of the youth can serve as a powerful incentive to reform.

These pressures are having an effect on juvenile procedures throughout the nation. Currently, approaches to the publicity of juvenile proceedings range from discretionary disclosure to certain circumscribed groups of individuals, such as teachers and counselors; to public disclosure for all serious offenses; to public disclosure of any proceedings on charges that would be considered criminal if the perpetrator were an adult. In all but a few states, the decision to open a juvenile proceeding to the public is mandated by law or left to the discretion of the juvenile judge. Only a few states allow the accused juvenile to determine whether to open the proceeding or keep it private.

Although the Supreme Court has not ruled on the issue of an accused juvenile's right to a public or private trial, it has ruled on the First Amendment rights of news media to report on juvenile proceedings. On this issue, it has fallen squarely on the side of the public's right to know. These holdings result in an odd inconsistency in states in which juvenile proceedings are held in private. There, the right of the public to attend a juvenile delinquency proceeding is not the same as the right of the news media to report on the developments in the case. Thus, while it is well settled that juvenile judges may exclude members of the public from coming into the courtroom and observing the trial, it is far from settled that the judge can bar the news media from attending and/or from reporting the story. Although many states have so-called shield laws, which make it illegal to publish the names of juveniles who are the subject of juvenile proceedings, recent rulings by the Supreme Court leave the constitutionality of these laws in doubt. [*Oklahoma Publishing Co. v. District Court* (1977); *Smith v. Daily Mail Publishing Co.* (1979)]

Generally, if the news media have discovered information about a juvenile proceeding, they may not be forbidden from publishing it. However, court restrictions on what the participants or others with knowledge may say to the news media about a juvenile case have been upheld by courts. In other words, a court may order persons with knowledge of a case not to discuss the case with the news media, but a court may not order the news media not to print information it has received, whether or not obtained illegally. The issue of whether juvenile courts may close their doors to representatives of the news media as they may to the general public is also not resolved. A number of states allow juvenile courts to exclude the news media if the judge thinks that the rights of the participants, particularly the accused youth, will be compromised by the reporting. Most courts have held that the press does not have an absolute right to attend juvenile court proceedings. Even the laws of most states that have such restrictions tend to make an exception for high profile cases in which the alleged crime is very serious and the public has a high degree of interest. Whether or not the law allows news reporting of juvenile cases, many news organizations choose voluntarily to forgo printing the names and addresses of juvenile delinquents or their juvenile victims, feeling that it could damage the youths' chances to reform and live normal, productive lives.

RELIGIOUS FREEDOM Parents have a right to determine the religious upbringing of their children. The government usually may not interfere with parental decisions based on religious beliefs unless the child's life is thereby threatened. The most common instance of this occurs when parents refuse medical treatment for their children because of their belief that prayer alone will heal the child. Under certain circumstances, the government may intervene to order medical treatment for the child, against the parent's wishes. See **neglect.**

Generally, minors have no independent rights to act on their own religious beliefs when these differ from those of their parents. A court will not order parents, for example, to allow their children to attend or join a church of their choice if the parents object. On the other hand, the government will not usually intervene to force children to obey their parents with regard to attending a church of the parents' choice. An exception may be made if the minor runs away from home to live in a religious community. In such a case, police may be called to return the minor to his or her parents under the usual laws concerning runaway children. An unresolved issue concerns whether parents may hire independent "deprogrammers" to physically restrain their children from joining a religious organization and attempt to change their minds. At least one court has allowed this.

Although the general rule is that children must accede to their parents' wishes in religious training, there has been some judicial recognition of children's independent religious rights when some other aspect of their lives is also implicated. This is particularly the case where the state and the child's parents have different views as to what is best for the child. For example, courts will frequently consider a mature minor's independent religious views when deciding whether to order life-saving medical treatment for him or her against the parents' religious beliefs. [See also **abortion; medical treatment.**] In addition, in the Supreme Court case of *Wisconsin v. Yoder,* in which it was decided that people in an Amish community could choose to teach their children at home in contravention of a state law that required children to attend school, Justice Douglas noted in dissent that perhaps the children should have been allowed to state their preferences as to where they may choose to be schooled. In the justice's opinion, the moral and intellectual development of the fourteen-year-old children involved in the case was sufficient that they should be heard on the issue in court.

RELIGIOUS HOLIDAYS   The First Amendment to the U.S. Constitution prohibits the government from promoting or inhibiting the practice of any religion. However, it is well established that the public schools do not violate these injunctions by permitting students time off from school in order to take part in religious observances. Rather than promoting any religious belief, this accommodation is viewed as facilitating the free exercise of religion by students, which is guaranteed by the First Amendment.

The public schools are not *required* by the Constitution to give any time off for religious activities. If a school chooses to do so, the Constitution requires only that it give similar privileges to students of all established religions. Moreover, time off for religious occasions need not be automatically granted. A public school may restrict the option only to those students whose parents request their children's presence at observances taking place during school hours.

The fact that public schools operate on a schedule that routinely gives Christian and Jewish students time off on their respective Sabbath days does not mean that adherents of religions with Sabbath observances on other days of the week can choose not to attend school on those days. At least one court has held that, by choosing to send their children to public schools, parents have agreed to the standard schedule. If they feel strongly about the Sabbath observance, their option is to send their children to a private school in keeping with their views.

REPORTING LAWS   Laws that require certain persons to report reasonable suspicions of **child abuse** to a state child welfare agency responsible for the investigation and prosecution of such acts. Reporting laws have been in existence only since the early 1960s, when national attention was focused on the problem of child abuse by the medical

community's recognition of identifiable symptoms suffered by battered children. A groundswell of legislation in all fifty states, the District of Columbia, and American protectorates around the world attempted to bring the hitherto quietly ignored epidemic of child abuse into the open and eradicate it.

All states with one exception require reporting on the condition of children up to the age of eighteen. Wyoming ceases to require reporting on children over the age of sixteen.

Reporting laws differ on the point of which persons are required to report. Generally, any one who regularly sees children in a professional capacity is required to report suspected abuse. This includes physicians, dentists, psychologists, psychiatrists, and other medical personnel—such as nurses—who treat children. Many states also include guidance counselors, teachers, day care providers, social workers, residential care workers, and police officers. Some states also require attorneys and clergymen to report suspicions of child abuse. In about half of the states, everyone is obligated to report suspected child abuse. In most states that do not require everyone to report, anyone *may* report.

In order to induce compliance, mandatory reporting laws usually immunize those persons who are required to report suspected child abuse from legal liability if their suspicions turn out to be wrong. So long as a reporter has a good faith belief that child abuse may be occurring, he or she is shielded from lawsuits for libel, slander, invasion of privacy, or breach of confidentiality for reporting suspicions to an appropriate agency. The duty of attorneys, physicians, and clergy not to disclose the confidences of their clients has been abolished in some states for the narrow purpose of reporting to an appropriate agency that child abuse may be occurring. If a person makes a knowingly false report, however, or if he or she spreads allegations of abuse to persons other than a state law enforcement or child welfare agency, immunity from legal responsibility for such statements may not be granted.

Persons who are required by a reporting law to inform authorities of suspected child abuse may be prosecuted under the criminal law if they fail to do so. However, there have been relatively few such prosecutions—probably because it is so difficult to prove that someone had knowledge of child abuse. In some states, a child welfare agency that receives a report of suspected child abuse may be sued for negligence if it fails to investigate properly and a child is injured as a result. See *DeShaney v. Winnebago County Department of Social Services.*

▥ **RESIDENCY REQUIREMENTS** Public schools may impose residency requirements on children seeking to enroll. In *Martinez v. Bynum*, 461 U.S. 321 (1983), the U.S. Supreme Court heard a challenge to a Texas statute that denied free attendance in public school to a child who was living in McAllen, Texas, with his adult sister for the sole purpose of attending the public school there. The child's parents lived in Reynosa, Mexico. Although they were Mexican citizens, the child was a citizen of the United States by virtue of being born in Texas. The statute in question limited enrollment in McAllen public schools to children who "resided" there for any reason other than solely to attend school.

The Court noted that residency requirements serve a legitimate purpose in limiting state services to residents, who presumably pay taxes and contribute to the economic and cultural base of the society. It is not unconstitutional for a state or district within a state to prefer its own residents for receiving benefits and largess funded by state resources. If a school were required to take any child that showed up on a free basis, important planning for the best use of school resources could be negated, classrooms could be overcrowded, and the quality of education could suffer. In addition, the traditional and cherished role of local control over educational processes could be compromised if significant numbers of students from outside a local district were admitted into public schools within the district. The Court ruled that the Constitution permits a state to restrict eligibility for tuition-free education to its bona fide residents.

Although residency requirements "discriminate" against persons who do not reside within a state or district, this type of discrimination is not based on "immutable" characteristics, such as race or gender, or on matters of protected beliefs, such as religion. Rather, a person may receive the benefits of a free public school education simply by becoming a resident. Generally, to be a resident requires nothing more than physical presence in a locality and the intention to stay and make the community one's home. In order to prove an intention to stay in a community, some states have passed laws requiring domicile in a state or district for a certain length of time. These types of residency requirements have been struck down as not legitimate, because the length of time one has lived in a place does not always correlate with whether one intends to make that place home.

Interestingly, although a state may require children to reside, or live, in a certain district in order to attend schools there, the state may not deny entry into public schools to children who are living there illegally; that is, illegal alien children whose parents are nevertheless residents by virtue of their physical presence and an intention to remain indefinitely have a right to attend public school on the same basis as do citizens or legal aliens. See *Plyler v. Doe.*

RESTITUTION A popular **disposition** in juvenile delinquency cases, restitution requires the delinquent minor to pay compensation or make reparations to the victims of his or her delinquent acts. Many believe that restitution is a particularly appropriate rehabilitative option for juvenile delinquents because it shows them the human consequences of their destructive acts and teaches them that they are directly accountable for a remedy. At the same time, restitution provides relief to the victims of juvenile crime.

Restitution may be made in several ways. The delinquent youth may be ordered to pay a sum of money to the court or directly to the victim of the delinquent act. The delinquent may be ordered to repair damaged property himself or herself, or to do an amount of work for the victim equivalent in value to what it would cost to have a third person make the repairs.

Restitution is used most frequently to amend acts of vandalism and theft. Violent crime against persons is not usually subject to remedy by payments of money or equivalent work, although medical bills are sometimes ordered paid by a juvenile offender who causes personal injury. Victims of violent acts perpetrated by youths are often all too glad never to see the person who injured them again. Moreover, youths who resort to physical violence are not normally considered candidates for rehabilitation by means of restitution, unless it is coupled with serious efforts at psychological counseling and behavior modification.

The law regarding restitution for youthful offenses is not complicated. Basically, the amount of restitution required must be reasonably related to the amount of damage done by the child. At the same time, however, it must not be "excessive." If the sum required is so far in excess of what the youth is able to pay—even though commensurate with the damage caused—restitution will be merely punitive, rather than aimed at rehabilitation, as required by the mandate of juvenile court.

In addition, the law prohibits making restitution a condition of receiving **probation,** unless it may be paid off by means of work, rather than a lump sum of money. Although a youth has no entitlement to probation, a minor cannot be denied probation merely because he or she is too poor to pay an amount of money in restitution. In some states, a juvenile delinquent's parents may be liable for the payment of restitution. Again, however, the youth may not be denied probation because his or her parents are too poor to pay.

RUNAWAY AND HOMELESS YOUTH ACT First passed in 1974, this federal law is designed to set up a network of care services for homeless and runaway children that operates outside the juvenile justice system.

In the last decade of the twentieth century, the problem of homeless juveniles has overwhelmed the social support systems of many urban areas and has been felt in smaller communities. Children flee intolerable home situations, only to find a worse fate on the streets: they become drug addicts, prostitutes, and thieves and are prey to the most depraved criminals and contagious diseases, including AIDS.

To remedy this situation, the act requires the federal government to develop a network of emergency shelters and services and set up long-term residential care for troubled youths. Grants are made available to both public and private agencies to carry out these mandates. To be eligible for this financial aid, institutions must demonstrate that they reach an area known to be frequented by homeless youth and that they have a maximum capacity of twenty persons.

The act attempts to reach out to the itinerant youths themselves by offering aid in attaining and adapting to life off the streets. A youth must be between sixteen and twenty years of age and have no other place to turn to live (for example, no relative must offer a place to live). These "transitional services" may last up to 540 days.

The act also funds programs that aid runaways in communicating with their relatives, usually through free and untraceable telephone contacts.

SCHALL V. MARTIN Fourteen-year-old Gregory Martin of New York was arrested on 13 December 1977, accused of hitting another youth in the head with a loaded gun and stealing his jacket and shoes. The juvenile authorities decided to keep Martin in **preventive detention** pending his trial in **juvenile court.** A state law allowed such custody for children believed likely to commit another delinquent act if released before trial. Martin and two other minors challenged this restriction of their liberty on the grounds that it was forbidden by the Fifth Amendment to the Constitution.

In 1984, the case reached the Supreme Court, which ruled that the practice of keeping accused juvenile delinquents in custody prior to adjudication does not violate the Constitution. To reach this conclusion, the Court balanced the interests of society in having possibly dangerous suspects kept off the streets prior to their trials with the juveniles' interest in retaining their liberty during this time. The interests of society were considerable, said the Court, and not affected by the age of the alleged perpetrator: the victim of a crime committed by a minor is not any less injured than the victim of an adult offender. Moreover, said the Court, the high rate of recidivism—or repeat crimes—among youthful offenders was another justification for keeping accused juveniles locked up before their trials.

On the other hand, the Court acknowledged that juveniles who are accused of crimes but not yet found guilty have a substantial interest in being free of government restraints on their liberty—even when that restraint lasts only a very short time. Nevertheless, a minor's interest in this liberty is not as strong as an adult's, explained the Court, because the minor's "interest must be qualified by the recognition that juveniles, unlike adults, are always in some form of custody. . . . Children, by definition, are not assumed to have the capacity to care for themselves. They are assumed to be subject to the control of their parents, and if parental control falters, the State must play its part as parens patriae." An additional reason argued in favor of keeping an accused minor in custody: the welfare of the accused child himself or herself. A juvenile who is released from custody pending trial might be hurt if a later victim of the juvenile's delinquent behavior fights back, or if the juvenile resists arrest. Keeping the juvenile temporarily out of the pressure of peers who could lead him or her into a "downward spiral of criminal activity" was also a reason the Court cited in favor of the practice.

Having thus decided that legitimate reasons—in favor of protecting both society and the accused child—outweighed the child's liberty interest, the Court concluded that pretrial detention in general would not violate the Constitution. It still remained to examine the New York law in question to determine whether it really served these legitimate goals or was merely designed to punish youth who were still entitled to the presumption of innocence. On this score, the Court noted that under New York law at the time the maximum time a juvenile could be detained before trial was seventeen days, including a three-day limit between arrest and the **preliminary hearing** and a fourteen-day maximum between that hearing and the actual adjudication. Moreover, in this case, the detained juveniles were housed in facilities separate from adults, in dormitories with children of roughly their own ages. They were allowed to wear street clothes and were offered educational, recreational, and counseling services. Misbehavior at the facility was punished by confinement to the child's room. From this the Court concluded that punishment was not the true purpose behind the New York preventive detention law. Furthermore, the Court was satisfied with the due process accorded each child before detention was ordered: each was given notice of the charges, informed of his or her rights, and required to appear with a parent or responsible adult. Juvenile judges were required to consider the nature and seriousness of the alleged offense, the likelihood that the child would be proved guilty at trial, any prior record, and the adequacy of the parents' supervision of the child. In Martin's case, the fact that he was arrested at 11:30 at night, that he lied about his address, and that the crime involved a loaded weapon induced the judge to order him detained. The Supreme Court did not find this unreasonable.

Three justices dissented: Marshall, Brennan, and Stevens. They believed that the vaunted "hearings" given children prior to ordering detention were, in fact, perfunctory and that detention of any kind before trial was harmful—including exposure to bad influences and even physical assault by other detainees. Worst of all, the dissenters believed, the very detention itself could lead impressionable youth to doubt their self-worth and view society as hostile and oppressive—a recipe for more serious offenses to come.

🏛 **SCHOOL DROPOUT DEMONSTRATION ASSISTANCE ACT OF 1988** A federal law designed to help lower the rate of high school dropouts by providing grants to local school districts. Receipt of these funds is conditioned upon a district setting up programs to identify youth at risk of dropping out and designing early intervention programs to stave off this eventuality. Funds for schools to set up summer remedial programs to keep students on track for graduation are also available. Grants may be given for schools to study the factors—academic, cultural, or societal—that correlate with high dropout rates and to try to mitigate them. School districts are also encouraged to adopt programs that track dropouts, to find out why they decided to drop out, and to encourage them to reenter school and earn a diploma.

🏛 **SCHOOL PRAYER** The First Amendment to the U.S. Constitution provides that "Congress shall make no law respecting an establishment of religion or prohibiting the free exercise thereof." Thus, the government must neither promote nor inhibit the practice of any religion. These two mandates, known respectively as the "establishment" and "free exercise" clauses, impose a very narrow road down which the government must tread. Because public schools are funded by tax dollars, they can be viewed as an arm of the state. They must, therefore, be careful not to take any action that might be viewed as promoting particular religious beliefs or inhibiting the practice of any. The subject of the rights of children to engage in, or be free of, religious influences in the public schools is one of the most litigated and complicated areas of the law.

Although the rules regarding school prayer are far from clear, the following rules generally apply. The administration and teaching staff of public schools may not take any actions that even appear to be sponsoring religious activities in the school. Clearly, requiring students to recite prayers in school is a violation of this policy. This was the holding of the first Supreme Court case to examine the issue in 1962. *[Engel v. Vitale]* Since that time, the courts have invalidated school policies permitting teachers to offer prayers in school, even when those students who object are excused from attending. Teachers must keep their religious views to themselves, lest their very position of authority imply to the students that the teachers' views are necessarily the "correct" ones. Thus, teachers may not even speak privately to students during breaks in instruction in order to discuss their own religious views. Teachers have no right of free speech that outweighs their obligation to refrain from any display of religious preference while on school grounds during school hours. Teachers instead have a duty to stick to the curriculum chosen by the school authorities in their districts. In one case, a teacher was forbidden to read the Bible silently to himself at his desk during breaks, because this action could be interpreted by students as sanctioning the Christian religion over others. A period of silent meditation sponsored by the school is also impermissible, if students are made to believe that they should engage in prayer during that time.

Schools may not teach courses that espouse a religious doctrine, even if attendance at such courses is strictly voluntary. However, schools may teach courses about religion, if the material is presented in an objective fashion intended to foster an understanding of the role of religion in cultural perspective, and provided they are presented only as part of a balanced secular study. Similarly, school libraries may include religious books and books about religion, so long as they present a reasonable balance of books from various religious traditions.

Religious displays, programs, and pageants in public schools have also been the subject of much litigation. The general rule is that if a reasonable observer would believe that the activity imparts a school-sponsored approval of religion, it is unconstitutional. For example, a large portrait of Jesus Christ on permanent display outside a school principal's office has been deemed impermissible. However, seasonal displays—such as Christmas trees, nativity scenes, and programs of seasonal religious music—are not violations of the Constitution provided they are accompanied by nonsectarian instruction regarding the origins and cultural significance of the events and provided an effort is made to present the traditions of other religions as well in an even-handed manner. The clear intent of these activities must be to enrich the students' understanding of various religious heritages, rather than to indoctrinate students in a particular view. Students who object to the activities must be permitted not to attend. See also **curriculum choices**.

Religious prayers or invocations at school-sponsored sports events or graduation ceremonies may be allowed only if they are initiated entirely by students.

Having considered the many ways in which school authorities are obligated to refrain from any activity that might appear to promote or "establish" a religious preference in the schools, it is also important to remember that school policies may not inhibit the free exercise of religion by their students while they are in school. See also **religious holidays.**

Hence, individual students are always free to pray privately in school. Students must be allowed to discuss religious issues among themselves during periods in which classes are not in session, provided they do so at their own initiative. High school students may also hand out religious tracts and conduct group prayers under the same conditions that *all* students are allowed to pass out other types of literature. Similarly, if the school allows any extracurricular student groups to meet on school property after school hours, it must allow student-formed religious groups to meet also under the same conditions. [See **Equal Access Act.**] However, schools need not allow students to attend voluntary religious classes at the school during school hours, even if voluntary classes that are secular in nature are also allowed at those times.

Schools may always enforce reasonable rules against student activities that distract from the educational mission of the schools, provided they enforce these rules even-handedly against all disruptive behavior, and not just those student activities that are religious in nature.

For the most part, the government cannot interfere with religious instruction in private schools. Yet, the state can insist on certain standards with regard to the teaching of nonreligious material in private schools.

SCHOOL RULES Because public school authorities stand **in loco parentis** to the children in their charge, schools have a recognized broad authority to set rules of conduct necessary to prevent disruption of the educational purpose of the school. These rules are many and varied, but most seek to maintain order, safety, and an atmosphere conducive to learning.

The first important legal challenge by a student to a school rule occurred in 1923 when a certain Miss Pugsley, eighteen years old, defied a rule in her Arkansas high school prohibiting "immodesty in dress." The prohibition included "[t]he wearing of transparent hosiery, low-necked dresses . . . , or the use of face-paint or cosmetics." Caught with talcum powder on her face among other sartorial transgressions, Pugsley was expelled from school. Her challenge to the rule was memorialized in the case of *Pugsley v. Sellmeyer*, which set the standard for the legality of school rules until the U.S. Supreme Court decided *Tinker v. Des Moines Independent Community School District* in 1969.

In its opinion in the Pugsley matter, the Arkansas Supreme Court held that the dress code rule was valid and the school could enforce it. Local school boards must have broad authority to govern education in their districts and courts must not interfere in matters of detail, including school rules, said the court. Admonishing that courts "have more important functions than hearing complaints of disaffected pupils," the *Pugsley* judges held that school rules need only be "reasonable" to be valid. Moreover, courts were not to be concerned with whether school rules were wise or expedient. Only unreasonable, arbitrary, or capricious actions by school officials would be subject to review by the courts. "It will be remembered also that respect for constituted authority, and obedience thereto, is an essential lesson to qualify one for the duties of citizenship, and that the schoolroom is an appropriate place to teach that lesson," said the court.

The court then attempted to define just what type of school rules would be "unreasonable, arbitrary, and capricious" and, hence, vulnerable to challenge. According to the Pugsley court, school rules would be found invalid only if they: (1) resulted in oppression or humiliation of a student; (2) required an expenditure of time or money in order to comply; or (3) required the student to take affirmative actions to comply (rather than merely to refrain from certain conduct). Moreover, even reasonable rules would be invalidated if they were enforced in an arbitrary or discriminatory way. In Pugsley's case, the rule against "immodest dressing" did not result in any humiliation, did not require time or money to comply with, and did not require that Pugsley take any affirmative steps. It was therefore proper.

Under the "Pugsley principles," as these standards became known, the student challenging a school rule had the burden of proof to show that the rule should be struck down. The school board need not even advance any reasons in favor of the rule.

For forty-six years the "Pugsley principles" were followed by courts hearing challenges to school rules. The Supreme Court decision in *Tinker v. Des Moines Independent Community School District* in 1969 changed this somewhat. Under the *Tinker* standard, school rules that affect a student's protected constitutional right to freedom of speech can be justified only if they are absolutely necessary to prevent conduct that "interferes materially and substantially" with the educational mission and operation of the school. Moreover, the burden of proving that a rule is necessary, and thus valid, has been shifted in these instances to the school board. This is a considerably higher threshold that must be met before school rules affecting student expression are permissible.

In 1985, the Supreme Court spoke again in regard to school rules affecting children's right to privacy while in school in the case of *New Jersey v.*

T. L. O. In that case, a majority of the justices allowed a slightly lower standard than that enunciated in *Tinker* to determine whether searches of students' property on school grounds were permissible. Under *T. L. O.*, school officials can promulgate rules allowing them to search students or their property upon a "reasonable suspicion" that they will find evidence of violations of other school rules or illegal conduct. Lower federal courts have since held that it is permissible for schools to restrict students' privacy still further if they notify the students in advance that their lockers, desks, and other school property used for storing students' things are subject to searches. However, students' personal effects, such as backpacks, purses, wallets, pockets, and sport bags are still subject to the "reasonable suspicion" rule of *T .L. O.*

School rules that do not affect the constitutional rights of freedom of speech and freedom from unreasonable searches and seizures are still basically subject to the Pugsley principles. Of course, it can be argued that nearly all "behavior" is expressive, and must be protected. The twenty-first century will undoubtedly see a number of challenges to school rules alleging that the student conduct involved was the students' attempt to "express" themselves. However, schools can at least take comfort in the fact that government authorities, including schools, have always been permitted to restrict the exercise of constitutional rights, including freedom of speech, to reasonable times, places, and manners of expression. Thus, even with the expansion of students' rights in the last three decades, the sum effect is still to leave the vast majority of school rules soundly in place.

For example, schools are within their authority to forbid on their premises all student activities that would be illegal if conducted elsewhere. Moreover, they can ban the possession of weapons, including guns, on school property. (A student challenge to these rules based on the constitutional right of citizens to bear arms found in the Second Amendment is unlikely to be successful!) In addition, drugs, alcohol, and cigarettes can be kept off school property. Roughhousing, vandalism (including graffiti), damaging property, use of obscene or insulting language or epithets, and fighting all may be proscribed. During class periods, teachers may enforce rules against talking, making noise, or engaging in disruptive behavior. Rules against public displays of affection and **dress codes** are also common and usually legal. Schools may also establish attendance standards and discipline students who fail to show up.

It may seem to go without saying that schools are entitled to make and enforce these basic rules for civilized behavior, were it not for the amazing fact that somewhere, sometime, a student (or a parent) has sued a school district for enforcing such minimal standards of decency. The following is a list of student activities that courts have found school authorities justified in cracking down on: using a "stun gun" on a fellow student, having sexual intercourse with another student on school property, phoning in bomb scares, setting off false fire alarms, assaulting teachers, using obscene language to refer to teachers in their presence, using drugs on school property, fighting, coming to school drunk, setting fires, stealing school property.

Occasionally, courts do find that school rules are arbitrary, discriminatory, or impinge on basic rights possessed by the students. For example, behavior of students off school premises is usually not grounds for school discipline. A court found that a school was not justified in disciplining a student who made an obscene gesture at a teacher when both were off school property and after school hours. Likewise, rules that prohibit students from expressing themselves in a civil manner during times and in places on school grounds that do not disrupt classroom work have been invalidated as impinging on students' First Amendment rights. Ultrasevere rules on hair length or dress have also been found to be arbitrary by courts, because they do not really advance school order and discipline in any important way.

Sanctions that schools may impose to enforce valid rules are necessarily flexible. Generally, they involve denying privileges to students—from participating in recess to graduating. Participation in sports or extracurricular activities sponsored by the school, membership in school honorary societies, and entitlement to a certain grade advancement can all be withheld from students who break school rules. In addition, teachers can assign extra work or temporary detention to miscreants. **Corporal punishment** has specifically been held not to be unconstitutional when used on public school students. See also **Ingraham v. Wright**. Suspension and **expulsion** are also possible punishments, as is a transfer to another school. When disciplinary sanctions involve suspension or expulsion, special procedures to ensure **due process of law** may be required.

SCHOOL SAFETY It is settled that children are entitled to attend school under reasonably safe conditions. School facilities must be well maintained, sanitary, well lighted, and free from hidden dangers, such as slippery steps or defective playground equipment. The remedy for violations of these requirements is problematic, however. In many states, agencies of the government have what is known as "sovereign immunity," which means they cannot be sued for breach of their official duties. Therefore, children who suffer harm at school—an agency of state government—may be left without compensation in states with sovereign immunity. In these states, an injured child may have to sue an individual teacher or school official instead. In order to recover in such a case, the child must show that the teacher's (or official's) conduct caused his or her injury *and* that the conduct was not part of the teacher's official job duties. If the teacher's exercise of his or her official duties caused the injury, the teacher also has immunity from lawsuits as an agent of the government.

Many states have abolished the doctrine of sovereign immunity as it relates to public schools. In these states, students who are injured at school as a result of the school's negligence may sue the school or school district directly. Such lawsuits are civil in nature and depend on a state's tort laws. (A tort is a private wrong for which money damages may be awarded in a court of law.) Over the years, there have been many such lawsuits alleging improper supervision or unsafe physical conditions and equipment in schools. Many of these lawsuits concerned injuries caused to students participating in extracurricular sports. In addition to such private lawsuits, at least one court has ruled that students may be exempted from **compulsory attendance laws** if the school to which they are assigned is demonstrably unsafe.

It is clear that schools must take steps to protect their students. From this premise, two major legal issues dominate discussions of public school safety: how far *may* a school go and how far *must* a school go to ensure the safety of students?

The issue of how far a school *may* go in protecting its students concerns the competing constitutional rights of the students, such as the right to be free of unreasonable searches and seizures, the right to free expression, and the right to associate with people of one's choice. In the late twentieth century, schools all over the country have been forced to take drastic steps to keep their students safe—some of which raise constitutional questions. For example, schools have resorted to banning the wearing of gang insignia and colors, even when this means that students may not wear sweatshirts with the logos of popular universities because they have somehow acquired a "secondary" meaning in the world of gang warfare. Schools have resorted to searching lockers, testing for drugs, using metal detectors, and other measures that clearly restrict students' freedom of action. See, for example, **dress codes, school rules,** and **search and seizure.**

The issue of how far a school *must* go to protect the safety of its students is of more recent origin. With the rise of student violence directed at fellow students, some parents have demanded that schools take more responsibility for student misbehavior. Naturally, schools must enforce rules to keep order and discipline in schools, but they are placed in a difficult position. If they crack down too hard on individual freedoms, they run the risk of violating the students' constitutional rights. If they do too little, they may also be accused of violating students' constitutional rights. Parents have alleged that, because students are required to attend school, the schools have a "special relationship" with the students that requires the schools to virtually guarantee the students' safety as an aspect of constitutional law. So far, courts have resisted this argument [see *DeShaney v. Winnebago County Department of Social Services*]. Students are not like the inmates of prisons or mental institutions who are helpless to go elsewhere if their environment is unsafe. Rather, students may change schools if they wish. Moreover, students have access to the outside community, where their complaints of danger in the schools can be more readily heard and remedied. Nevertheless, this issue is likely to arise again in the coming century.

SEARCH AND SEIZURE The Fourth Amendment to the U.S. Constitution protects citizens against "unreasonable searches and seizures." With the exception of searches conducted at school, children are entitled to the same protections as adults in this regard.

Generally, the police may search any person, or his or her property, only after obtaining a search warrant from a judge. The judge may issue a warrant only if there is "probable cause" to believe that the items sought will be found in the places to be searched. "Probable cause" basically means a "very high likelihood." A search warrant must be very specific, describing the person, place, or thing to be searched and the item or items for which the police are looking.

The police may conduct searches and seizures without a warrant only in limited circumstances. First, police may search a suspect, or his or her possessions, after a "hot pursuit" when it is likely that evidence of a crime may be destroyed before a warrant can be obtained. Police may search a person they have just arrested. If there was probable cause to arrest the person, there is probable cause to search him or her. Police also do not need a warrant to "stop and frisk" someone they have probable cause to believe may be carrying concealed weapons that create an immediate danger of harm to them or third persons. The police may also search anyone or any place if they obtain permission to do so from the person to be searched or the owner of the place or thing to be searched. Because children and their property technically are under the control of their parents, it is the law in most states that a parent or guardian may give consent for the police to search a child's room or possessions. In some states, parents may not give consent for a search of a child's most intimate possessions, such as purses, papers, diaries, computer files, or wallets.

A recent development in some communities involves parents giving a "blanket" permission to police to enter their premises when they are away to check up on a juvenile who has been left in charge. Parents who are worried about their teenager throwing wild parties at which underage drinking or other illegal acts may occur when they are gone can arrange to have the police stop by at any hint of trouble. Since the permission is voluntarily given by the property owner, there should be no issue about the legality of the practice. Some question the wisdom of issuing a standing invitation to the police to enter one's home, however.

Evidence that is seized by the police as a result of an unlawful search may not be used in court to prosecute a person. This is known as the "exclusionary rule." It is designed to discourage the police from engaging in illegal searches, because they will not be able to use the fruits of their labors to convict criminals.

The Fourth Amendment protections regarding searches and seizures apply only to those places or things in which a person normally has an "expectation of privacy." Of course, people expect their houses and apartments to be private, as well as their purses, briefcases, suitcases, pockets, clothing, papers, files, diaries, and bodies. The issue of to what extent police may search an automobile that they have stopped for some valid reason has been extensively litigated. Generally, the police may search the passenger compartment of the car, including any bags or containers within reach of the car's occupants. They may also search the glove compartment. The police, however, may not usually search the trunk of the car without a warrant. Nevertheless, the police may impound the entire car and take it away for the time necessary to obtain a warrant to search the trunk.

If, in the normal course of their duties, the police see evidence of a crime in a place they are lawfully entitled to be, they may seize it and use it to prosecute the owner. This is known as the "plain view" doctrine. A person has no expectation of privacy regarding items he or she has left out in plain view. If the police find evidence of a crime unrelated to the crime for which they are conducting their search, they usually must apply for another search warrant in order to seize the new evidence. Of course, if they have reason to believe that the delay in getting a search warrant for the new evidence will enable a criminal to hide or destroy the evidence they have seen, they are justified in seizing it at the moment they see it.

The prohibition against unreasonable searches and seizures applies only to actions of the government. Thus, only government officials or government employees are forbidden from warrantless searches. With regard to juveniles, this raises several issues. First, the Fourth Amendment does not restrain parents, guardians, siblings, friends, or any other people from searching a minor's private possessions and turning in evidence of crimes they find to the police. Searches like these may subject the searcher to civil liability for trespass or invasion of privacy, but they do not violate the Constitution. Evidence seized in this way may be used in a criminal or delinquency proceeding.

Second, the issue of whether school employees are government employees who must abide by the Fourth Amendment in dealing with students has been very important in recent years. A few courts have held that school personnel are not agents of the government and therefore, the Fourth Amendment does not apply to their actions. Under this view, teachers and other school personnel may conduct searches of students and their possessions unrestrained by the Constitution. However, most courts concede that school employees, at least public school employees, are agents of the government because they are paid from public tax monies. Thus, the power of school officials with respect to searching their students is not unlimited. At the same time, the law recognizes that schools are engaged in the vital task of educating the young, and must be able to maintain safety, order, and discipline among the students. Therefore, the rule is that school personnel may search the papers, possessions, and person of a student when they have a "reasonable suspicion" that the student has broken the law or a school rule and that evidence of the misconduct will be found in the place to be searched. The school may also require individual students to take drug tests when they have a reasonable suspicion that the student has been using drugs. The "reasonable suspicion" that must exist before school offi-cials may search a student is less stringent than the "probable cause" the police must have in situations outside school. [See *New Jersey v. T. L. O.*] One exception to this looser standard for a valid search is when school officials conduct a search on the request of the police. If the school officials did not have reason to suspect any evidence of a crime themselves, the higher standard for police searches—probable cause—must exist before the school officials may search at the request of the police.

Normally, schools may not conduct broad searches of all of the students in order to find evidence of wrongdoing by some of them. The reasonable suspicion necessary for a school to conduct a search must be focused on a particular student or small number of identified students. This means, for example, that a school may not conduct across-the-board drug tests of all of the students. An exception exists for extracurricular activities. The school may require students who wish to engage in these activities to take quali-fying drug tests.

Some schools feel that the need to keep a safe and disciplined environ-ment requires them to conduct sweep searches. These schools have reserved the right to search school property used by students at all times. In order to avoid misunderstandings about privacy at school, many schools have re-sorted to a broad notification to students on the first day of every school year that the school reserves the right to search students' lockers and other storage areas at the school. This notice negates any expectation of privacy the students might have with regard to storage spaces owned by the school. However, the personal effects of students are still subject to an expectation of privacy while on school grounds.

As schools have become more dangerous places in the last years of the twentieth century, the rule that schools may not subject the entire student body to routine searches is changing. For example, many schools now have metal detectors at their doors that subject all who enter to a search of their person and property, with or without suspicion. Although this is clearly a "search," courts have held that it does not violate Fourth Amendment rights in most cases. Schools arguably have an affirmative duty to keep their stu-dents safe from violence perpetrated by other students, or outsiders who come onto school property. In order to discharge this duty, the use of metal detectors to detect weapons is usually seen as a reasonable precaution that does not impose on the privacy rights of students unduly. After all, it is calculated to discover large metal objects, few of which students have any legitimate reason to bring to school, especially not weapons. Small, intimate items are not discovered by metal detectors.

The protections of the Fourth Amendment are designed to keep citizens safe from intrusive prying by the government and from the seizure of their private effects. Oddly, in the final years of the century, some parents and citizens are clamoring for the schools to take on the affirmative duty of protecting their children. There is some support for the idea in the Constitution. The Supreme Court has held that where the government takes charge of citizens and deprives them of the means to protect themselves, such as when a person is incarcerated in prison or a mental institution, the government then takes on the affirmative duty to protect them. Some have argued that this is true of the public schools. Generally, courts have rejected this argument, because students are free to leave the schools and go to another school, unlike inmates in prison or mental hospitals. However, if the trend toward violence in the schools continues, it is possible that the courts will rethink their position on this matter.

SEXUAL ABUSE Any forced sexual contact of a child by an adult who is the child's caretaker or stands **in loco parentis** to the child. Under some circumstances, an older child who molests a younger one in his or her care may be charged with sexual abuse. Generally, "sexual abuse" is defined as touching or fondling a child's genitals, or forcing the child to touch the adult's genitals. Oral sex and the penetration, or attempted penetration, of the child's vagina or anus are sexual abuse. In addition, forcing a child to look at the adult's genitals or to disrobe and expose himself or herself is also sexual abuse. Adults who force children to have sexual contact with each other may also be committing sexual abuse. An adult who has consensual sexual relations with a minor generally has not committed sexual abuse (unless the child is very young) but may be charged with **statutory rape.**

In the 1990s, a movement is afoot to amend the definition of "child abuse" under state laws to include the sexual exploitation of children. This would provide a potent new weapon against child pornographers, who most often are not the caregivers of the children they exploit. Under traditional child abuse laws, only a parent or other caretaker can be charged with child abuse for engaging in sexual exploitation of the child. See also **child pornography; Sexual Exploitation Act.**

SEXUAL ACTIVITY   It is well settled that states may outlaw sexual activity between older individuals and young people under a specified age. [See **statutory rape.**] However, it is unclear whether young people under the age of majority have a constitutional right to engage in consensual sexual activity with each other.

Part of the uncertainty in this area arises because the law is still unsettled regarding how far states may go in regulating the sexual activity of adults. Many states have old statutes on the books that outlaw homosexual acts or heterosexual intercourse between people who are not married to each other, even if the activity is consensual and occurs solely within the privacy of the participants' homes. These laws are sometimes called "antifornication" statutes. Because of strong statements by the Supreme Court in the latter half of the twentieth century regarding an individual's entitlement to privacy in matters involving reproduction, procreation, and reproductive health, many Court watchers believe that these types of state statutes would be found unconstitutional if challenged. However, a 1986 ruling by the Court that let stand a Georgia statute making consensual homosexual acts in the privacy of one's home a crime [*Bowers v. Hardwick*] makes it difficult to tell how the Court of the twenty-first century may rule. One thing is fairly certain, though: if a law regulating adult sexual conduct is constitutional, it will also be constitutional when applied to teenagers.

Even assuming that the Supreme Court will find antifornication laws unconstitutional in the future because they infringe on adult individuals' rights to privacy in sexual matters, it does not follow that such laws directed specifically at minors will also be found unconstitutional. An assumption that children need additional protection from the consequences of their immature decisions, as well as an interest in reducing teen pregnancy rates, may supply the justification for upholding these laws. As of the 1990s, eleven states have laws making sex between consenting teenagers a delinquent act for which the participants may be prosecuted. These states are Arizona, Florida, Illinois, Kansas, Massachusetts, Michigan, Montana, New Hampshire, Tennessee, Utah, and Vermont.

Legal scholars who foresee the Supreme Court striking down laws prohibiting consensual sex between teenagers base their reasoning on the fact that the Court has recognized a teenager's right to privacy in making decisions regarding procreation. [*Carey v. Population Services International* (1977)] Thus, they reason that if a teenager has a right to decide to have a child, it follows that he or she must certainly have a right to engage in sexual intercourse. Other observers do not agree that the right to have sex follows from a right to decide whether to have a child. The latter right may simply be a recognition that if a young female "gets into trouble" after breaking a law against underage sexual activity, she should at that point have the right to decide the course of the pregnancy. As of the 1990s, Court watchers predict that a small majority of Supreme Court justices would vote to uphold laws prohibiting teenage sexual activity if such a challenge reached them.

Even if antifornication laws are upheld in the abstract, teenagers who are prosecuted under them may attack the validity of the laws if they are not uniformly enforced. Studies have shown that young unmarried females are much more likely to be the targets of prosecution for "fornication" than are young males. A young female might therefore legitimately argue that the law was a violation of her right to **equal protection** under the Constitution.

SEXUAL EXPLOITATION ACT A federal law, passed in 1977 and amended numerous times, that prohibits the production, transportation, sale, or possession of **child pornography.** Specifically, the law makes it a federal offense to use anyone under the age of eighteen as a model or actor for visual depictions of sexual conduct, or in sexually suggestive poses, if the material will be transported across state lines. It is illegal to transport (including via computer modem), mail, sell, reproduce, or even possess such materials in the privacy of one's own home. The "selling" or "buying" of children to be used in the production of child pornography is also a federal offense. Moreover, parents, **guardian**s, and anyone else with custody or control of a child violates federal law if he or she knowingly permits the child to engage in sexually explicit acts for the purpose of producing child pornography. It is not necessary to prove that the producer, transporter, or possessor of the pornographic material actually knew that the people depicted in it were under the age of eighteen, as the fact that any model was underage is sufficient for conviction.

Unfortunately, it is often difficult to police the act because the young people depicted in such materials are unknown, frequently foreign, and of uncertain ages. Therefore, the act also requires that persons who produce visual material depicting sexually explicit conduct ascertain the true identities and ages of the actors who model for them. The producer must keep a record of this information and make it available for inspection by federal officials.

Violators of various provisions of the act are subject to fines and imprisonment, which may include life imprisonment in the case of child selling or buying.

SINGLE-SEX SCHOOLS Children in the public schools are entitled to be free of discrimination based on their gender. In general, this means that there can be no single-sex public schools. In the last decade of the twentieth century, there has been renewed interest in single-sex schools because of claims that they tend to focus students' attention more on education and less on social status. Proponents of single-sex schools also say that they promote a sense of team endeavor among boys and give girls an opportunity to participate more in class discussions in which they are allegedly ignored and intimidated when boys are present. The validity of these claims has not been proved. Nevertheless, in a few school districts, single-sex programs have been instituted. In one case, a federal court found that separate schools for academically gifted boys and girls in Boston violated the Constitution. Because the boys' program was much larger than the girls', the admissions criteria for the girls' program was much stricter, thereby cutting out many more female applicants than males. The court held that admissions criteria must be the same for both sexes.

Another federal court found that single-sex high schools for academically gifted students are not inherently unequal and, hence, discriminatory, when enrollment is voluntary, coeducational public schools exist, and the opportunities provided in each school are the same. This court accepted the argument that single-sex schools aid students in concentrating and found, therefore, that there was a public interest in creating these types of schools that outweighed students' interests in having all schools coeducational.

The Supreme Court has not yet ruled on whether single-sex schools are automatically unconstitutional when schools exist for each gender and the programs in them are essentially the same. However, it is quite clear that a state may not run a single-sex school for one gender only.

Private schools are generally exempt from constitutional requirements for equal protection, unless they accept funding from government sources. Private schools that segregate the sexes for religious reasons have added protection for their policies because of the First Amendment right to the free practice of religion.

SPEEDY TRIAL In most states, minors taken into custody for delinquent acts are entitled to a speedy resolution of the charges against them—exactly the same as for adults charged with crimes. However, a minority of states hold to the view that juvenile delinquency adjudications are not criminal proceedings, but civil proceedings. Because there is no constitutional right for the speedy adjudication of civil matters, a juvenile charged with delinquent acts in those states has no right to a speedy trial.

There are two components to a delinquency proceeding that are subject to the speed requirement: first comes the **preliminary hearing.** During this phase, the accused minor is brought before a judge or magistrate and the charges against him or her are formally entered. This is the official start of a delinquency proceeding. The second part of the requirement concerns the trial itself. That is the procedure during which evidence is taken and weighed and the court decides the merit of the charges. Although the right to a speedy trial applies to both procedures, what is considered speedy may vary for each, particularly depending on whether the accused minor is being held in detention. Generally, all procedures must be expedited whenever an accused is being held in custody, because the deprivation of liberty is considered an extremely great penalty to pay—especially if the accused is found not guilty.

Most states' laws set a particular number of days within which an accused juvenile must be formally charged or brought to trial. Usually, the official charging must occur within a few days of the juvenile's arrest at the most, even if he or she has been released into the custody of parents. The period within which the actual trial must take place varies greatly, from ten days in some states for juveniles who are being held in custody to six months or longer if the juvenile is not in custody. A few states specify that the statute of limitations for trying an adult for the same behavior with which a minor is charged will apply to the minor's case as well. The trial must take place within that period. In some states, this can be three years or more.

Some states' laws merely provide that trial of a juvenile must take place within a "reasonable" amount of time, leaving it up to a trial judge to determine whether the particular circumstances of a case justify a delay or violate the minor's constitutional rights.

STANFORD V. KENTUCKY   Following on the heels of *Thompson v. Oklahoma* in 1988, this case, decided one year later, represents the Supreme Court's further refinement of the Eighth Amendment rights of juveniles. In *Thompson*, the Court decided that the constitutional prohibition on "cruel and unusual punishment" precludes the execution of persons for crimes they committed while under the age of sixteen. In *Stanford*, the Court held that the Eighth Amendment does *not* prohibit execution for crimes committed by persons between the ages of sixteen and eighteen.

Two separate appeals from death sentences were consolidated in *Stanford*. In each case, a youth of sixteen or seventeen had committed a brutal murder accompanied by aggravating circumstances. Both defendants were repeat offenders. One had previously tried to kill his own mother with insecticide placed in capsules of pain relievers. Each defendant had shown no remorse for the crimes, expressing matter-of-fact justifications or even glee at the killings. They had been sentenced to death by juries in state courts. Their appeals, based on the Eighth Amendment's ban on "cruel and unusual punishment" reached the Supreme Court.

Predictably, the same four justices who had dissented from the holding in *Thompson* stuck to their belief that the Constitution was not violated by sentencing persons who commit murder while minors to death. Rejecting the argument that minors have diminished culpability because of their immature judgment, Justice Scalia writing for the majority noted that there is no reason that someone under the age of eighteen cannot be responsible for a murder: "[I]t is absurd to think that one must be mature enough to drive carefully, to drink responsibly, or to vote intelligently in order to be mature enough to understand that murdering another human being is profoundly wrong and to conform one's conduct to that most minimal of all civilized standards."

The fifth justice voting to uphold the death sentences in *Stanford* was Justice O'Connor, who had cast the deciding vote against the death penalty in *Thompson*. O'Connor's switch was based on her observation that every state with a minimum age below which murderers may not be punished by execution sets that minimum age at sixteen. Therefore, she reasoned, there is no national consensus that execution for crimes committed at age seventeen or eighteen is cruel or unusual.

The dissenters in *Stanford*, Justices Stevens, Brennan, Marshall, and Blackmun, had been in the majority in *Thompson*. Their arguments against execution for crimes committed by persons between sixteen and eighteen years old were the same as in the earlier case: diminished culpability because of immature judgment.

STATUS OFFENSE   An activity that is illegal when engaged in by a minor, but not when done by an adult. Typical status offenses are truancy from school, violating curfew ordinances, running away from home, or habitually refusing to obey one's parents. Status offense laws are very old and intended to keep youth on the path of virtue by curbing unruly behavior and reinforcing parental authority.

A status offense is not a crime. Nevertheless, commission of a status offense can land the offender in juvenile court, where he or she may be ordered to undergo counseling, submit to an officially appointed guardian, or even be committed to a reformatory or detention facility. A juvenile court record is generated that can be the basis for more severe penalties if the minor engages in illegal behavior in the future.

Conduct forbidden by status offense laws is generally of a type traditionally viewed as unwholesome and likely to corrupt the morals of the young. Typical statutes prohibit young people from "living in circumstances of manifest danger of falling into habits of vice or immorality"; from "being in danger of leading an idle, dissolute, lewd, or immoral life"; from "associating with immoral, vagrant, vicious, criminal, notorious persons"; from being "morally depraved," "unruly," and "incorrigible"; or simply from being "ungovernable." Statutes that are as broadly worded as these are vulnerable to constitutional challenges for being too vague to give young people a clear warning about what is actually forbidden. Exactly what is "morally depraved" behavior, for example?

Other typical status offense statutes are very specific and usually stand up to objections on constitutional grounds. Laws that forbid truancy from school, set certain hours during which young people are not to be on the street [see **curfew**], or forbid minors from entering bars and other places from which they may lawfully be excluded are all usually clear enough to withstand challenges for vagueness. Similarly, laws making it a status offense for an underage minor to attempt to marry without parental consent are not unconstitutionally vague [see **marriage rights**]. In one case, it was held that a law prohibiting minors from being "beyond the power and control of [their] parents" was clear enough to survive a constitutional challenge. Ostensibly, children know when they are not heeding their parents' commands.

Even when status offenses are clearly defined, the way in which they are enforced can lead to constitutional problems. In some jurisdictions, there is a history of sex discrimination in the state's choice of whom to prosecute. Frequently, young women are the target of prosecutions, while young men have been allowed to violate the status offense laws with little consequence. If proved, such discrimination may result in the law's invalidity for denying females **equal protection** under the law.

A youth who has been charged with a status offense must generally appear before a juvenile court judge. If he or she is not charged with any more serious criminal offense in addition to the status offense, the court has various options:

1. The judge may dismiss the case after an informal agreement has been reached that the child will improve his or her behavior in the future.

2. The judge may decide that the child's problems are better addressed by another arm of the state's child welfare agency and refer the case there. Typically, that agency will enroll the youth in some type of counseling or psychotherapy.

3. The judge may decide that the real problem in the child's life is an abusive home situation. In that case, the court may order an investigation of the child's parents to determine whether **child abuse** or **neglect** charges against the parent are in order. Even without a finding of abuse, the court may change the child's custody from one parent to another or may appoint an unrelated guardian for him or her. Other options include placement in a foster or group home away from the child's present troubled home. Occasionally, a court may find the minor to be emancipated, or partly emancipated, and therefore legally beyond the parents' control. [See **emancipation.**] Placing the offending youth in a different living situation is frequently the best solution, even though it means that the child has been found "guilty" of the offense charged. Troubled teenagers may be better behaved away from parents with whom a dynamic of clashing wills is perpetuated. Ironically, parents are often the ones who file status offense charges against their own children in an effort to regain control over them, or sometimes in order to legally get them out of their homes.

4. If the youth's behavior has been particularly egregious, the judge may sentence him or her to attend a state reform school or even be institutionalized in such a place for periods of time ranging from a few weeks to years. This option is usually resorted to only on a second or third offense, and, in some states, only if the child has also been charged with activity that would be considered criminal if he or she were an adult. [See **juvenile delinquent.**] This last option has been greatly

criticized for not being in the minor's best interests. Critics claim that time spent with hardened juvenile delinquents may encourage delinquent conduct.

The federal government frowns on reform institutions as a place for youthful status offenders. If a state receives federal funding through its juvenile justice and delinquency prevention program, it may not send status offenders to secure detention. Some states have specialized institutions just for status offenders. The option of institutionalization, however, is less accepted for status offenders in the last decade of the twentieth century.

It is not clear whether a minor has a right to be represented by an attorney in a status offense proceeding. Arguably, any time a person's (including a minor's) personal liberty is at stake, he or she should have the opportunity for counsel by a legal professional. Another reason it is important to provide a juvenile accused of a status offense with legal representation is the possibility that the child's interests may differ from those of his or her parents. In a large percentage of status offense cases, the juvenile's parents were the ones who filed the complaint about their child's behavior. Therefore, it would seem naive to assume automatically that the child's legal representation in the status offense case could safely be left in the hands of the child's parents to arrange.

In recent years, criticism has been directed at the entire system of status offenses because of its focus on the juvenile's behavior alone, rather than on the dynamics of his or her family. Many professionals who work with children believe that habitual problematic behavior of the type proscribed by status offense laws is an indication that the entire family is dysfunctional. In fact, public officials confronted with status offense complaints against minors frequently investigate whether child abuse of some type may be at the root of the child's misbehavior. Some states have therefore shifted away from handling such cases by punishing the child. Rather, they work with the entire family to make it functional. A few states, such as Florida, have abolished the status offense entirely and make the child welfare agency responsible for handling the child. Usually this involves counseling of some sort that can include the entire family.

STATUTE OF LIMITATIONS A law that sets a time limit for initiating lawsuits. Statutes of limitation are important because they serve to set a finite time beyond which a person will not be liable to compensate another for wrongfully caused harm, thereby instilling some certainty in the unpredictable affairs of life. Because children are considered incapable of protecting their own legal interests, most states defer the running of the limitations period for children until the child reaches the age of **majority.** This special consideration is believed necessary to ensure that injured parties are not deprived of their chance to recover just compensation for wrongful acts merely because they were not old enough to understand their rights at the time the injury occurred. On the other hand, a child does not need to wait until the age of majority to initiate a lawsuit. Provided he or she is represented by an adult, a child may sue or be sued just as any other citizen. See also **guardian ad litem.**

The deferral of the running of the period of time set in a statute of limitations is called tolling. Suppose a statute of limitations allows a person to bring a lawsuit two years following an injury caused by someone else's negligence. If a child was injured at age ten, the statute of limitations would not begin to run until the child reached majority at eighteen. He or she would have two more years, or up to his or her twentieth birthday, in order to file a lawsuit to recover for the injury.

The tolling of a statute of limitations for children does not apply for some types of lawsuits. Generally, medical malpractice suits must be initiated within the normal limitations period, even if the plaintiff is a child. Some states have extended the limitations period for medical malpractice claims involving children to allow extra time for them to file suit, but not necessarily until they have attained majority. For example, New York allows children ten years following negligent medical treatment to file a medical malpractice suit. For adults in New York this period is two and one-half years. However, this period may still be within the child's minority depending on how old the child was at the time of injury. Lawsuits against state and federal government agencies are also an exception to the tolling provisions for children. These types of lawsuits must be initiated within the normal limitations period, regardless of the age of the plaintiff.

Paternity actions present a problem for states seeking to set reasonable statutes of limitations. Generally, if the action is brought by an illegitimate child's mother or a child welfare agency, the normal limitations period applies. In most states, the illegitimate child himself or herself will have a longer time to bring a lawsuit to establish paternity. This is in keeping with the Supreme Court's view that illegitimate children should not suffer discrimination that legitimate children do not. If illegitimate children were kept from seeking enforcement of the **support obligation** from their fathers because of an unreasonably short statute of limitations for establishing paternity, such discrimination would exist. Nevertheless, there are a few states that do not allow children to toll the normal statute of limitations on a paternity action. These states reason that it would be unfair to hold a putative father who may not have had any knowledge that he had a child liable to pay support for the child retroactively eighteen years or more after the child was born.

STATUTORY RAPE The criminal offense of having sexual intercourse with a person who is under a certain age. Statutory rape laws have been on the books in most states from their earliest days. The rationale behind them is that young people are incapable of understanding the full significance and consequences of certain acts in which they might willingly engage—sexual intercourse chief among them. Because full understanding of the act is lacking, the theory is that there can be no true "consent" to it in the sight of the law. Therefore, in order to protect young persons from their own inexperience, statutory rape laws punish older individuals who have sex with a person under a specific age, regardless of whether the younger person agreed to the act. Statutory rape is a felony, just as is rape.

Most statutory rape laws set the age under which sex with a minor is a felony at sixteen, although a few states go as low as twelve and others as high as eighteen. Traditionally, statutory rape laws applied only to adult men who engaged in sex with young females. Today, most of these laws are gender neutral, applying equally to men and women who seduce underage sexual partners. However, a recent Supreme Court ruling upheld laws that penalize men only, finding that it was not impermissible gender discrimination. In *Michael M. v. Superior Court* (1981), the Court found that there were compelling reasons for treating men and women differently with regard to statutory rape: (1) the state interest in preventing teenage pregnancies was furthered by targeting the older male seducers of underage females for prosecution; (2) males and females are not in similar circumstances with respect to the risks of having sexual intercourse, because only women can become pregnant; and (3) targeting only males for prosecution tends to equalize deterrence to engaging in unwed sexual intercourse as to both sexes, the risk of pregnancy already being a deterrent to young females but not to males. A minority of Supreme Court justices dissented from this holding. They would have found the law targeting only males for prosecution of statutory rape to be unconstitutional because it discriminated against men.

In some states, the prosecution of statutory rape is directed at adults only. Some other states' laws provide that the perpetrator of a seduction must be a certain number of years older than the victim before statutory rape has been committed. In these states, a minor may be guilty of statutory rape by seducing another minor who is younger by a certain number of years. Minors who engage in sex with other minors of the same or close age may be guilty of lesser criminal offenses, depending on the state's law, but they will not be guilty of statutory rape. See also **age of consent; sexual activity.**

STEPPARENT The spouse of the **biological parent** of a child, who is not himself or herself so related to the child. Generally, stepparents have no legal rights or duties with respect to their stepchildren. However, a few jurisdictions do place a statutorily imposed obligation to support minor children on any stepparent standing **in loco parentis** to the child. In addition, stepparents can formally agree to accept some parental responsibilities delegated to them by their spouse, the biological parent. The stepparent will be bound by any duties he or she has voluntarily assumed as well as those imposed on him or her by law in a few states. Concomitantly, the stepparent will also enjoy rights of control over the child that are necessary to fulfill these duties.

The first way a stepparent may acquire parental rights over a stepchild is to adopt him or her. In this case, the stepparent becomes an **adoptive parent** and will enjoy full **parental rights** and duties consistent with that status.

Short of **adoption,** a stepparent may accept responsibilities for the stepchild's welfare by a separate agreement in which he or she agrees to provide financial support of a particular type for the child. For example, the stepparent may agree to pay for the child's education. Such agreements do not necessarily relieve the child's biological parents of their duty to support the child. Additionally, the biological parent with custody of the child (usually the spouse of the stepparent) may officially delegate some of his or her authority to make decisions regarding the child to the stepparent. For example, the biological parent may execute a power of attorney to the stepparent to make important medical decisions for the child in the event the biological parent is not able to do so.

If the stepparent has not officially assumed any responsibility for the child, he or she will still have some authority over the child's activities, which the biological parent delegates in an informal manner. Thus, an informal understanding usually prevails that a stepparent is the authority figure in a household when the custodial biological parent is absent. In the same way that a baby-sitter has responsibility and corresponding authority to see that the children left in his or her care are safe and adequately provided for, a stepparent assumes the authority of a stepchild **in loco parentis.** For example, a stepparent may not sit by and let minor children play with matches and set fire to the house merely because he or she has not assumed any official, legal duties with respect to the children.

When a family composed of a biological parent and a stepparent splits up, the stepparent usually has no right to custody of the child. However, some states will give a stepparent custody if it is in the child's best interests. This may occur when the stepparent and the child have established a close and stable relationship; the biological parent agrees with the arrangement, has died, or has had his or her parental rights terminated; and there are no other close biological relatives who wish to assume responsibility. The child's preference to live with the stepparent may also tip the balance in his or her favor. See also **child custody.**

As with custody, a former stepparent typically has no **visitation rights** with former stepchildren, unless the biological parent agrees to the visits. Recently, however, courts have been granting former stepparents visitation rights with former stepchildren if it can be shown that this is in the best interests of the child.

STUDENT FEES   There is no right under the federal Constitution for children to attend school free of charge. States may offer public education if they please. And, once having decided to offer education through public schools, states must provide it to all children who wish to enroll. All states today do offer tax-funded public education. Most state constitutions require that this schooling—elementary through high school—be offered free of charge to all the state's residents. (Schooling does not have to be offered free of charge to nonresidents [see **residency requirements**].)

This means that any courses needed to graduate from public school must be free, but conflicts occasionally arise as to whether fees may be charged for optional courses offered through the public schools. At least one court has held that any course for which credit is given that may be used toward graduation must be free.

Another issue that arises with some frequency is whether textbooks and supplies used by public school children must always be provided free of charge. Courts have decided both ways. Optional extracurricular programs in public schools may charge fees or require students to supply their own equipment.

Usually, if a student cannot afford the necessary supplies or fees for school courses, the fees are waived. In at least one case in which a school system was challenged for not providing textbooks free of charge, the court held that, because no students were provided books, there was no basis for a charge that the government was discriminating unfairly. This was true, despite the fact that poor students who could not buy the needed books would necessarily receive an education of lower quality than wealthier students who could buy the books. Other courts have decided similar cases differently.

SUPPORT ENFORCEMENT The collection of funds owed by a parent for support of his or her children that are extracted through resort to the legal system. Technically, the **support obligation** is owed to the child, but because children cannot sue in their own names, the parent having legal custody of the child will usually be the one to initiate support enforcement on the child's behalf. A **guardian ad litem,** child welfare agency, or district attorney may also file suit for enforcement of court-ordered child support. A custodial parent who sues to collect arrearages in child support after the child is grown is usually entitled to keep whatever funds are collected as compensation for extra expenses he or she was forced to make to counter the shortfall in support from the noncustodial parent during the child's minority. However, a child who has reached the age of **majority** may initiate support enforcement to collect money to which he or she is presently entitled as part of a parental agreement to support him or her beyond the age of majority.

Normally, child support obligations are enforced through a procedure known as a civil contempt proceeding that is brought in the same court that granted the parents' divorce and issued the initial order for payment of child support. The purpose of the proceeding is to coerce the defaulting parent to pay the sums owed according to the order. To this end, the court has the power to order the nonpaying parent to go to jail until he or she makes the required payments. Challenges to the constitutionality of this power have been made based on the argument that imprisonment for debt has not been legal since debtors' prisons were outlawed in the nineteenth century. However, courts generally hold that imprisonment for failure to support a child is not imprisonment based on a monetary debt, but based on a breach of duty to support one's family. Thus, it is constitutional. After the child reaches the age of majority, the ability of the court to threaten the defaulting parent with jail time disappears. A custodial parent suing to collect arrearages in child support after the child is grown must be content with collection through normal civil judgment means—usually the seizing and selling of the owing parent's property.

A civil contempt proceeding is initiated by the custodial parent's filing a petition with the court. A hearing will be held at which the custodial parent has the burden of proving the existence of an order for support and the noncustodial parent's failure to pay. There is a rebuttable presumption that the noncustodial parent is able to make these payments. The burden of proof then shifts to the owing parent either to pay the money owed or to prove that he or she is financially unable to make the required payments. As civil contempt will be found only if nonpayment is willful and deliberate, a showing of insolvency will usually absolve the owing parent of the support obligation until he or she is again able to pay. However, if the noncustodial parent deliberately became insolvent merely to avoid the support obligation, civil contempt will be found.

Because of poor success with civil contempt proceedings as a means to enforce child support obligations, many states have been experimenting with alternative methods of collection. Some states require parents to post bonds, or pay money into a special account, before they will rule on custody and child support issues. This money is then used to pay support obligations if the noncustodial parent defaults. Alternatively, some states authorize family courts to place liens on the property of the owing parent, and to sell the property and pay support from the proceeds if that parent defaults. Another method of collecting support that has achieved some success in the last years of the twentieth century is the garnishment of the owing parent's wages. A court will order the parent's employer to withhold a certain percentage of the parent's wage and pay it to the custodial parent for support of the child. State laws usually forbid employers from firing a worker whose wages are garnished in this way in order to save the trouble and expense of the special accounting involved, or to punish what the employer may see as a moral lapse on the employee's part. In some states, a parent owing child support may voluntarily direct his or her employer to withhold the required amount monthly and pay it to the other parent for child support. This is known as a voluntary assignment of wages. Other state laws authorize the seizure of the owing parent's tax refunds, pension or retirement funds, unemployment compensation, life insurance payments, or other entitlements in order to satisfy his or her support obligation.

With the crisis in nonsupport of the nation's children, some states are taking a creative approach. In New York City, for example, a proposal has been made to allow the city to sell several hundred million dollars of bonds that would be backed by the assets of deadbeat parents. The city would use the proceeds of the bond sales to pay support to the entitled children, then the city would use every legal means to seize the assets of parents who did not pay the required support. Investors in the bonds would be paid interest from the sale of these seized assets. [*The Wall Street Journal*, 12 June 1996, C1]

If the state legal system is unable to force an owing parent to pay child support, the custodial parent has the last resort of turning to private collection agencies for help. This is a growing business in the 1990s, as arrearages on child support payments are at an all-time high. This method of collecting the funds is the least attractive to the custodial parent, since such private collection agencies can keep up to 30 percent of whatever they collect from a "deadbeat" parent. But sometimes a custodial parent may consider that even the 70 percent remaining is better than nothing.

SUPPORT OBLIGATION The legally enforceable duty of a **biological parent** to provide for the material well-being of his or her children until they attain the age of **majority** or achieve **emancipation,** or until some other legally significant event occurs to absolve the parent from further obligation. For example, an **adoption** usually—although not always—serves to extinguish the support obligation of the adopted children's biological parents and transfer it to the new **adoptive parents**. A court-ordered termination of **parental rights** also ends the obligation to support the children in most states. A man who provides sperm for the conception of a child by a married couple has no support obligation toward that child whatsoever, provided the mother's husband consented to the procedure [see **surrogate parent**].

A support obligation may be imposed on persons who are not the biological parents of a child in a few circumstances. The husband of a woman to whom children have been born during the marriage is presumed to be the biological father of those children and must support them even if he is not the father—unless a **paternity action** proves the identity of the real father. Also, absent a paternity ruling to the contrary, a man who has acknowledged children as his own, by word or deed, is obligated to support them. In a few jurisdictions, a **stepparent** must support minor children with whom he or she lives.

The legal duty to support one's children is a relatively recent phenomenon. Prior to the mid-1800s, a parent's obligation to support his or her children was a moral duty only, and was not enforceable by law. Moreover, this moral duty devolved mostly upon the father—the reason being that children were virtually deemed to be the property of their fathers at the time. (Women were also virtually the property of their husbands, could not own property, and did not usually earn money outside the home. Thus, it was reasonable not to impose a duty to support children on them.) Today, all fifty states and the District of Columbia have statutes imposing legally enforceable obligations on parents to support all their minor children, including illegitimate ones. In most cases, these statutes place the obligation on both mothers and fathers, although a few states still hold that the father has the primary duty of support. The constitutionality of this arrangement is in doubt because of its discriminatory nature.

The obligation to support is basically the duty to nurture, protect, and shelter the children. It includes providing adequate nutrition, clothing, and housing, as well as medical treatment and educational opportunities. These obligations continue throughout the minority of the children, and possibly into adulthood if a child is disabled.

Both parents share these support obligations jointly and equally. This does not mean, however, that each parent must contribute the same amount of money to the family's upkeep. Rather, it means only that the obligation to provide the necessities of life for the children is the same for both parents. Indeed, when the family is intact, the monetary contribution of each parent to the children's welfare is usually not an issue at all, provided the necessities listed above are available to each child. However, when the parents divorce, family courts are left the dilemma of how to translate the support obligation into a purely monetary sum in order to ensure that the custodial and noncustodial parent are contributing equally to the upbringing of their children.

Courts consider numerous factors when assigning a monetary figure for support payments from divorced parents. Pursuant to federal law, all states have promulgated support guidelines, which typically introduce a formula based on the parent's income and the number of children to be supported. However, most state courts retain a great deal of discretion to fashion a support payment tailored to the specific needs of the family. Most courts go beyond mere "survival" sums in making a support determination. Usually, they try to set a sum that will enable the children to enjoy the same standard of living they would have had if the parents had not divorced. Other factors that will be thrown into the mix include the ability of both parents to pay—with reference not only to their present earnings, but also their earning potential and the local job market—the children's special needs, and the relationship of the children with the parents. The custodial parent may not be required to contribute as much monetarily, since courts usually take into account the value of that parent's time spent caring for the children in other ways. In addition to money, courts may require "in kind" payments of support, such as requiring a noncustodial parent to carry the children on his or her health insurance policy.

Divorcing parents may agree among themselves as to the monetary contributions each will make to supporting the children. A court must approve such agreements, or they are considered void. Because the support obligation is owed to the children and not to the other parent, neither parent may bargain away the children's right to support from either. Parents may bind themselves contractually to support their children beyond the age of majority if they wish. Usually, this is done to ensure that a child will have the means to finish college or some type of higher education. For the most part, courts have held that children have no automatic right for parental support through college. Nonetheless, some courts have been known to order support for a child to go to college when the child displays the aptitude for higher education and he or she could reasonably have expected support through college if his or her parents had remained married. The fact that married parents are not required to support their children through college, while a divorced parent may be ordered to do so, has not been held to be unconstitutional discrimination.

Once support obligations have been set by a court, they cannot be changed without the court's further order. Ordinarily, only a major change in circumstances in the family will support a modification of child support obligations, and they generally do not result in lowered payments. For example, a parent's unemployment or change of job to a lower pay scale does not justify a modification of child support payments, but a new job with greater pay may merit an increase in ordered support payments. The fact that one parent has remarried and has new family support obligations also typically will not serve to diminish the amount of support he or she owes to children from a prior marriage. Conversely, the fact that the custodial parent has remarried and is getting some other type of support from his or her new spouse is not a reason to decrease payments of child support from the noncustodial parent. Even the emancipation of one child may not justify a decrease in owed payments for the other children. A change in the children's needs is one reason a modification of support may be ordered. For example, a medical problem may require additional payments. Some support awards include "accelerator clauses" that order payments to increase in step with inflation.

In most cases, the payment of child support is not to be conditioned on observation of visitation rights. The two obligations are considered to be completely separate. Therefore, a noncustodial parent may not cut off support payments because he or she has been thwarted in attempting to exercise visitation rights. In rare cases, courts have terminated support obligations where older children have refused visitation and cut off all contact with the parent owing support.

If a parent falls behind in support payments, the amount in arrears remains due and owing at any time and is not erased by the child's reaching the age of majority. See also **Aid to Families with Dependent Children; criminal nonsupport statute; Parent Locator Service; support enforcement.**

SURROGATE PARENT A man or woman who provides the egg or sperm, or uterus, necessary for the conception and/or birth of a child that is intended to be given for **adoption** by specific known parents. The legal issues surrounding surrogate parenthood are confusing, and the law is in its infancy in this area. Although artificial insemination, in which a woman is inseminated with the sperm of a man who is not her husband, has been in practice for a relatively long period of time, ever newer methods of conception are appearing as science advances. Today, it is possible for conception to take place in a test tube, where donated sperm and eggs may be induced to meet and a child is conceived. The resulting fetus may then be implanted in the mother who donated the egg, or in another woman, who will carry the baby to term. In addition, couples who cannot have their own children may contract with a woman to become pregnant with the husband's sperm and carry the child to term.

A child conceived by a married woman whose husband consents to her impregnation by sperm from another man is the legal, legitimate child of the woman's husband under the laws of all states. The sperm donor, who is the child's biological father, has no parental rights or duties whatsoever. The husband, rather, is considered by the law to have all the rights and duties associated with fatherhood.

Following this rule, a surrogate mother (a woman who conceives through artificial means with the intention of giving up the child to known parents) is the legal, biological mother of the child she bears, and her consenting husband, if she has one, is the legal father of the child. The surrogate cannot be compelled to give up the child, since it is hers under the law. However, some states allow adults to agree by contract that a woman will bear a child in this manner and then give it to the other party for adoption. Most laws require that the agreement be approved by a court before conception of the child. Usually, the prospective adoptive parents agree to pay the expenses, including all medical costs, for the surrogate mother. The law generally prohibits payments of unearmarked funds, because this smacks of "baby selling," which is illegal in all states. If, after the birth of the child, the surrogate mother refuses to give the baby up, this is her right. She may be liable for damages for breach of the adoption contract, and most likely she will be required to pay back all monies she received under the contract. Some states refuse to recognize surrogacy contracts at all. In these situations, not only may the surrogate mother change her mind, but she is not liable for a breach of contract at all.

The situation in which a surrogate mother does not provide the egg for conception of the child but merely provides the uterus in which the fetus develops is newer, rarer, and more complex legally. At least one court has ruled that the biological parents, that is, those who donated the genetic material for the child through a sperm and an egg are the legal parents of the child. The woman who bore the child has no legal rights to it. Other courts have held that the best interests of the child should prevail in such a case, opening the possibility that the woman who gave birth could keep the child although she has no biological relation to it.

A case decided in California in 1996 illustrates the disparity between the capabilities of technology at the end of the century and the glacial development of the law. Jaycee Buzzanca was born in 1994. She was the product of in vitro fertilization of an egg and sperm from anonymous donors, which was then implanted into a surrogate mother who gave birth to her as part of an arrangement to provide a child to another couple—the Buzzancas. However, the Buzzancas divorced before Jaycee was born. Mr. Buzzanca claimed he was not the father of the child and that the child was not "born of the marriage." The child was left with Mrs. Buzzanca, who also seemed not to want her, as she took no steps to officially adopt Jaycee. The court hearing Mrs. Buzzanca's claim that Mr. Buzzanca should pay child support ruled instead that Jaycee was without any parents at all. Arguably, six adults could be Jaycee's parents: the man and woman who donated her genetic material; the surrogate mother and her husband; or the Buzzancas. In 1998, the case is being heard by an appellate court in California. [Davis, Ann, "High-Tech Births Spawn Legal Riddles," *The Wall Street Journal*, 26 January 1998, at B1] In 1998, a California court of appeal ruled that the origin of Jaycee's genetic material was not relevant. What mattered was that she would not have come into being without the intent and willful actions of the Buzzancas. Therefore, Mr. Buzzanca as well as Mrs. Buzzanca have the obligation to support Jaycee. [Davis, Ann, "Status of 'High-Tech' Parents Is Clarified" *The Wall Street Journal*, 11 March 1998, at B2]

TENDER YEARS DOCTRINE A presumption that the best interests of very young children require their placement in the custody of their mothers following a divorce. This judicial doctrine was first espoused in the United States in 1830. It is similar to the **maternal preference rule,** which prefers the mother's custody for any child because of supposedly superior skills in child care. Unlike that rule, however, the tender years doctrine may be rebutted by evidence that the mother is unfit [see **unfit parent**], or that the father is the better and more nurturing parent for the child at issue. While less severe than the maternal preference rule, the tender years doctrine also places obstacles in the way of fathers who wish to retain custody of their children after a divorce. Changing attitudes in the late twentieth century are mitigating the doctrine. Many states' laws relegate it to the status of "tie-breaker"—meaning that it will only be brought into play if the parents' qualifications for **child custody** are otherwise equal.

As its name implies, the tender years doctrine presupposes that a child's need for a mother's care diminishes as the child grows older. While there is no fixed age at which a child is no longer of tender years, children under the age of five are universally within the definition of "tender years." States differ in their perspective on children between the ages of five and ten. And all states seem to have set thirteen as the upper limit of tender years, unless the child is developmentally handicapped.

TERMINATION PROCEEDING A legal procedure through which **parental rights** are terminated. A termination proceeding totally severs the parent-child relationship. The parent whose rights have been terminated no longer has any control over the child and has no right to visit, communicate with, or have any contact whatsoever with him or her forever after. In most states, a termination of parental rights also ends the parent's duty to support the child [see also **support obligation**].

A procedure to terminate parental rights is initiated through the filing of a petition with a family court. Usually, it is brought by a child welfare agency that has already worked with the parent or parents to remedy abusive or unwholesome conditions in the family. Indeed, most states allow termination of parental rights only after intervention by a child welfare agency in the family's affairs has failed to remedy bad parenting practices. Hence, a child welfare agency is almost always the one to bring the petition. However, some states allow other parties to petition as well, such as a parent, **foster parent, guardian,** or **guardian ad litem** for the child. A child may not initiate a termination proceeding on his or her own volition.

Because of the importance of parents' rights to raise their children and children's need for a parental relationship of some kind, parental rights may be terminated only in the most extreme of circumstances—and only when it is in the best interests of the child. [See also **best interests of the child rule.**] Statutes in all states prescribe the procedures that must be observed before parental rights may be terminated. A special court order following a formal hearing is necessary in most jurisdictions, and the full panoply of due process rights must be provided to the parents before such an order may issue. A parent must have notice of the pending termination and the right to call and cross-examine witnesses through an attorney. In most states, an indigent parent must be provided an attorney at the state's expense. Most statutes also require that the child have a **guardian ad litem** to represent his or her separate interests in the matter.

There are two phases to a termination proceeding. In the first phase, the parent's fitness to raise a child is examined. If the parent is found unfit [see **unfit parent**], the court (in the second phase) then considers whether the child's particular circumstances make a termination of the parental relationship in his or her best interests. The state has a heavy burden of proof in both phases of the proceeding. Generally, it must prove by clear and convincing evidence that the parent is unfit and that the child's interests require the termination. This is a more exacting standard than the usual requirement, in civil cases, that a matter be proved by a mere preponderance of the evidence.

A finding of **abandonment** or **neglect** is sufficient to support a termination of parental rights in most cases, especially if the parent was given a chance to reform and failed to do so in a reasonable time. A single instance of **child abuse** may be enough to terminate the parental relationship, particularly if the court believes the child is in physical danger from the parent. A mental or physical impairment that renders the parent incapable of caring properly for the child will also justify a termination of parental rights. Parental rights will never be terminated simply because the court finds that the child would be "better off" being raised by someone other than his or her parents.

If the court finds sufficient cause to terminate parental rights, it must then determine whether the child's best interests lie in cutting off all contact with the unfit parent. In some cases, the court may decide that termination is not in the child's best interests, but that a circumscribed relationship with some contact with the parent will best serve the child's emotional needs. Generally, if the parent is not found unfit, parental rights will not be terminated. However, in rare circumstances, extreme deterioration of the parent-child relationship will support a termination of parental rights, even though the parent is not unfit. Extreme deterioration may occur because of the child's unremitting hostility toward the parent or total emotional estrangement from the parent.

A termination proceeding should not be confused with a **child custody** proceeding. In the latter, the court is usually determining which of two fit, divorced parents would be the better caretaker. The parent who does not get custody usually still has parental rights to visit and communicate with the child and to decide issues involving his or her upbringing.

A termination of parental rights may also take place voluntarily. In this instance, a termination proceeding is not necessary. The parent wishing to terminate usually contacts the child welfare agency directly and arranges to place the child for **adoption.** The parent's consent for an adoption serves to terminate the parental relationship.

TESTAMENTARY RIGHTS   The right to bequeath, or give away, property in a will. Today, in most states, a person must be eighteen years or older in order to make a valid will. However, a child who has been emancipated [see **emancipation**] may dispose of property by will in some states before the age of eighteen. The property of a child who dies before the age of eighteen passes to his or her next of kin according to statutes regulating how the property of persons who die without making a will is to be given away. These statutes are known as laws of intestate succession. The property of a child who dies is distributed according to these laws, whether or not the child attempted to make a will. See **inheritance rights.**

Generally, the next of kin under intestate succession statutes will be the child's biological parents, unless the child was married. If the child was married, the property goes to his or her spouse. If the minor has children, but no spouse, the property will go to the children. If the biological parents of the deceased child are not alive, the child's property will pass to his or her biological siblings. If there are no siblings, the child's grandparents will inherit.

In keeping with the rule that an **adoption** severs all ties with the adopted child's biological relatives, the property of an adopted child who dies will go to his or her adoptive family. An exception to this rule occurs when the child was adopted by the spouse of his or her biological parent. In such a case, the biological parent would inherit, because his or her **parental rights** over the child were never severed. Some states follow the source rule with respect to property left by a deceased adopted child. Under this rule, property that was given to the child by his or her biological parents would be returned to those parents, even though the child was later adopted and all other ties to the biological parents were severed.

TESTIMONIAL COMPETENCY Possession of the qualities necessary to give testimony in a court of law. These may be summarized as the abilities of observation, memory, narration, and truthfulness. In other words, a witness must be able to observe events, remember them, and retell them truthfully. In the case of young children, one or all of these abilities may be lacking. For this reason, courts have traditionally required a special hearing on the competency of potential child witnesses before they are allowed to testify at a trial.

A competency hearing usually takes place at a separate session of the court away from a jury, and sometimes in the absence of the parties and their attorneys. Usually, the judge questions the child in order to be assured that the child can understand questions and relate cogent answers. The judge also questions the child as to whether he or she understands the difference between the truth and a lie, and the importance of telling the truth. Sometimes, the parties' attorneys will also question the child, or a child psychologist may be asked to question the child and report an expert opinion on the child's competency.

At a competency hearing, a child may be asked simple questions about his or her family, or what happened on a special occasion, such as a birthday. As stated earlier, the child will almost always be asked directly if he or she understands the difference between the truth and a lie. The child may be asked to give an example of both. The child will then be quizzed about the importance of telling the truth, and how lies are "bad." The child's ability to formulate coherent answers and relate them forthrightly is important to a finding of competence. The child may be tested for consistency by repeated questions about an event. Sometimes leading questions that suggest an answer are asked, in order to test whether the child is suggestible. If the child is able to withstand this questioning and maintain the consistent ability to relate events, he or she will usually be allowed to testify.

In recent years, commentators have questioned the necessity of a pretrial competency hearing for small children. They reason that the members of a jury are able to decide for themselves whether a child is capable of forming and remembering observations and relating them truthfully during the course of normal examination and cross-examination. Some states have, in fact, abolished competency hearings for children. In these states, virtually all children who can talk are allowed to testify.

A determination that a child is competent to testify does not mean that he or she will be able to do so effectively in the actual trial. Children can become intimidated by the courtroom surroundings, the presence of an audience, and the fact that unfamiliar adults are quizzing them—sometimes in a rather unfriendly way. If the child is the victim of the crime being tried, the trauma of facing the defendant may be emotionally distressing, or even psychologically damaging. All of these factors can distract an otherwise intelligent and competent child witness and make him or her unable to relate events coherently.

In order to protect the emotional health of child witnesses, and to help ensure that the quality of their testimony will not be impaired by the intimidating atmosphere of a trial, many states' laws allow special measures to be taken for the testimony of children. For example, some states allow children to give testimony in a separate room, connected to the courtroom by one- or two-way closed circuit television. Others allow children to testify in a place other than the courtroom and have their testimony preserved on videotape, to be played back at the actual trial. In some states, the courtroom may be closed to the public at the time the child is called to testify. Or, the child's testimony may be heard in the relative calm of the judge's chambers. Some states allow the child to sit on a parent's (or other adult's) lap or to testify from a less imposing location than the witness box.

In drafting laws that give special prerogatives to child witnesses, states walk a fine line between protecting children and safeguarding the constitutional rights of criminal defendants. The Sixth Amendment to the U.S. Constitution provides that a person accused of a crime must have the opportunity to face witnesses against him or her and cross-examine them. Thus, if children are allowed to testify at remote locations out of the presence of the defendant, this right may be infringed. Generally, the Supreme Court has held that it is permissible to exclude the defendant from a pretrial competency hearing. In *Kentucky v. Stincer* (1987), the Court reasoned that the defendant would still have an opportunity to cross-examine a child who passed such a competency hearing when he or she testified at trial.

The same is not true for testimony at trial. Generally, the defendant, or at least his or her attorney, must be present and allowed to cross-examine at any session at which a child is allowed to testify outside of open court. The important factor seems to be that the defendant be able to see the child testifying against him or her. In one case, the Supreme Court ruled that it violated a defendant's right to a face-to-face confrontation with a witness to allow the child to testify from behind a screen in the courtroom. [*Coy v. Iowa* (1988)] The defendant's rights were violated even though he could hear the child's testimony and the child was questioned by his attorney. However, in another case, the high Court ruled that it was permissible to isolate a child witness with the parties' attorneys in a room equipped with a one-way closed circuit television channel. The defendant could see the child testify from where he sat in the courtroom, but the child could not see him. [*Maryland v. Craig* (1990)] One factor influencing whether remote testimony violates the defendant's rights seems to be whether the court has found that the particular child testifying in the case needs extraordinary protective measures in order to give cogent testimony. In other words, a blanket rule allowing every child to testify from another location is probably not constitutional.

Another special concession commonly made to child witnesses that raises constitutional issues is the use of leading questions. Normally, questions that already suggest an answer, such as "Did the defendant tell you not to tell anyone?" are not allowed in court. Forcing a witness to narrate his or her story without such prompting is considered a far better way to ferret out the truth at a trial. However, in the case of small children, most courts will allow some form of leading questions. Children may be too timid or embarrassed to find their own words for the events to which they are testifying. Nonetheless, judges have discretion to decide when leading questions are actually putting words in the child's mouth that he or she would not have chosen. In such instances, leading questions may be barred. See also **Child Victims' and Child Witnesses' Rights Act; hearsay statements.**

THOMPSON V. OKLAHOMA In this 1988 case, the U.S. Supreme Court considered the constitutionality of executing persons for crimes they committed when they were minors. William Thompson was fifteen years old when he and some older friends killed Thompson's former brother-in-law, allegedly because the victim had been abusing Thompson's sister. The crime was particularly brutal, amounting to torture and execution, and evidence indicated that it was premeditated: Thompson announced to his girlfriend as he left the house on the night of the murder that he and some others were going to kill the victim. He then bragged about the crime afterward. A jury sentenced Thompson and his friends, who all were tried separately, to death. Thompson's appeal reached the Supreme Court.

In the appeal, Thompson argued that the Eighth Amendment's prohibition of "cruel and unusual punishment" forbids execution as a penalty for crimes committed while under the age of sixteen. A very narrow majority of the high Court agreed. Justices Stevens, Brennan, Marshall, and Blackmun believed that "it would offend civilized standards of decency to execute a person who was less than 16 years old at the time of his or her offense." In reaching this conclusion, the majority attempted to discern the "evolving standards of decency that mark the progress of a maturing society." The Court noted the many states that have outlawed the death penalty entirely, as well as the states that set a minimum age of sixteen for death-eligible crimes. The majority pointed out that only eighteen or twenty people had been executed for crimes committed under the age of sixteen in the United States in the twentieth century, and that the last such execution had taken place in 1948. They noted that only 5 of 1,393 persons sentenced to death between the years 1982 and 1986 were under sixteen at the time of the offense. In addition, the majority listed the nations of the Anglo-American tradition and nations in Western Europe that had either outlawed the death penalty completely or forbade its use on criminals whose crimes were committed when they were minors. The fact that numerous professional organizations, such as the American Bar Association, advocated the abolition of the death penalty for minors was also presented by the majority as evidence that modern opinions of justice were moving away from executions for crimes committed by minors.

The justices in the majority then went on to explain the trend as they saw it. Juveniles are not as culpable as adults, said the Court, because they have "less experience, less education, and less intelligence" than adults. This makes teenagers less able to evaluate the consequences of their conduct, while at the same time makes them more apt to be motivated by emotion or peer pressure than adults. Moreover, teenagers still have a capacity for growth, so that rehabilitation, rather than retribution, should be the byword for their treatment. The justices expressed skepticism that someone under sixteen could make the cold-blooded cost-benefit analysis about the possibility that he or she might be executed for a crime and be deterred from it by that possibility. Thus, the death penalty does not even serve a deterrent purpose where juveniles are concerned. Society has a very high obligation toward its youth, concluded the Court, which does not permit execution.

Justice Sandra Day O'Connor was the fifth justice to vote against Thompson's death sentence. Although she concurred with the result of the majority opinion, she had different reasons for voting to vacate the sentence. She believed that the fact that Oklahoma law did not set a minimum age for crimes warranting the death penalty meant that juveniles who were tried as adults, as was Thompson, were unintentionally made subject to execution. O'Connor felt that the seriousness of the result—execution for juvenile-committed crime—could not be sanctioned unless the state legislature had actually considered the issue.

Three justices dissented from the majority view. Justices Scalia, Rehnquist, and White (Justice Kennedy did not take part in the case) believed not only that Thompson's sentence was fair, but that the social trend regarding punishment for juvenile criminals was actually moving in the opposite direction than the majority of justices believed. Writing for the dissent, Justice Scalia wryly observed, "[T]he risk of assessing evolving standards is that it is all too easy to believe that evolution has culminated in one's own views." The dissent pointed out that state and federal laws were increasingly *lowering*, rather than raising, the ages at which minors could be tried for crimes in adult courts. This showed, in the dissent's view, less tolerance by society for misbehaving juveniles and a desire for more punishment. Moreover, statistics showed increasing numbers of violent crimes committed by juveniles, who were often "cynical, street-wise, repeat offenders," and "indistinguishable, except for age, from their adult counterparts." Furthermore, said the dissent, this trend was not really a departure from long-standing Anglo-American tradition: the great English legal commentator, Blackstone, wrote in 1769 that the age of seven was the age below which a person was conclusively unable to have the mental capacity to commit a capital crime. Above that age, a person could be shown to have knowledge of both the wrongfulness of an act and the intent to commit it. In America, between 1642 and 1899, there were records of twenty-two executions for crimes committed under age sixteen.

The dissent went on to say that Thompson was sentenced to death only after careful, individualized consideration of his case at numerous levels in the justice system. First, juvenile court authorities studied Thompson's background and concluded that rehabilitation through juvenile procedures was not viable. Thompson was a repeat offender of numerous serious, violent crimes. The jury who convicted and sentenced Thompson also considered his age, relative maturity, lack of remorse, and chance for rehabilitation when deliberating his fate. Thus, Thompson had received all the due process required for any citizen in a criminal proceeding.

TINKER V. DES MOINES INDEPENDENT COMMUNITY SCHOOL DISTRICT

The first case in which the U.S. Supreme Court recognized that children, as well as adults, have a constitutional right to express themselves, *Tinker* (1969) involved a challenge to the validity of a school policy banning the wearing of armbands in class.

Several students brought suit in federal court, through their parents, claiming that their civil liberties had been denied when they were suspended from school for wearing black armbands in protest of American military involvement in Vietnam. After conducting its hallmark balancing test—weighing the legitimate interests of each side in the controversy—the Court agreed with the students. It stated that the wearing of armbands was a form of symbolic speech that was protected under the Constitution. As a preliminary matter, the Court made the now famous pronouncement that recognized for the first time the constitutional rights of schoolchildren to freedom of speech:

> First Amendment rights, applied in light of the special characteristics of the school environment, are available to teachers and students. It can hardly be argued that either students or teachers shed their consti-

> tutional rights to freedom of speech or expression at the schoolhouse gate. . . . [at 506]
>
> Students in school as well as out of school are "persons" under our Constitution. They are possessed of fundamental rights which the State must respect, just as they themselves must respect their obligations to the State. . . . In the absence of a specific showing of constitutionally valid reasons to regulate their speech, students are entitled to freedom of expression of their views. [at 511]

Having acknowledged this, however, the Court went on to emphasize that these rights were subject to reasonable restrictions by school authorities if it were necessary to prevent disruption of the educational activities of the school. After all, education is also a very important societal and individual interest. Upon examining the facts of the case, the Court concluded that the school district did not have good reason to believe that the educational process would be disrupted by the mere wearing of armbands by students. Rather, it appeared that the school merely wanted to avoid "the discomfort and unpleasantness that always accompany an unpopular viewpoint." [at 509] This was not sufficient to justify infringing on the students' rights to engage in symbolic speech by wearing the armbands.

It is fitting that children's constitutional rights should be first recognized in a case involving freedom of speech, since that is the area in which the Supreme Court has been most zealous in protecting rights. *Tinker* can also be viewed as important for the rights of parents. Notably, the students in this case shared the political views of their parents. Some commentators have questioned whether the outcome would have been the same if the students had held views contrary to those of their parents.

TITLE IV-D AGENCY Sometimes simply called "four dee" agency, this is the state institution responsible for enforcing child **support obligations**. [See also **support enforcement**.] The name *IV-D* derives from the Federal Child Support Enforcement Act, which is also known as Title IV-D. That act directed the states to create agencies for the purpose of enforcing child support orders. In addition to taking measures to collect child support payments, IV-D agencies may set procedures for establishing the paternity of illegitimate children. See also **illegitimacy; paternity action.**

TITLE IX The section of the Education Amendments of 1972 [20 U.S.C. §§ 1681 et seq.] that prohibits discrimination on the basis of gender in the public schools is usually simply known as Title XI. It provides:

> No person in the United States shall, on the basis of sex, be excluded from participation in, be denied the benefits of, or be subjected to discrimination under any education program or activity receiving Federal financial assistance.

In addition to the **equal protection** clause of the Fourteenth Amendment, this law is one of the major sources of protection for the rights of females in education. Of course, it also applies to prevent discrimination against males, although practically speaking, the greatest discrimination in schools has been against females. The "big stick" for enforcing Title IX's ban on gender discrimination, of course, is the threat of withholding federal money from schools that do not comply. In the latter decades of the twentieth century, virtually every public institution of learning from grade schools through college accepts some type of federal funding. The only schools specifically exempted from Title IX are private undergraduate colleges.

After Title IX was passed, a dispute arose as to whether the act's prohibition of sex discrimination applied only to the departments within schools that actually received federal money, or whether it applied to all programs in a school in which at least one department received the federal money. The issue was crucial to determining the breadth of the act's protection. If the ban on discrimination were only "program specific," that is, if it applied only to the program that actually received the federal money, schools could circumvent the act's provisions through creative accounting. For example, a school could choose to accept only federal money that was not earmarked for a particular program and could shift that money to programs that did not discriminate, leaving more money in the general fund to support programs that do discriminate. This is precisely what a number of institutions did, particularly with regard to athletic programs that traditionally provided a far greater number of opportunities to male students than to female students.

In 1984, the Supreme Court put an end to the uncertainty in the case of *Grove City College v. Bell*, 465 U.S. 555 (1984), when it held that the provisions of the act relating to federal funding are program specific. This significantly narrows the scope of Title IX protection. Nevertheless, students who feel they have been discriminated against on the basis of gender in a particular school program that receives federal funding can sue the school for a court order to stop the discrimination.

TOBACCO PRODUCTS   Currently, all states prohibit the sale of tobacco products to minors under the age of eighteen. A 1996 initiative by the Food and Drug Administration (FDA) recommended zero tolerance for sales of tobacco products to minors. It also proposed banning vending machine sales and self-service racks in retail stores. The distribution of "free samples" of cigarettes would also be banned under its recommendations. In addition, the FDA initiative proposed sweeping new restrictions on cigarette advertising designed to discourage youthful smokers.

The restrictions on sale to minors include every form of tobacco, from cigarettes and cigars to chewing tobacco. Like laws regulating alcohol, these age-based restrictions on products that can be freely purchased by adults are believed necessary for the protection of children's health. Because of the natural belief of children in their own invulnerability, they are thought incapable of making a wise choice with regard to a product that can addict them and result in devastating health problems many years later.

Despite decades of warnings about the hazards of tobacco use, studies in the last years of the twentieth century indicate that cigarette use among the nation's youth is increasing, particularly among young women. The public agencies of the federal government, the states, and many local government and nonprofit organizations are engaged in an effort to "deglamorize" the use of tobacco among the young and present the devastating effects of tobacco induced illnesses.

At the federal level, an initiative is afoot to make tobacco products subject to regulation by the FDA. This depends on the classification of tobacco as a drug, a possibility that is increasingly likely with the results of new studies on the effects of nicotine on the human nervous system.

In 1997, major representatives of the tobacco industry have themselves proposed a settlement, whereby they will offer billions of dollars in compensation for injuries suffered by smokers as a result of the use of their products, a self-imposed ban on advertising that attracts children, affirmative measures to discourage underage smoking, and the submission of their product to regulation by the FDA, among other things. In exchange, the tobacco companies will continue to be able to market cigarettes in the United

States and abroad and will be immune to punitive damages in future lawsuits. It is unclear whether the federal government will accept the proposal at this point, and some critics are skeptical. First, they point out that regulation by the FDA may prove to be a great advantage to the cigarette companies, since it is likely that the first step the FDA will take will be to order the amount of nicotine in cigarettes lowered. Studies of sales of low-nicotine cigarettes that have already been on the market show that, to compensate for the smaller amount of nicotine in the cigarettes, consumers frequently resort to smoking more of them. Thus, regulation by the FDA may, ironically, result in increased sales of the regulated product. Moreover, critics of the federal anticigarette campaign are fond of pointing out that the reason children begin smoking in the first place is often to show a defiance of authority and, ultimately, a defiance of death, which can only be made more attractive by the frantic efforts of adults to deprive them of this symbol.

Tort Responsibility

A tort is a wrongful act (or sometimes an omission to act) that causes harm to another person, for which the person responsible must compensate by a payment of money to the injured person. A tort is not the same thing as a crime, although some tortious behavior may also be considered a crime. Generally, a crime is wrongful behavior that the public authorities (the police and public prosecutor) will investigate and prosecute at public expense. The person found guilty of a crime may be punished by imprisonment or payment of a fine to the public treasury. However, the victim of a crime is not compensated by the criminal justice system. By contrast, a tort does not concern the public authorities, but the person injured by a tort may sue the person who caused the harm in a court of law. If the court finds that the person being sued, the defendant, was responsible for the harm, he or she will be ordered to pay a sum to compensate the injured party.

Questions often arise as to who is responsible for a child's behavior that causes injury to others. The general rule is that children may commit torts and are responsible for harm they cause in exactly the same way as adults. However, children's behavior is not usually judged by the same standards as adult behavior in determining whether it is wrongful and tortious.

The standards used to determine the legal responsibility of children for tortious conduct may depend on the type of tort involved. There are two broad categories of torts: intentional and unintentional.

Intentional torts require an intent to commit the act. In some states, this also includes the intent to cause harm. Battery, slander, and deceit are examples of intentional torts. A child may be old enough to intend to throw rocks, but not old enough to specifically want to injure the other child at whom he is throwing them. In some states, the intent to throw rocks would be enough to hold the child liable for harm, but some states' courts would also require some evidence that the child had a malicious desire to hurt the victim through his or her actions. Since there is no particular age at which the ability to form a malicious intent arises, the court will consider the capacities of the individual child in each case. However, it appears from a study of these legal cases that the ability to desire to hurt another and to know what types of actions will do so develops remarkably early in the human species! One court found that a child of six could have had the intention to burn down a building when he caused a fire.

Unintentional torts do not require any finding of intent to cause harm. Negligence of some sort is the touchstone of unintentional torts. In other words, it is necessary to find that the harm was caused because someone was not as careful as the situation required. In the case of adults, the test is whether a reasonable, average adult would have been more careful in the situation that led to the injury. In the case of children, the test will be subjective. In other words, it will be necessary to show that the particular child who caused harm was capable of understanding the possibility of harm occurring in the situation, and, in fact, usually acted with greater care. This proven, it is then possible to conclude that the child was negligent for not having acted with greater care at the time the harm was caused. For example, if a child who caused a fire by playing with matches normally was aware that playing with matches might cause a fire, the child may be found negligent because he played with matches on this occasion.

Although there are no specific age limits at which a consciousness of the consequences of dangerous actions develop, some states still follow an arbitrary, traditional common law system of determining a child's capability of negligence. In these states, children under seven are presumptively incapable of negligence, because they are assumed incapable of the type of foresight necessary to appreciate risks of specific behaviors. Children over the age of fourteen are presumptively capable of this thought. Between the ages of seven and fourteen, there is a rebuttable presumption that the child is capable of negligence. This means that evidence that the particular child is either extraordinarily bright or dull is useful to show either negligence or the incapacity to be negligent at those ages. Naturally, as the child approaches the age of fourteen in these states, the presumption of negligence grows stronger.

A special exception is made in the law of torts when a minor is engaged in activities that are normally undertaken only by adults. In these situations, the minor will be judged by the higher standard of careful conduct used to judge the behavior of adults. Such activities include the operation of automobiles, airplanes, motorboats, and recreational off-road vehicles such as dirt bikes and snowmobiles. Using firearms, playing golf, and hunting are also examples. Thus, if a minor hurts someone with a gun, the objective, higher test of negligence used for adults will be applied to the minor.

Although children are theoretically legally responsible for the harm they cause others, whether intentional or not, in reality it does little good to sue a child for compensation because children rarely have any money. Therefore, those injured by the acts of children usually try to find some way to make their parents liable for the harm. Contrary to common perception, parents are not automatically responsible for harm caused by their children. The parent must be shown to have been negligent in his or her own right with regard to controlling the child who caused the harm, before the parent will be required to pay. Or, it must be shown that the child was performing some service at the request of his or her parent when the child caused harm. Then it is possible to argue that the child was the parent's agent, and under the traditional rules of agency law, the parent would be liable for the agent's transgressions. Thus, someone hurt by a child's negligence will usually sue the child's parents for negligent supervision of the child. In the alternative, growing numbers of states have **parental responsibility statute**s, which make parents automatically liable for some types of harm caused by their children, although the amount that may be recovered under such statutes is usually limited.

TRANSPORTATION RIGHTS   Beyond the issue of **busing** to achieve racial integration, parents have occasionally sued public school districts claiming that their children have a right to be transported from their homes to the public schools at taxpayer expense. The U.S. Supreme Court heard such a challenge in 1988, when, in *Kadramas v. Dickinson Public Schools* (1988), the Court ruled that the federal Constitution does not require a school district to provide transportation to the public schools. Moreover, if a school district does provide transportation, the transportation does not have to be free of charge. However, if the district does provide transportation, the Constitution requires that it do so on an equal basis to all students who are similarly situated. In other words, if the district decided to provide transportation to all students outside a certain mileage limit distance from the schools, it must do so on an equal basis. Generally, a school district that provides transportation to public schools is under no obligation to transport children to parochial or private schools. Some states, however, have laws requiring such transportation.

Children who refuse to abide by rules and regulations on school buses may lawfully be denied the privilege of riding them.

TRIAL AS ADULT In certain cases, a minor who is accused of committing criminal acts may be tried as an adult in adult court, instead of juvenile court. This occurs after a juvenile court "waives" jurisdiction, or "certifies" the youth for trial as an adult.

Generally, juveniles are tried as adults when it appears that rehabilitation through juvenile procedures is unlikely, or when the crime was particularly vicious. Although the juvenile who is "waived" into adult court is subject to adult penalties for the crimes of which he or she is accused, there are some advantages to trial as an adult. For one thing, the juvenile in adult court now has the full complement of constitutional due process protections available to adult criminal defendants. The juvenile is eligible for bail and is entitled to a jury trial and a public trial. In addition, juries and some judges are often more likely to be lenient toward a youth who is on trial in adult court, because they know that the minor could end up in the notoriously brutal environment of an adult prison. In fact, some studies have shown that the juvenile tried as an adult spends less time incarcerated than a juvenile who proceeds through an adjudication in juvenile court.

In addition to the nature of the crimes committed by the juvenile, other factors that a court considers when determining whether to try a juvenile as an adult include:

1. The age of the accused. Generally, the older the child, the more likely he or she is to be transferred to adult court. Older juveniles are believed less likely to gain from the rehabilitative efforts of juvenile agencies, either because they are less malleable or because they will be beyond the jurisdiction of the juvenile system before any progress toward rehabilitation can be made.

2. The maturity and sophistication of the accused.

3. The nature of the crime. Was it a crime against property, or did it involve violence against a person? Was the crime committed after planning or premeditation? The more serious, violent, or premeditated the offense, the more likely the accused will be tried in adult court.

4. Any prior offenses committed by the accused. Prior offenses committed by a child are also considered an indicator that he or she is not amenable to rehabilitation in juvenile court.

Before a child's case may be transferred to adult court, a hearing must be held on the appropriateness of the transfer. [See *Kent v. United States.*] Evidence generally is restricted to the above factors. The issue of the child's guilt or innocence of the underlying charges is not to be addressed. After all, that is the purpose of the eventual trial—whether in juvenile or adult court.

The accused is entitled to have an attorney at the transfer hearing. The hearing does not need to comply with all the same procedural safeguards of a regular trial. However, the state must present some evidence as to why the child is not a good candidate for the juvenile system. The burden of proof, while on the state, is not a high burden: in most states it is necessary only to show that there are "reasonable" grounds to believe the child cannot be rehabilitated in juvenile court. Either the child or the state may appeal a ruling on which court will hear the juvenile's case.

TUITION VOUCHERS   In an effort to improve educational opportunities, some states have recently experimented with giving parents "vouchers" that entitle them to receive a sum of money that can be used toward paying tuition at a school of their choice. The "vouchers" are paid for by tax dollars. Although at first blush such schemes are attractive because they seem to give all children the opportunity to attend schools of their own choice, in reality these systems discriminate against poor people. Invariably, the amount of the voucher is only sufficient to cover part of tuition at a private school. The better the private school, of course, the less of the cost of tuition a voucher will provide. Therefore, in order to enroll one's child in such a school, a parent must be able to make up the difference in the cost of tuition. Affluent families can do this much more easily than the poor. Hence, the poor's choices of schools are still limited—often to the same public schools they would have attended before the voucher system. However, with vouchers in place, all the students whose families can now afford it go to other schools. The public schools are drained of funds and draw only the poorest students. Because the public schools now have even fewer resources and funds to count on, the quality of education there spirals downward. In effect, the voucher system may well serve to institutionalize a class system of education based on wealth. It remains to be seen whether courts will step forward to find that systems such as these are unconstitutional because they violate the rights of poor people to equal protection of the laws.

UNDERGROUND NEWSPAPERS

UNDERGROUND NEWSPAPERS Students in public schools have the right to communicate their views to others by any medium, including written media, so long as their activities do not "substantially interfere" with the educational objective of the school. Therefore, students generally have a right to hand out their own written materials, including so-called underground newspapers, within schools. In *Hazelwood School District v. Kuhlmeier,* the Supreme Court ruled that school officials may censor school publications, that is, they may require submission of the written material for their approval and may prohibit publication of objectionable material. However, *Hazelwood* dealt with publications that were "official" student newspapers. It involved a paper put out by students in a journalism class that was part of the class's curriculum. The Court said that such a newspaper, because it was sponsored by the school, was not a "public forum" in which anything goes. The school had no obligation to disseminate a paper it sponsored if it disagreed with the content. On the other hand, underground newspapers are not sponsored by the school. Can they be censored by school officials?

One thing is clear. School administrators can restrict the dissemination of any materials to times and places within the school that will not interfere with classes. The question of whether a school can require that students submit purely private material that they wish to pass out to school administrators for prior approval has not yet been decided by the Supreme Court. Federal courts at lower levels are divided on the issue. Some hold that requiring the prior approval of school authorities for purely private material is a violation of the First Amendment. Others have held that such restrictions are permissible. In those jurisdictions that permit a prior restraint on private student disseminated material, it is unclear what standards will justify disapproval. Some courts have held that the content of the material must be such that its dissemination at school would cause a "substantial" disruption of the educational process. This is the test set forth by the Supreme Court in *Tinker v. Des Moines Independent Community School District.* Other courts have held that school authorities may ban the distribution of private material if it contains vulgar language (even if it is short of "obscene") or libelous material. One court has held that it was permissible for a school to ban the distribution of private student material that contained advertisements for items that could not legally be sold to children. Another permitted the ban on an underground newspaper that contained a "sex survey" of students because it arguably could cause emotional distress and psychological harm to some students. In general, however, schools cannot prohibit the distribution of private material by students just because it deals with controversial matters, or because it is critical of school administrators. The burden of proof is always on the school to prove that there is a reasonable cause for prohibiting particular material from distribution.

UNFIT PARENT   A parent whose inability to care properly for his or her child justifies a temporary or permanent termination of **parental rights,** if this is in the best interest of the child. See **best interests of the child rule.**

There are many ways a person can demonstrate unfitness for parenting. Generally, if a parent engages in any behavior that can be defined as **child abuse, abandonment,** or **neglect,** he or she is arguably unfit. There are other situations in which a parent may be considered "unfit" as well:

- Severe physical or mental illness. A physical or mental condition that prevents a parent from providing for a child's basic needs may render the parent unfit even though he or she has demonstrated love and affection for the child. A mentally retarded parent may be unfit if he or she is unable to understand or carry out proper parenting duties. However, the mere fact that someone is retarded or physically handicapped is not reason in itself to find a parent "unfit." A judicial determination must be made on the basis of evidence of the parent's abilities before this fact will justify removal of a child from the retarded or handicapped parent.

- Addiction to alcohol or drugs. If a parent's addiction to drugs or alcohol interferes with the ability to give the child proper care, the parent may be judged unfit. Some courts find that the parent's refusal or inability to recognize his or her own addiction indicates "unfitness" for parenting. Similarly, the failure of addicted parents to undertake rehabilitation may make them "unfit" in the sight of the law, even though the child has not suffered apparent abuse or neglect because of the parent's habit.

- Criminal record. A parent's criminal record in and of itself may result in a finding of "unfitness" even if the criminal conduct did not involve the child. Generally, the parent must have been convicted of numerous or particularly serious crimes before he or she is automatically "unfit." Of course, if the parent is in prison, he or she will not be able to care for the child adequately. However, if the incarcerated parent makes every effort to maintain meaningful contact with the child, he or she may not be judged "unfit" upon release.

Poverty alone is not an indicator that a parent is "unfit," even if the parent is unable to provide the necessary food, shelter, clothing, and medical care required to properly parent a child. If poor parents are caring and responsive to the child's needs, they are not unfit unless they refuse material help from a child welfare agency or other source.

A parent's unfitness may be only a temporary condition, and most courts will give the parent an opportunity to reform before taking steps to restrict or terminate parental rights. An exception may be where the child is in imminent danger of physical harm or where he or she has suffered **sexual abuse** at the hand of the unfit parent.

Currently, if a parent's behavior is not a crime and does not affect his or her ability to provide a child with the necessary material and emotional supports of life, the parent is not "unfit" in most jurisdictions. Thus, a parent's homosexuality, promiscuity, dishonesty, laziness, or any other trait that may be considered a "character flaw" will not result in a finding of unfitness. However, these factors may be considered when a court determines which parent is most "fit" to have custody of a child. See **child custody.**

▥ UNIFORM CHILD CUSTODY JURISDICTION ACT (UCCJA)

A law passed by all fifty states that sets forth rules as to which state's court will have jurisdiction to decide **child custody** cases when the participants live in different states. The UCCJA also applies to determine jurisdiction of parental termination, guardianship, visitation, and dependency proceedings. [See **juvenile court; termination proceedings; visitation rights.**]

The importance of this law for increasing the stability of the lives of countless children from broken homes after the mid-1970s can not be overstated. Before that time, parents jockeying for advantage in a custody fight, or trying to have established custody orders modified, could "shop" for a forum state to hear the case. They frequently dragged their children from their established homes to the chosen state, where they could petition to have their custody case heard in hopes of a more favorable resolution.

The UCCJA prevents this by setting rules for which state should have the final say in custody determinations. Under the act, the states may negotiate among themselves, considering which is most appropriate to hear the case. Usually, the state with jurisdiction will be the one in which the child has resided for six consecutive months, or with which the child has had the greatest meaningful "contact." This may mean the state in which the child lived for most of his or her life, where he or she goes to school, or where he or she has the most family and friends.

Once it is determined which state has jurisdiction, under the UCCJA no other states may hold legal proceedings on the same issue. After custody is determined, all other states must recognize and abide by the custody decree. States other than the state that originally had jurisdiction in the matter are also restricted in their ability to modify custody decrees. In addition, the UCCJA authorizes courts to impose fines on parents who take their children to inappropriate or inconvenient forum states in an effort to influence custody decisions.

The provisions of the UCCJA vary slightly from state to state, but they generally resemble the federal **Parental Kidnapping Prevention Act** (PKPA). Where the UCCJA provisions differ from that of the PKPA, the latter, being a federal law, will prevail.

UNIFORM INTERSTATE FAMILY SUPPORT ACT (UIFSA)   A model law intended to aid in the collection of child support payments from parents who reside in another state. Drafted in 1993 by a panel of legal experts, the model law was intended to replace and to improve upon both the Uniform Reciprocal Enforcement of Support Act (URESA) and the Revised Uniform Reciprocal Enforcement of Support Act (RURESA). The UIFSA had been adopted by twenty-one states by the end of 1994.

Prior to the creation of URESA in the 1950s, it was very difficult to force a parent who lived in a different state than his or her dependent child to live up to the obligation to support the child. At that time, a court in the state where the child lived could not exercise jurisdiction over the absent parent. Unless the owing parent returned to the child's state, or was officially extradited to the child's state, there was no way to bring him or her before the court to determine or enforce a **support obligation.**

Both URESA and RURESA created what is known as long-arm jurisdiction to bring the absent parent to court in the child's state in order to answer to demands that he or she support the child. This provision has been further strengthened by the UIFSA. Long-arm jurisdiction under the UIFSA means that if the absent parent has any significant contacts with the child's home state, a court in the child's state can require the absent parent to show up personally and answer to charges that child support is owed.

In cases in which it is still not possible to bring the absent parent to a forum in the child's state, the UIFSA provides that a forum—a court or administrative tribunal—in the absent parent's state can decide the case. Typically, the custodial parent, as a representative for the child, files a petition with a court in the child's home state alleging that the absent parent owes support. The home state court forwards the petition to a court (or administrative tribunal) in the absent parent's state. The absent parent will then be required to appear in that forum and answer to the charges that support is owed. The case will be prosecuted by a district attorney in the absent parent's state, and neither the custodial parent nor the child is required to be present. The absent parent may cross-examine the custodial parent or other witnesses from the child's state through a written deposition, or out-of-state witnesses can testify by means of a telephone conference call.

If a support order has already been issued by one state, the UIFSA provides simplified means for it to be enforced in another state. First, an order can be sent directly from a court in the child's home state to the absent parent's employer in another state, requiring that wages be withheld from the absent parent's paycheck and sent directly to the child. Second, an administrative tribunal in the absent parent's state can issue an order directly to the absent parent requiring payment of the overdue support.

Prior to passage of the UIFSA, the law allowed courts in the absent parent's state to modify support orders that came from courts in the child's home state. Under the UIFSA, this is no longer possible. The order issued by the original court that had jurisdiction over the child support matter must be enforced in all states exactly as it was when first issued. This change ameliorated the confusion of having multiple support orders issued by different states with differing provisions, all intended to address the same case.

The UIFSA also has similar provisions to enforce orders to pay alimony or spousal maintenance, and to determine the paternity of an absent father prior to adjudicating support issues. [See also **paternity action.**] The UIFSA cannot be used, however, to determine **visitation rights.**

 VACCINATION REQUIREMENTS States may require children to be vaccinated against certain diseases as a prerequisite to attending school. When considered together with **compulsory attendance laws,** this virtually amounts to a command by the state that children receive vaccinations. Objections have been raised to these laws because they invade the most private realm of human rights: namely, the right to determine what will happen to one's body.

Despite this objection, vaccination requirements have been ruled constitutional. Courts reason that the state's interest in protecting the health of all its citizens is a compelling reason to require vaccinations for common, highly communicable diseases, some of which can be dangerous. The requirement that all schoolchildren be vaccinated protects each single child from contagion from others, as much as it protects others from contagion from any single child. Thus, it is considered equally applied.

In most states, a parent whose sincerely held religious beliefs contradict the mandate for vaccinations may obtain a waiver for his or her child. It is unsettled, however, whether *any* sincere belief against vaccination will qualify for the waiver, or whether the belief must be part of the doctrine of a particular recognized religion. In one case, the highest court in New York held that it was unconstitutional as a violation of the First Amendment for a state to grant waivers only to parents who could prove allegiance to an organized religion. The court held that this violated the prohibition on establishing a religion. Rather, any "religious" belief would qualify. However, it had to be a religious belief. A scientific belief, or a prejudice, was not sufficient.

In addition, statutes usually permit a waiver of the vaccination requirement if a parent can show that it is medically contraindicated for the child.

VISITATION RIGHTS The legally enforceable rights to associate with one's child or parents with whom one does not reside. Usually, visitation rights are asserted by a divorced noncustodial parent or the parents of a child who has been placed in foster care. Under certain

311

circumstances, visitation rights may also exist with respect to persons other than a child's parents, such as siblings, grandparents, or stepparents.

Initially, it should be noted that the law is unclear as to whom visitation rights belong—the child or the parent. Numerous courts have held that parents have a constitutionally protected interest in continued association with their children following a divorce or separation, even where decisions regarding the child's upbringing have been delegated to someone else. At the same time, most courts have held that a child has an important interest in maintaining a relationship with his or her parents, regardless of whether the family remains intact. Some courts characterize the primary right of association as belonging to the child, and not the parent. Regardless of the technical answer to this dilemma, all states' laws recognize that visitation by anyone must be in the child's best interests. See **best interests of the child rule.**

Visitation rights encompass not just the right to physical custody of a child for a temporary period of time, but the right to be in the physical presence of the child and to maintain telephone or postal contact with him or her. During the time that a noncustodial parent has visitation privileges with the child, the custodial parent is usually not permitted to intervene. For example, if a child visits his noncustodial father for six weeks during the summer, the child's mother—the custodial parent—has no rights to "visitation" during that period. In special circumstances, however, a court may order that visitation only take place in the presence of the custodial parent, or some other caretaker of the child.

Usually, enforceable visitation rights exist only in regard to a biological or adoptive parent. Grandparents, siblings, and other relatives, including stepparents, have no automatic right to association with a child following a breakup of the child's family unit. In some states, however, grandparents do have a right to maintain contact with the child under the provisions of a **grandparent visitation statute.** Also, in recent years, courts have been more willing to order visitation for stepparents who have been divorced from the child's biological parent. In such cases, the stepparent has the burden of showing that visitation would be in the best interests of the child. Usually, this involves proving that the stepparent and the child had a particularly close and loving relationship and that the stepparent was involved in the child's day-to-day care. Some states allow others to seek visitation, but they must show a very close emotional contact with the child. In the case of adoption, unless a biological parent reserved rights of visitation prior to placing a child for adoption, that parent will have no visitation rights once the adoption is finalized.

When visitation is granted, it is usually stipulated that it is to be on a "reasonable" basis. This type of court order leaves it up to the parents to decide among themselves when and where visitation is to take place. If the parents cannot agree on visitation, the court will set the terms and conditions. On rare occasions, a court will leave the determination of the time, place, and frequency of visitation entirely up to the custodial parent.

Given that the law places a very high value on the continued association of parents with their children, denial of visitation rights may be made only under the most compelling circumstances. In order to show that visitation of a noncustodial parent would not be in the best interest of the child, a custodial parent must show that the noncustodial parent is unfit in some way. [See **unfit parent**.] This may be due to an ongoing substance abuse problem, past physical or sexual abuse of the child, or unstable mental health that could endanger the child.

Courts are divided as to whether the noncustodial parent's associations with third parties are relevant in granting or denying visitation. Usually, courts hold that, unless the noncustodial parent's conduct with others is likely to have a detrimental impact on the child, visitation for that reason cannot be denied. For example, some courts have held that the fact that a noncustodial parent is a homosexual does not, in itself, disqualify him or her from visitation. Instead, a parent's sexual conduct with a lover of either sex might be considered a disqualifying factor if it takes place in front of the child.

In the past, courts were more willing to pry into the "moral character" of the noncustodial spouse. Behavior that was not so extreme as to support a termination of all parental rights might nevertheless result in denied visitation. However, today regular contact by a child with his or her parents is considered so important that courts go to great lengths to preserve it, even if this means careful fashioning of the conditions under which it may take place. If a court believes that direct contact between a parent and child will be deleterious to the child, contact may be restricted to telephone or mail correspondence. In some circumstances, such as when a noncustodial parent has threatened violence against the child or former spouse, or when there is reason to believe that the parent may try to kidnap the child instead of returning him or her to the custodial parent, visitation may be denied entirely.

A failure to pay child support is usually not considered a justification for disallowing visitation. The rights and duties of child support and visitation are considered to be completely separate. First, courts find it unseemly to condition a visit with the child on the payment of a sum of money.

Second, to deny the child association with his parent is considered unfair punishment of the child, since visitation with a parent is as much the child's right as the parent's. Moreover, a child whose parent has not paid support has already undergone a material deprivation. It would be cruel to impose the emotional deprivation of withholding the company of the parent as well.

Although a court's discretion in ordering visitation to take place under certain circumstances is broad, a court usually may not condition visitation on the noncustodial parent's agreement to continue the child's religious training in the faith chosen for him or her by the custodial parent. This is true even though the custodial parent may have been given the power to determine the child's religious upbringing. Because a parent has a constitutional right to practice his or her own religion, requiring the parent to train the child in another faith is considered an infringement of those rights. Nevertheless, a court can order a noncustodial parent not to *interfere* with the training given to the child by the custodial parent by trying to indoctrinate the child in another faith during the period of visitation.

Since visitation rights are as much the right of children to continued association with their parents as vice versa, it would seem a given that the child's wishes in the matter should be consulted. This is, in fact, the case. However, the wishes of the child are not always the deciding factor. Particularly in the case of young children, the state may determine whether visitation is in the child's best interests, regardless of his or her wishes. Generally, unless the child's welfare is endangered, courts feel that the opportunity to foster close relations between parent and child is more important to preserve than giving in to the whims of the child—who in some cases is influenced by the animosity of the custodial parent against the noncustodial parent. An older child's wish to have visitation will usually be respected and given greater weight than resistance to visitation. Some states have statutes determining at what age a child's wishes in the matter will be considered. For example, in Ohio, that age is eleven.

Once visitation is granted, its conditions cannot be too onerous. This creates problems when one parent moves out of state. For the most part, courts will not force a parent to live in a certain area simply to make visitation more convenient. An exception is made when a parent's relocation appears to be a deliberate attempt to prevent visitation by the other parent. The burden of proof is on the noncustodial parent to show that the custodial parent's move was made in bad faith and is not in the best interests of the child.

VOCATIONAL TRACKING It is illegal for public schools to refuse a student admission into a vocational course based on the student's gender. Gone are the days when only boys could take "shop" or auto mechanics courses and only girls were allowed to take home economics and typing. **Title IX** of the Education Amendment of 1972 is the law most responsible for this development, although there are other statutes, both federal and state, that address the issue of gender tracking in vocational programs. In addition to banning outright refusals of admission to students into the vocational course of their choice on the basis of gender, Title IX forbids sex discrimination in guidance counseling services and the tests used for placing students in vocational training programs.

Despite these laws, gender stereotyping and tracking persist in schools in more subtle forms. Peer pressure, faculty hostility, and biased advice from counselors are all factors in keeping cross-enrollment of students in vocational classes that are not traditional to their gender very low. In general, students need to be aware that subtle pressures based on gender may influence their choice of vocational classes, and they must be prepared to act in accordance with the dictates of their true desires.

WEST VIRGINIA BOARD OF EDUCATION V. BARNETTE

In this important decision, the U.S. Supreme Court in 1942 ruled that a state could not compel public school students to pledge allegiance to the national flag. A West Virginia law made it mandatory for schoolchildren to say the familiar "Pledge of Allegiance" as a part of their school program. Students who refused to pledge were expelled from school. Their absence from school for this reason was considered unexcused and they were subject to prosecution for being "delinquent." In addition, the children's parents were subject to fines and jail terms. Several children and their families, who belonged to the Jehovah's Witnesses, objected to the pledge on the grounds that it contradicted their religious beliefs, which taught that the law of God is superior to those of men and forbade oaths to "images" such as the flag. They appealed their expulsion and subsequent prosecutions.

In the Supreme Court's decision, Justice Jackson was careful to point out that the issue in the case was not whether sincere religious objections were sufficient to make an exception to a valid law, but whether the law was valid in the first place. The Court said it was not. The Court noted the irony of the fact that "[t]o sustain the compulsory flag salute we are required to say that a Bill of Rights, which guards the individual's right to speak his own mind, left it open to public authorities to compel him to utter what is not in his mind." The protection of constitutional principles in this case, admonished the Court, was particularly important because the state's rationale for the practice was to teach the "ideals, principles and spirit of Americanism." Said the Court: "That they are educating the young for citizenship is reason for scrupulous protection of Constitutional freedoms of the individual, if we are not to strangle the free mind at its source and teach youth to discount important principles of our government as mere platitudes." The Court concluded its discussion with a paragraph that has been much quoted in later opinions.

> If there is any fixed star in our constitutional constellation, it is that no official, high or petty, can prescribe what shall be orthodox in politics,

nationalism, religion or other matters of opinion or force citizens to confess by word or act their faith therein.

This case in many ways foreshadowed the famous decision in *Tinker v. Des Moines Independent Community School District,* which formally recognized that the First Amendment's right to free speech applies to schoolchildren. In *Barnette,* the Court was concerned with forcing students to say something that did not coincide with their beliefs. From there it seems a small step to recognize students' rights to affirmatively speak something that does reflect their beliefs. However, this next step took another twenty-seven years.

WISCONSIN V. YODER An important case in which the U.S. Supreme Court was confronted with the question of whether a state could compel children to attend school beyond the eighth grade in contravention of their parents' devout religious beliefs. The 1972 case involved Amish parents who were convicted in criminal court for failing to send their children to school as the law required.

As in all its family law discussions, the Court engaged in a careful balancing of the competing interests of the parties. On the one hand, the state has a very compelling interest in fostering an educated citizenry. Educated citizens with a capacity for critical thinking are essential for the functioning of a democracy, and for the preservation of a civilized and productive social order. On the other hand, one of the most sacred rights guaranteed under the Constitution is the free exercise of religion.

In spite of the very important state interest in having children educated to take their responsibilities in a free society, the Court decided that the law requiring compulsory education for Amish children was too restrictive of the rights of the Amish to practice their religion. The Amish believed that if their children attended school past the eighth grade they would be exposed to influences that would conflict with their lifestyle, and the Amish culture would be threatened. They contended that their religion and the simple life they led were one and the same.

Most of the Court's ruling in the Amish's favor depended on a respectful review of their nearly 300-year history in America and the important values they tried to live by, including honesty, hard work, nonviolence, and self-reliance. The Court concluded that the Amish society, rather than being harmful to the children's ability to contribute to society, actually helped it. Thus, the state's interest in an educated citizenry was still being served, without the intrusion on the Amish freedom of religion.

The *Yoder* holding is said to be very narrow. The same decision would probably not be made for any other religious group, unless it could demonstrate as long a history of religious faith reflected in a disciplined and insular lifestyle.

The case was also interesting because of a dissent by Justice Douglas, in which he objected to the holding because it gave total deference to the parent's religious beliefs and did not consider the beliefs of the children. The effect of the ruling was to impose the parents' views on the children, according to Douglas, and he questioned whether the state should be able to override the parents' religious objections if an Amish child wished to attend public high school.

WRONGFUL LIFE This is the name given to a highly controversial type of lawsuit to recover compensation for a private wrong, or tort, based on the notion that some birth defects are so deleterious that a child afflicted with them would be better off not to have been born. If the lawsuit is successfully prosecuted, the medical professional who negligently failed to help prevent the child's birth is liable to pay compensation to the child for his or her suffering as a result of being brought into being. The lawsuit is usually directed at a doctor or a genetic counselor who failed to warn prospective parents of the possibility of grave birth defects, or to aid the couple in preventing the birth. In the closing days of the twentieth century, only a small minority of states recognize this claim at all. States that do not recognize this claim base their position on a number of potent arguments, including:

- At the time of the alleged negligence, the plaintiff (the afflicted child) was not in existence, therefore the medical professional did not owe a duty to him or her to be careful in preventing him or her from coming into existence.

- It is not the province of the law to determine whether it is better not to exist than to have gross disabilities of any magnitude. Such matters can only be left to religious and philosophical conjecture.

- It is impossible to measure the amount of compensation due to a person with an impaired life because it is impossible to know if this life is better or worse than no life at all.

- The defendant medical professional's negligence in failing to prevent the birth of a defective human being was not a proximate cause of the injury, since the real injury is not the birth, but the birth with the defects, and the defects are caused by genetic factors beyond any physician's control

- It is contrary to public policy to allow a lawsuit based on a failure to negate life when the entire purpose of the tort laws is to protect life.

- Recognizing this lawsuit is tantamount to recognizing a right not to be born.

The lawsuit known as wrongful life should not be confused with wrongful *birth*. In a wrongful birth action, it is the parents of the defective child who are suing to recover compensation for the expenses of caring for him or her. The injury consists in being forced to have a child with deformities, when the birth could have been prevented by proper medical screening and counseling. Similar are lawsuits for wrongful conception brought against medical personnel for negligence in performing sterilization procedures, leading to the birth of an unwanted child.

Wrongful life should also not be confused with a lawsuit to recover for prenatal injuries. In that type of lawsuit, a child born with preventable birth defects alleges that a physician was negligent in not taking steps that would have prevented the defects. By contrast, in a wrongful life suit, there was no known medical procedure that could have prevented the birth defects. Lawsuits to recover for prenatal injuries might include allegations that a physician did not adequately monitor the fetus for signs of distress and oxygen deprivation, did not perform a cesarean section when one was called for, prescribed drugs to a pregnant mother that were known to cause birth defects and the like. In a few unusual cases, a child born with defects resulting from their mother's use of alcohol or drugs during pregnancy have been allowed to sue their own mothers for negligence. However, like wrongful birth, not all states recognize lawsuits to recover for prenatal injuries, whether caused by medical personnel, the child's parents, or third parties.

For Further Reading

Alley, Robert S. *School Prayer: The Court, the Congress, and the First Amendment*. Buffalo, NY: Prometheus Books. 1994.

Mr. Alley painstakingly reconstructs the thinking of James Madison and the founding fathers responsible for the First Amendment's religious freedom clause in this excellent history of prayer in the public schools. Spanning two centuries, from the first days of the republic to the election of Clinton as president in 1992, this discussion includes the major Supreme Court decisions on the issue, as well as an overview of the activities of Congress and the presidents, and evokes the general tenor of the times in which the activities took place.

Coontz, Stephanie. *The Way We Never Were: American Families and the Nostalgia Trap*. New York: Basic Books. 1992.

A fascinating look back at the American family that dispels some of the myths about the "good old days."

Hempelman, Kathleen A. *Teen Legal Rights, A Guide for the '90s*. Westport, CT: Greenwood Press. 1994.

Presented in a simple question/answer format, this book addresses basic legal concerns of modern teenagers—school rules, jobs, relationships with parents, drugs, sex, teen crime, and beyond. Although the answers to each question are necessarily short (usually no more than one or two paragraphs in length), the author provides a short list of additional reading on each subject that should prove useful to the reader who wishes more in-depth discussion.

Hogan, John C. *The Schools, the Courts, and the Public Interest*. 2d ed. Lexington, MA: D.C. Heath and Company, Lexington Books. 1985.

Covering major issues such as race, religion, individual rights, and economic disparity as they relate to the public schools, this book provides an excellent starting point for understanding the evolution of legal thought in education.

Kramer, Donald T., ed. *Legal Rights of Children*. 2d ed. Colorado Springs: Shepard's/McGraw-Hill. 1994.

Intended for legal professionals, this three-volume set provides a very comprehensive, if technical, discussion of all major legal issues involving children, including the latest court cases and major federal and state legislation.

Mezey, Susan Gluck. *Children in Court: Public Policymaking and Federal Court Decisions*. Albany: State University of New York Press. 1996.

An excellent in-depth analysis of how litigation in the arena of family issues has affected children's lives in America. Mezey examines the areas of constitutional rights, welfare and entitlement programs, and the child support enforcement system to conclude that, despite increased activity on behalf of children in the courts, the overall welfare of the nation's youngest citizens has not been advanced in the last half-century and, indeed, has been backsliding.

Purdy, Laura M. *In Their Best Interest? The Case against Equal Rights for Children*. Ithaca, NY: Cornell University Press. 1992.

A thought-provoking rebuttal of the notion that children should enjoy the same rights as adults. Purdy painstakingly sets out her opponents' positions, based on the argument that justice requires the same freedoms be accorded to everyone, regardless of age. She then shows why this would lead to a society more dysfunctional than our present one. Along the way, she elucidates her arguments with examples drawn from historical experiments with permissive child-rearing techniques. She also makes a case for maintaining strong public school systems, and touches on moral issues of all sorts—including the need for some sort of "moral" teaching in children's lives, even if it must come from secular schools that are plagued with the current theory that anything other than strict neutrality on moral issues constitutes an impermissible "indoctrination."

Stevens, George E., and John B. Webster. *Law and the Student Press*. Ames: Iowa State University Press. 1973.

Dated because it does not contain the latest pronouncements on student expression by the Supreme Court, but gives a good basic description of the various issues facing schools and students when students express themselves, including censorship, libel, obscenity, contempt, advertising, copyright, and access to information. Sections on libel, contempt, and obscenity should still be pretty up to date. Good history of pre-Kuhlmeier cases.

Whitman, Mark, ed. *Removing a Badge of Slavery: The Record of* Brown v. Board of Education. Princeton: Markus Wiener Publishing, Inc. 1993.

The saga of the battle to abolish segregated education in the United States as told in the words of the actual participants. Mark Whitman has collected original materials from legal cases challenging separate schools as far back as 1849, including actual testimony, and oral and written arguments on both sides of the issue. The book culminates in the historic 1954 decision of *Brown*, which finally laid to rest the doctrine of "separate but equal" in education. The background and broader meaning of the decision, which Whitman calls "probably the most far-reaching and the most morally significant Supreme Court decision in American history," is concisely profiled by the author's brief introductions to each step in the battle as well as illuminated by selected writings from legal experts and others involved.

Other Sources

Berrick, Jill, and Gilbert Neil. *With the Best of Intentions: The Child Sexual Abuse Prevention Movement.* New York: Guilford Press. 1991.

Besharov, Douglas, ed. *Protecting Children from Abuse and Neglect: Policy and Practice.* Springfield, IL: Charles C. Thomas. 1988.

Cahn, Rhoda, and William Cahn. *No Time for School, No Time for Play: The Story of Child Labor in America.* New York: Julian Messner. 1972.

Davis, Samuel M., and Mortimer D. Schwartz. *Children's Rights and the Law.* Lexington, MA: Lexington Books. 1987.

Friedman, Scott. *The Law of Parent-Child Relationships.* Chicago: American Bar Association. 1992.

Gross, Beatrice, and Ronald Gross, eds. *The Children's Rights Movement: Overcoming the Oppression of Young People.* Garden City, NY: Anchor Books. 1977.

Hawes, Joseph M. *The Children's Rights Movement: A History of Advocacy and Protection.* Boston: Twayne Publishers. 1991.

Hewlett, Sylvia Ann. *When the Bough Breaks: The Cost of Neglecting Our Children.* New York: Free Press. 1991.

Kfoury, Paul R. *Children before the Court: Reflections on Legal Issues Affecting Minors.* 2d ed. Salem, NH: Butterworth Legal Publishers. 1991.

Lindsey, Duncan. *The Welfare of Children.* New York: Oxford University Press. 1994.

McCarthy, Martha M., and Nelda H. Cambron-McCabe. *Public School Law: Teachers' and Students' Rights.* 3d ed. Needham Heights, MA: Allyn and Bacon. 1992.

Mason, Mary Ann. *From Father's Property to Children's Rights: The History of Child Custody in the United States.* New York: Basic Books. 1990.

Mnookin, Robert, ed. *In the Interest of Children.* New York: W. H. Freeman. 1985.

Myers, John E. B. *Legal Issues in Child Abuse and Neglect.* Newbury Park, CA: Sage Publications. 1992.

Ordover, Eileen L., and Kathleen B. Boundy. *Educational Rights of Children with Disabilities.* Cambridge, MA: Center for Law and Education. 1991.

Rose, Susan J., and William Meezan. "Defining Child Neglect: Evolution, Influences and Issues." *Social Service Review* (June 1993).

Terkel, Susan Neiberg. *Understanding Child Custody.* New York: Franklin Watts. 1991.

Table of
Cases

Table of Statutes

Adoption and Safe Families Act of 1997, Pub. L. No. 105-89 (1997)
Adoption Assistance and Child Welfare Act of 1980 (AACWA), 42 U.S.C. § 672
Aid to Families with Dependent Children (AFDC) Act, 42 U.S.C.S. §§ 601–615
Bilingual Education Act, 20 U.S.C. §§ 3281–3283
Child Abuse Prevention and Treatment Act, 42 U.S.C. § 5101–5106
Child Victims' and Child Witnesses' Rights Act, 18 U.S.C. § 3509
Children's Television Act of 1990, 47 U.S.C. §§ 303a, b, 394 (Supp. IV 1992)
Education Amendments of 1972, 20 U.S.C. §§ 1681 et seq.
Equal Access Act, 20 U.S.C. §§ 4071–4074
Fair Housing Act, 42 U.S.C. § 3604
Fair Labor Standards Act, 29 U.S.C. §§ 201 et seq.
Family Educational Rights and Privacy Act, 20 U.S.C. § 1232g
Federal Child Support Enforcement Program, 42 U.S.C. §§ 651–669
Gifted and Talented Students Education Act of 1988, 20 U.S.C. §§ 3061–3068
Indian Child Welfare Act of 1978 (ICWA), 25 U.S.C. §§ 1901–1903
Individuals with Disabilities Education Act of 1990, 20 U.S.C. § 1400 et seq.
Juvenile Delinquency Act, 18 U.S.C. § 5032
Juvenile Justice and Delinquency Prevention Act, 42 U.S.C. 5601 et seq.
Missing Children Act, 28 U.S.C. § 534(a)(3)
National School Lunch Program (NSLP), 42 U.S.C. §§ 1751 et seq.
Parental Kidnapping Prevention Act, 18 U.S.C. § 1073; 28 U.S.C. § 1738a; 42 U.S.C. §§ 654, 663
Runaway and Homeless Youth Act, 42 U.S.C. §§ 5701 et seq.
Sexual Exploitation Act, 18 U.S.C. §§ 2251–2258
Telecommunications Act of 1996, Pub. L. No. 104-104, 110 Stat. 56 (1996)

Index

Boldfaced page numbers refer to entries on that subject.

Since her graduation from Stanford Law School in 1979, Lauren Krohn Arnest has served on the writing staffs of major legal publishers, including the Bureau of National Affairs, Inc., and Shepard's/McGraw-Hill. Mrs. Arnest presently does freelance writing and editing on legal and other topics from her home in Colorado Springs. She and her husband, composer Mark Arnest, run Seat of Our Pants Productions, a creative services enterprise that produced its first original musical theater offering *All about Love,* an adaptation of Plato's *Symposium,* in 1997.